HOLLINGSWORTH ARMS

Azure, on a Bend. Argent. 3 Holly Leaves. Slipped. Vert.

CREST: *A Stag Lodged, p.p.r.*
MOTTO: *Disce Ferenda Pati*

TINCTURES OR ARMORIAL COLORS, ETC.

Colors	Tinctures	Precious Stones	Planets	Virtues
Blue	Azure	Sapphire	Jupiter	Loyalty
White	Argent	Pearl	Luna	Innocence
Green	Vert	Emerald	Venus	Love

DESCENDANTS

of

Valentine Hollingsworth, Sr.

By

Joseph Adger Stewart

Louisville, Kentucky

JOHN P. MORTON & COMPANY

INCORPORATED

1925

I have with pleasure and with the assistance of many members of the family added to the memoranda of names collected by Wm. B. Hollingsworth of Baltimore and printed in 1884, corrected some errors, and no doubt made others. Corrections and additions will be appreciated.

There are thousands of the descendants of Valentine Hollingsworth, Sr., not included, because I did not have their addresses.

It is to be hoped that some member of the family will, some day, write a "History of the Hollingsworths," as many of them have helped to make history in the United States since 1682.

J. ADGER STEWART.

4780 Ashbottom Road
Louisville, Ky.
December 1924

HOLLINGSWORTH HALL

THE Hollingsworths have held their own all along the ages. They were an old Saxon family said to have settled in the North-eastern part of Cheshire, as early as 1022, in which year the ancestral estate, Hollingsworth Manor, in Cheshire, was purchased. The name represents a locality, from the estate of that name, near Mottram, in the county in question. The name comes from the two words, "holly" and "worth," a farm, meaning a farm of holly trees. Annals dating from the Norman conquest, speak of "the hundred of Macclesfield or Maxfield," known in the Domesday survey as "the hundred of Hamstan," and one of the Manors mentioned in these ancient books is that of Hollingsworth Manor, situated on the edge of the great woods of Macclesfield. The visitation of Cheshire by the official herald in the year 1580 includes "John Hollingsworth, Gent," and "Robert Hollingsworth," among the gentry residing in the hundred of Macclesfield." A further record speaks of Robert Hollingsworth of Hollingsworth Hall, from whom the family is descended, and who was Magistrate for the counties of Chester and Lancaster. The church of the family and the hall, both several centuries old, are still standing, and upon both are emblazoned the family Coat of Arms. The late owner, Captain Robert Hollingsworth, the last representative of the English branch of the family, died in 1865. The estate is said to include 625 acres and to be valued at 20,000 pounds. Picturesque red-berried holly trees abound upon the estate, and when one realizes its nearness to the edge of the Macclesfield woods, the arms and crest handed down for generations acquire a picturesque significance. The tinctures of the shield are azure, suggestive of the blue sky, argent, of the silvery streams that flow through the woodlands, and vert, of the green leafage of the forest trees. The virtues of these colors are equally beautiful, expressing loyalty, innocence and love. The Crest is a stag, recalling the Saxon Earls of Cheshire and merry hunting scenes, and three glistening holly leaves suggest Christmas in merry England. Motto—Learn to suffer what must be borne, or, bear patiently what must be borne. The usurpation of that Saxon shire by the Norman Earl, Hugh Lupus, no doubt suggested the motto. At any rate the records state that these freemen of Hollingsworth and the seven other manors that make up Macclesfield, paid their yearly tax to the usurping earl and held their manors in undisturbed possession.

It is probable that the Hollingsworths went over to Ireland from England with other planters, early in the 17th century.

The name Hollingsworth, so widely known and honored in the United States, is spelled severally: Hollingworth, Hollonsworth, and Hollingsworth. The last spelling has been clung to by a large majority of the descendants of the founder of the family in America, who was Valentine Hollingsworth and who came to the New World from Ireland, in 1682, the year in which William Penn arrived in the Delaware, in front of which is now the city of Philadelphia, Pa. The Hollingsworth family was noted for its enterprise and industry, and many of its members were largely engaged in the manufacture of flour, and were the owners of a number of mills on the branches of the Elbe River in Cecil Co., Md., New Castle Co., Del., also in Virginia, South Carolina, and in other states, and later of shipyards, steel mills, etc.

* * * * *

The family flower or tree is the holly tree. In Kentucky and neighboring States, the holly should be transplanted in the month of August.

VALENTINE HOLLINGSWORTH, SR.

THE original immigrant ancestor of the American family of Hollingsworth was a member of the Society of Friends, and many of his descendants adhere to that faith. He was the son of Henry Hollingsworth of Belleniskcrannel, Parish of Legoe, County Armagh, Ireland, and of Catherine, his wife, was born at Belleniskcrannel "about the year 1632," and was married April 7, 1655, to Ann Ree, daughter of Nicholas Ree of Tanderagee, County Armagh. She was born about 1628, at Tanderagee, and died February 1, 1671. He then married, April 12, 1672, Ann Calvert, daughter of Thomas Calvert, of Dromgora, Parish of Segoe, County Armagh, and of Jane, his wife.

In 1682, Valentine Hollingsworth, Sr., and his family, accompanied by his son-in-law, Thomas Connaway, and by John Musgrave, an indented servant, sailed from Belfast for the Delaware River, arriving a few months after William Penn's arrival in the good ship "Welcome." He settled on a large plantation of nearly a thousand acres on Shelpot Creek in Brandywine Hundred, New Castle (now Del.) Co., about five miles northeast of the present city of Wilmington, and not far from Port Christian, or Christiana of the Swedes. Not long thereafter a monthly meeting was established, the sessions being mainly held at Hollingsworth's House. In 1687 he granted "unto friends for a burying place half an acre of land for ye purpose, there being already friends buried in the spot." The section in question soon became known as the "New Worke" or "New Ark," now the thriving town of Newark, Del. That Valentine Hollingsworth was a man of extraordinary ability and influence is demonstrated from the fact that almost immediately after his arrival in the New World, he was called upon to hold office and participate in public affairs. He was a member of the first Assembly of the Province of Pennsylvania, shortly after William Penn's advent, that of 1682-3; also of the Grand Inquest empaneled October 25, 1683, to consider the famous case of Charles Pickering and others charged with counterfeiting. He served in several subsequent sessions of the Assembly, those of 1687, '88, '95 and 1700, from New Castle County, and was a Justice of the Peace from the same county. He was also a Signer of Penn's Great Charter and a member of the Pro-Provincial Council. He died about 1711. His second wife, Ann Calvert, died August 17, 1697. Both were buried in the old burial ground at Newark, Del., which he had presented to the Friends in 1687.

Issue 1st Marriage (Ann Ree)

I. Mary[1]—Born January, 1656, at Belleniskcrannel, Ireland. Died 1746. She first married Thomas Conoway, about 1684, who died July 17, 1689, and then Randal Malin, in 1693. More of Mary later.

II. Henry[1]—Born September 7, 1658, at Belleniskcrannel, Ireland. Died at Elkton, Cecil Co., Md., 1721. He married Elizabeth Atkinson, August 22, 1688. More of Henry later.

III. Thomas[1]—Born March, 1661. More of Thomas later.

IV. Catherine[2]—Born May, 1663. Died June 29, 1746. Married George Robinson, November 2, 1688. More of Catherine later. Issue 2nd marriage (Ann Calvert).

V. Samuel[2]—Born January 27, 1673, in Ireland. Died 1748. Married Hannah Harlan, 1701. More of Samuel later.

VI. Enoch[1]—Born June 7, 1675. Died young, 1687.

VII. Valentine, Jr.[3], of Kennett, Pa.—Born November 12, 1677. Died 1757. Married Elizabeth Heald, 1713, Ireland. More of Valentine later.

VIII. Ann[1]—Born October 28, 1680, Ireland. Married James Thompson, 1700.

IX. John[2]—Born February 19, 1684, New Castle Co., Del. Died 1722. Married Catherine Tyler, in 1706.

X. Joseph[1]—Born May 10, 1686, New Castle Co., Del.

XI. Enoch[2] again—Born about 1688. Died September 26, 1690.

B-2. MARY HOLLINGSWORTH

Daughter of Valentine and Ann (Ree) Hollingsworth. Born January, 1656, at Belleniskcrannel, Ireland. She first married Thomas Conoway, about 1684, who died July 17, 1689. She then married Randal Malin, 1693.

Issue 1st Marriage (Thomas Conoway)

I. Elizabeth Conoway[2]—Born September 7, 1687. She first married Charles Booth, 1705. Married Thomas Crabb, 1720.

II. Ann Conoway[1]—Born about 1688. Married Philip Taylor, June 10, 1705.

III. Sarah Conoway[1]—Born about 1689. Married 1709 or '10, John Yearsley. A daughter married John Heald, 1744.

Issue 2nd Marriage (Randal Malin)

IV. Hannah Malin[1]—Died young.

V. Rachel Malin[1]—Born April 25, 1702.

B-2. HENRY HOLLINGSWORTH

Eldest son of Valentine[1] and Ann (Ree) Hollingsworth, Sr. Born at Belleniskcrannel, Ireland, September 7, 1658. Came to America, August 14, 1683, in the good ship "Lion of London"; died at Elkton, Cecil Co., Md., March, 1721. Will dated February 23, 1721, probated March 12, 1721. Was a surveyor. When only 18 years old, he assisted Thomas Holmes in laying out the City of Philadelphia. He was a large land owner in Chester Co., Pa., also in New Castle Co., Del. Was Sheriff of Chester Co., Pa., 1695. Coroner of Chester Co., and Clerk of the Court, from 1700 to 1708. He represented New Castle Co. in the assembly of Pa. in 1695, the same year with his father. In 1711-12 he removed to the head of Elk River, now Elkton, Cecil Co., Md., and was appointed Surveyor of the County by Lord Baltimore, March 9, 1712. He was the founder of the Hollingsworth family in Maryland. Married August 22, 1688, in the Parrish of Sligo, County Armagh, Ireland, Lydia Atkinson.

ISSUE

I. Ruth[2]—Born 1689. Married December 24, 1706, George Simpson.

II. Stephen[2]—Born 1690. Married Anne .... Was a Magistrate in Cecil Co., Md., in 1730. Removed to Virginia, and in 1734 obtained a grant of land of 472 acres on the west side of the Shenandoah River, Orange Co.

III. Zebulon[2]—Born in Chester Co., Pa., 1696. More of Zebulon later. Died August 8, 1763, in Cecil Co., Md.

IV. Catherine[2]—Married ..... Dawson, Kent Co., Md.

V. Abigail[2]—Married Richard Dobson, 1720.

VI. Mary[2].

B-2. THOMAS HOLLINGSWORTH

Son of Valentine[1] and Ann (Ree) Hollingsworth, Sr. Born in Belleniskcrannell, Ireland, about 1661. When on a visit to his son Abraham, who lived near Winchester, Va., in 1733, it is said he was killed by a buffalo near North Mountain, eight or nine miles north of Winchester, Va., having gone on a hunting expedition with some of the settlers. Will dated October 30, 1723. Filed Court House,

Wilmington, New Castle Co., Del. His home was always Rockland Manor, New Castle Co., Del., at that time a part of the Providence of Pennsylvania. He came to America with his father and settled in New Castle Co., west side of the Brandywine River, in 1682. He married first, Margaret ...., about 1684, who died August 1, 1687, and was buried at New Castle, Del. He married second, Grace Cook, of Concord, Pa., on January 31, 1692.

ISSUE 1ST MARRIAGE

I. Abraham[2]—Born January 19, 1686. He married Ann Robinson in 1710 and removed to Virginia. More of Abraham later.

ISSUE 2ND MARRIAGE

II. Isaac[2]—Born April 16, 1693. Died in 1699.

III. Elizabeth[2]—Born November 8, 1694. Married 1718, ... Stroud.

IV. Hannah[2]—Born January 17, 1697. Married 1718, ... Dixon.

V. Thomas[2]—Born December 23, 1698. Died September 1, 1753. He married December 28, 1732, Judith Lampley; more of Thomas later.

VI. Ann[2]—Born May 6, 1701. Died in 1708.

VII. Jacob[2]—Born January 4, 1704. Married September 23, 1729, Elizabeth Chandler—Born January 4, 1704. Purchased June 23, 1726, of James Aubrey, Attorney for Letitia Aubrey, daughter of William Penn, 225 acres of land in Mill Creek Hundred, New Castle Co., Del. He died intestate, leaving seven children. More of Jacob later.

VIII. Sarah[2]—Born August 7, 1706. Married 1724, John Dixon.

IX. Joseph[2]—Born March 11, 1709. Married in 1730, Martha Haughton. Removed to Virginia; more of Joseph later.

X. Grace[2]—Born March 9, 1712.

B-2. CATHERINE (HOLLINGSWORTH) ROBINSON

Daughter of Valentine, I, and Ann (Ree) Hollingsworth. Born in 1663. Died June 29, 1746. Married November 2, 1688, to George Robinson. He was born in the North of Ireland, 1666 or '67. He died August 8, 1738, in the 73rd year of his age.

ISSUE

I. Mary Robinson[1]—Born 1689. Married Thomas Jacobs, August 13, 1710, at the residence of Valentine Hollingsworth.
II. Ann Robinson[1]—Born 1701. Married Jonathan Ogden, 1720.
III. Valentine Robinson[1]—Born about 1705. Married Elizabeth Booth, 1740. After his death, his widow married Samuel Wilmer, 1749.

Catherine m Bryan. Dr. Donald.

C-3. ABRAHAM HOLLINGSWORTH

(Thomas[2], Valentine[1]), eldest son of Thomas[2] and Margaret Hollingsworth. Born at Rockland Manor, New Castle Co., Del., January 18, 1686. Died Frederick Co., Va., October, 1748. Will dated September 23, 1748, in which he willed 1,232 acres of land. Recorded Tuesday, November 1, 1748. Married March 13, 1710, to Ann Robinson, daughter of George Robinson. She died 1749. ("Abraham Hollingsworth of ye County of New Castell, and Manor of Rockland, to Ann Robinson, ye 13th day of ye 3rd month in ye year 1710 at ye house of Valentine Hollingsworth in ye said County.") Moved, in 1710, to Cecil Co., Md. In 1732 he bought of Alexander Ross, under his patent from the Governor of Virginia, 582 acres of land near Winchester, Frederick Co., Va., and in 1733, he moved with his family and some relatives to this grant. He fixed his home—"Abraham's Delight"—at a point southwest of the present town of Winchester, Va., on the branch of Abraham's Creek (named after him) which heads the Town Spring and Shawnee Springs, and there erected a flour mill, one of the very first in the county. He and his family were Friends, and attended meetings at East Nottingham, Pa., at least 150 miles distant.

ISSUE

I. George[4]—Born April 12, 1712. More of George later.
II. Margaret[4]—Born 1715. Married Benjamin Carter, of Virginia.
III. Lydia[4]—Born 1718. Married Lewis Neill, of Virginia.
IV. Isaac[4]—Born 1722. Married Rachel Parkins, of Virginia. More of Isaac later.

WILL OF ABRAHAM HOLLINGSWORTH[1]

I, Abraham Hollingsworth, of Opeckan, in Frederick County, in the Colony of Virginia, Yeoman being weak of body, but of perfect sound mind and memory, thanks be given to God therefore calling to mind the mortality of my body, do make and ordain this, my last will and testament. That is to say, principally and first of all, I give and recommend my soul into the hands of God, that gave it, and as for my body, I recommend it to the earth to be buried in a decent manner at the discretion of my Executors hereafter named and as touching such worldly goods wherewithall it hath pleased God to bless me with in this life I give and dispose of the same in the following manner and form.

Imprimis, my will and mind is that all my just debts and funeral expenses be first paid and discharged.

Item. I give and bequeath unto my well-beloved wife Ann one of my best feather beds with the furniture thereunto belonging, also I give unto her the household furniture, likewise I give unto my wife her riding horse and her saddle.

Item. I give and bequeath unto my son George Hollingsworth Two Hundred and Fifty Acres of land, being part of the One Thousand Two Hundred and Fifty acres of land lying joining to the land I gave to Benjamin Carter on both sides of the creek. I give it to him, his heirs and assigns forever.

Item. I give and bequeath to my son-in-law Benjamin Carter and to his heirs and assigns forever Four hundred acres of land lying on both sides the Creek called the Beaverdams.

Item. I give and bequeath unto my son Isaac Hollingsworth and to his heirs and assigns forever Five Hundred Eighty-two acres of land it being the old tract together with all and singular the buildings and appurtenances thereunto belonging or in any wise appertaining.

Item. I give and bequeath unto my son George Hollingsworth the sum of Seven pounds, Ten shillings of Current money which my son Isaac Hollingsworth shall pay to him twelve months after my decease.

Item. I give and bequeath unto my daughter Lydia Naill one of my feather beds and furniture thereunto belonging.

Lastly I do hereby nominate and appoint my wife and my son in law, Louis Neill and my son Isaac Hollingsworth my executors of this my last will and testament hereby revoking, annuling and utterly making void all former and other wills and by me heretofore made.

In witness hereof I have hereunto set my hand and seal the twenty-third day of September in the year of Our Lord One Thousand Seven Hundred and Forty Eight.

ABRM. HOLLINGSWORTH. (Seal).

Signed, sealed, published and
declared to be my last will
and testament in the presence
of   William Dobbin,
       James Dunbar,
       Joseph Lupton.

At a Court held for Frederick County on Tuesday the first day of November, 1748.

This will of Abraham Hollingsworth decd was presented unto Court by Lewis Neill and Isaac Hollingsworth, two of the executors therein named (Ann Hollingsworth the executrix having in open Court refused to take upon herself the burden of the execution of this said will) who made oath to the same according to law, and the said will being proved by the oaths of William Dobbin and James Dunbar two of the witnesses thereto who also made oath that they saw Joseph Lupton sign the same as an evidence it is admitted to record.

Teste.   J. Wood. C. C.

A copy teste:
    J. W. Baker, Jr.
        Deputy Clerk.

D–4. GEORGE HOLLINGSWORTH

(Abraham[3], Thomas[2], Valentine[1]), son of Abraham[2] and Ann (Robinson) Hollingsworth. Was born Cecil Co., Md., April 7, 1712. Moved with his father to Frederick Co., near Winchester, Va., 1733. In 1762 he sold all of his property in Virginia, and he and all his family except his son Robert and family, moved to South Carolina. He first married December 19, 1734, Hannah McCoy, daughter of Robert McCoy, Sr., of the Parish of Augusta, Frederick Co., Va. The following is taken from the records: "George Hollingsworth, son of Abraham Hollingsworth, late of Cecil Co., Md., now living on the North side of Opecken Colony, Va., married Hannah McCoy, daughter of Robert McCoy, Sr.

of same place, December 19, 1734, at the house of Isaac Parkins of
Virginia, in the presence of the following witnesses:

Abraham Hollingsworth (father)		William Hoge
Anne Hollingsworth (mother)		George Hoge
Margaret Hollingsworth (sister)		Richard Hiland
Lydia Hollingsworth (sister)		Samuel Bratton
Isaac Hollingsworth (brother)		Mary Buller
John Littler		Josiah Culbert
Daniel Rushen	Katherine Ross	Jacob Worthington
Thomas Eads	Katharine Thomas	Mary Littler
Josiah Ballinger	Mary Ballinger	Onan Thomas
Teran Kelly	Evan Thomas	Reuben Mills
Thomas Bab	Thomas Wilson	John Ross
Thomas Bransen	Hannah Mills	Mary Hollingsworth
Igt Sobt	Evan Thomas, Jr.	Isaac Parkins
Ellig Bensen	John Bullock	Mary Parkins
John Benters	John Wood	Benjamin Smith
William Smith	Esther Harrison	

ISSUE 1ST MARRIAGE (HANNAH)

I. Joseph⁵—Born 1735. First married ...... Frost. More of
  Joseph later. *m (2) Margaret Hammer newright — p.41*

II. Isaac⁵—Born 1737. Married Susanna Wright. More of Isaac
  later.

III. Abraham⁵—Born 1739. Married Margaret Wright. Moved to
  South Carolina. More of Abraham later.

IV. Ann⁵—Born 1741. Married ...... Brock.

V. Robert⁵—Born 1744. Married Susanna Rice, Winchester, Va.
  He died 1799. More of Robert later.

ISSUE 2ND MARRIAGE (JANE ELWELL)

VI. John⁵—Born 1755. Married Rachel Wright. More of John
  later.

VII. James⁵—Born about 1758 or '59. Married Sarah Wright. More
  of James later.

VIII. Henry⁵—Born 1760. Married Sarah Cook. More of Henry
  later.

IX. George⁵—Born 1762. Married Jane Henry. More of George
  later.

X. Nathan⁵—Born 1766. Unmarried.

XI. Susanna⁵—Born 1768. Married ...... Mote.

Indenture dated December 24, 1768, between George Hollingsworth[4], of Berkley in the Province of South Carolina, planter on the one part, and Jacob Hoge of the aforesaid County and Province, planter of the other part—

Whereas, in and by a certain grant bearing date the 28th day of August in the year 1767 and in the seventh year of his Majesty's reign under the hand of his Excellency, the Right Honorable Lord Charles Greenville Montague, Captain General, Governor and Commander in Chief in and over the said Province of South Carolina, and the great seal of the Province for that purpose appointed, did give and grant unto George Hollingsworth a plantation or tract of land containing 150 acres on Bush Creek in the County of and Province aforesaid, recorded in the Secretary of States office, now witnesseth, that the said George Hollingsworth for the sum of One Hundred pounds to him paid by the said Jacob Hoge, grants, bargains and sells and transfers the grant to him.

Witnesses: Signed:

    Jacob Brooks   George Hollingsworth[4]

    William Downs   Jane Hollingsworth.

    William Gary

E–5. ABRAHAM HOLLINGSWORTH

(George[4], Abraham[3], Thomas[2], Valentine[1]), of Laurens, S. C. Born near Winchester, Frederick Co., Va., 1739. Son of George and Hannah (McCoy) Hollingsworth. Resided Frederick County until 1774, when he removed to Dunmore (now Shenandoah) Co., Va. Resided there until 1777, when he removed to North Carolina, and later to Laurens Co., S. C. Married in Virginia, 1762, Margaret Wright.

ISSUE

   I. George[5]—Born October 3, 1763. Married Susannah. More of George later.

  II. Joseph[5]—Born September 22, 1765. Died April 8, 1844, Newton Co., Ga. Married 1789. Rosannah Nichols, of Laurens Co., S. C. Issue: 10 children. More of Joseph later.

 III. Robert[5]—Born November 22, 1767, Frederick Co., Va. Married 1791, Jennie Hamilton, of Laurens Co., S. C., Issue: 9 children.

  IV. Levi[5]—Born July 11, 1771, Frederick Co., Va.

   V. Jemima[5]—Born September 25, 1773, Frederick Co., Va.

VI. Hannah[1]—Born March 10, 1776, Dunmore (now Shenandoah) Co., Va.

VII. Richard[1]—Born July 12, 1778, North Carolina.

Abraham Hollingsworth[1], above, while a resident of Dunmore Co., Va., gives power to an attorney to sue, as below:

April 28, 1774.

Abraham[1] Hollingsworth, of the County of Dunmore, Colony of Virginia for divers good causes and considerations, does ordain and appoints Richard Campbell of the same county, to sue forth and cause to be executed a writ for docking the entail of one undivided half or moiety of a tract of land commonly known by the name of Joshua's Bottom, situate, lying and being in the same county devised to me by the will of my grand-father Robert McCoy, deceased. In witness whereof I have hereunto set my hands and seal this 28th day of September, 1774.

Witnesses: Signed:
  Abraham Keller   Abraham Hollingsworth
  Henry Nelson
  Burr Harrison
  Will Webb.

Indenture made by Abraham Hollingsworth[1], when a resident of the State of North Carolina, as below:

August 29, 1778.

Indenture made the 29th day of August, 1778. Between Abraham[1] Hollingsworth in the State of North Carolina, of the one part and Edwin Young of the County of Shenandoah of the Commonwealth of Virginia, of the other part. Witnesseth, that the said Abraham[1] Hollingsworth, for and in consideration of the sum of Two Hundred pounds current money of Virginia to him in hand paid by the said Edwin Young, conveys to him a certain piece or parcel of land situate lying and being in the South River of Shenandoah in the said County, called by the name of Job's Bottom, containing 216 acres, which was devised to the said Abraham[1] Hollingsworth, by his Grand-father, Robert McCoy, duly recorded in the County of Augusta will more fully appear, in Deed Book C, page 102, Woodstock, Shenandoah Co., Va.

In witness whereof Richard Campbell, Attorney in fact for the said Abraham[1] Hollingsworth, bearing the date the 28th day of September, 1774, duly recorded in the County Court of Dunmore, now Shenandoah County, hathe hereunto set the seal and affixed the name of the said Abraham[1] Hollingsworth, the day of year above mentioned.

Witnesses: Signed:
  Jet Hog Groots   Abraham[1] Hollingsworth (Seal).
  George Jones.

ALL OF THE SONS OF ABRAHAM¹ HOLLINGSWORTH ARE MENTIONED IN THE FOLLOWING DEED

February 10, 1792.

George¹ Hollingsworth and Susannah his wife of Laurens Co., S. C. of the first part and Levi¹ Hollingsworth of the said State and County aforesaid of the other part. George¹ and Susannah Hollingsworth for the sum of 750 pounds transfer to Levi¹ Hollingsworth, 150 acres lying in Laurens County, on a branch of Cane Creek adjoining Robert¹ Hollingsworth, Robert Hambleton, Widow Cunningham, Patrick Cunningham, and Richard¹ Hollingsworth, being part of the tract of land originally granted to Thomas North for 300 acres, commonly called and known by the name of Liberty Springs, and by the said Thomas North conveyed to John Williams by a lease and release bearing date, November 22 and 23, 1773, and by the said John Williams conveyed to Abraham¹ Hollingsworth by a lease and release bearing date, January 10 and 11, 1778, and devolving (going to) to the said George¹ Hollingsworth by Heirship, together with all and singular the ways, wells, water, and water courses, assessments and profits, commodities, advantages, emoluments, herediments and appurtenances whatever to the said Plantation, by Lord Charles Greenville Montague Governor and Commander in Chief of the Province of South Carolina. Signed and sealed and witnessed on the 10th day of February, 1792.

Witnesses:
    William Wheeler
    Joseph¹ Hollingsworth
    Robert¹ Hollingsworth.

Signed:
    George¹ Hollingsworth.
    Susannah Hollingsworth.

THE DAUGHTERS OF ABRAHAM¹ HOLLINGSWORTH ARE MENTIONED IN THE DEED BELOW

July 17, 1795.

Jemima¹ Hollingsworth and Hannah¹ Hollingsworth spinsters of the first part, of Laurens Co., S. C., released to George¹ Hollingsworth party of the first part, of Laurens Co., S. C., a Plantation consisting of 200 acres in Laurens Co., lying on Mud Lick Creek, granted to William O'Neal, December 23, 1771, and released to Abraham¹ Hollingsworth. Signed and witnessed July 17, 1795.

Witnesses:
    David Hollingsworth
    Joseph¹ Hollingsworth
    Simpson Warren.

Signed:
    Jamima¹ Hollingsworth
    Hannah¹ Hollingsworth.

F-6. JOSEPH HOLLINGSWORTH

(Abraham⁵, George⁴, Abraham³, Thomas², Valentine¹), son of Abraham⁵ and Margaret (Wright). Born September 22, 1765. Died April 8, 1844, Newton (now Rockdale) Co., Ga. Married 1789, Rosannah Nichols, and lived in a big old house with outside kitchen, on a farm in Laurens Dist., S. C. They moved to Georgia, after their children, about 1834, and both are buried at Smyra, Rockdale Co., Ga. Rosannah Nichols was born January 15, 1767. Died March 10, 1839.

- I. Jennie⁷—Born September 27, 1790. Married Billie Bailey. Lived and died in Laurens Dist., S. C.
- II. James⁷—Born September 13, 1792. Married Polly Rogers. Lived in Laurens, S. C., and stayed there. Issue: 1. Joseph⁸—Died unmarried at Griffin, Ga. 2. James⁸—Unmarried; killed in battle. 3. Letty⁸—Born at Walcott. 4. Rosannah⁸—Born at Culberson.
- III. John⁷—Born November 4, 1794. Married Rebecca Bailey, October 9, 1817. Lived in Laurens, S. C., and moved to Newton Co., Ga., about 1833. Died August 29, 1866. More of John later. Died June 13, 1859.
- IV. Joseph⁷—Born April 10, 1797. Married Elizabeth Ann Jane Carr Rogers, 1815, Laurens Dist., S. C., daughter of Andrew and Lattie (Franks) Rogers, and moved to DeKalb Co., Ga., 1815. Moved to Smyrna, Newton Co., now Rockdale Co., Ga., 1834. They had 5 children when they came to Georgia, and 4 more were born in Georgia. Lived in Griffin, Ga., several years. They are both buried in Heard Co., Ga., at Hollingsworth Ferry. More of Joseph later.
- V. William⁷—Born March 3, 1799. Married Permalia McDowell, January 11, 1826. Moved from Laurens, S. C., to Smyra, Ga., about 1828. Died March 28, 1883. More of William later.
- VI. Moses⁷—Born February 1, 1801. Married Elizabeth or "Betsey" Rogers, September 26, 1821. Came to Georgia, about 1824, from South Carolina. More of Moses later.
- VI. Aaron⁷—Born February 23, 1803. Married Ruth Rogers. Lived at Laurens, S. C. More of Aaron later.
- VIII. Mary⁷—Born October 11, 1805. Married Nathaniel Rogers January 13, 1825. Died June 13, 1847 or '48. More of Mary later.

CHURCH, NORTHEASTERN PART OF CHESHIRE, ENGLAND

IX. Martha[7]—Born September 11, 1808. Married George Rogers, December 24, 1829. Died March 30, 1888. More of Martha later.

X. George[7]—Born October 9, 1810. Married Elizabeth Jackson, about 1835. Married Nancy Johnson Rogers, about 1842. More of George later.

G–7. JOSEPH HOLLINGSWORTH

(Joseph[6], Abraham[5], George[4], Abraham[3], Thomas[2], Valentine[1]). Son of Joseph[6] and Rosanna (Nichols) Hollingsworth. Born April 10, 1797. Died June 13, 1859. Married Elizabeth Ann Jane Carr Rogers, 1815, Laurens Dist., S. C., and moved to DeKalb Co., Ga., 1825. Moved to Smyrna, Newton Co. (now Rockdale), Ga., 1834. She was born February 14, 1795, and died February 4, 1881. They had 5 children when they came to Georgia, and 4 more were born in Georgia. Lived several years in Griffin, Ga. They are both buried in Heard Co., Ga., at Hollingsworth Ferry.

Issue

I. James[8]—Born August 1, 1817, Laurens, S. C. Died September 23, 1864, Mobile, Ala. Married Joyce Eppison of Ebernezer, Ga. Family moved to Eastern Mississippi. More of James later.

II. Julia Ann[8]—Born February 9, 1819, Laurens, S. C. Moved to Georgia, in 1825. Died April 24, 1911, at Conyers, Ga. Married September 7, 1837, at home, near Ebernezer, Ga., (now Rockdale Co., Ga.) to John Lewis Stewart of Ebernezer, Ga. Born September 10, 1810, York District, S. C. Died April 30, 1886, at Conyers, Ga. He was a son of Alexander and Sarah (Striplin) Stewart and grandson of Alexander and Elizabeth (Barron) Stewart. More of Julia later.

III. Letitia[8]—Born in Laurens, S. C., about 1820. Moved to Georgia, in 1825. Married Benjamin Stewart in 18..... Moved to Randolph Co., Ala., and died in Coose Co., Ala. More of Letitia later.

IV. Levi[8]—Born December 25, 1822, Laurens, S. C. Married Betsey Echols of Heard Co., Ga., December 19, 1844. Died in Heard Co., Ga., on Chattahoochee River, May 23, 1899.

V. Rosannah[8]—Born June 7, 1825, Laurens, S. C. Died December 1, 1907, Powder Springs, Ga. Married William Scott. More of Rosannah later.

VI. Sarah[6]—"A beauty." Born DeKalb Co., Ga., March 10, 1828. Died in Macon, Ga., April 10, 1852. Married July 24, 1845, in Griffin, Ga., John McDonald. Then married Dr. Joshua Cherry, of Macon, Ga.

VII. Lizzie[6]—Born August 15, 1833, in Georgia. Married September 20, 1853, William W. Walcott.

VIII. Jane[6]—Born August 11, 1835, in Newton Co., Ga. Married Edward Mosely of Heard Co., Ga. Died December 23, 1909, Heard Co., Ga.

IX. Joseph A.[6]—Born in Newton Co., Ga., in July 1837. Died in Ensley, Ala., July 5, 1903. Married Lucy H. Mosely, of Heard Co., Ga. More of Joseph A. later.

H-8. JULIA ANN (HOLLINGSWORTH) STEWART

Daughter of Joseph[7] and Elizabeth Ann Jane Carr (Rogers) Hollingsworth. (Of Joseph[6], Abraham[5], George[4], Abraham[3], Thomas[2], Valentine[1]). Born February 9, 1819, Laurens Co., S. C. Died April 24, 1911, Conyers, Ga. Married September 7, 1837, at home near Ebenezer, Newton Co., Ga., John Lewis Stewart, who was born September 10, 1810, York Dist., S. C., and died April 30, 1886, at Conyers, Ga. He was the son of Alexander[2] and Sarah Striplin Stewart, and grandson of Alexander and Elizabeth Barron Stewart.

Issue

I. Sarah Elizabeth[9]—Born October 14, 1838, Ebenezer, Ga. Living 1924. First married Robert Jones, October 22, 1857, Conyers, Ga. Issue: 1 daughter, Bobbie.[10] Then married Hiram Henslee, October 16, 1864, Conyers, Ga. Issue: 1. Joseph[10]. 2. Lewis[10]. 3. Endox[10]. 4. Stewart[10]. 5. Atticus H[10]. 6. Mary Julia[10].

II. John Archibald Bellah[9]—Born December 2, 1840, Ebenezer, Ga. Married Kitty Tennessee King, Atlanta, Ga., April 4, 1867. Died June 2, 1891, Covington, Ga., and buried at Conyers, Ga. Issue: 1. Joseph King[10]. 2. Julia Hollingsworth[10]. 3. Eudox McCalla[10]. 4. Mary[10].

III. Julian Crawford[9]—Born February 17, 1843, Ebenezer, Ga. Married Robert Baggerly Etheridge, August 29, 1867, Conyers, Ga. Died November 12, 1887, Birmingham, Ala., and buried at Conyers, Ga. Issue: 1. Annie Stewart[10]. 2. Joseph Hamilton[10]. He married Belle Walker.

IV. Joseph Alexander[9]—Born October 17, 1845, Ebenezer, Ga. Married Carrie Julia Robinson, January 30, 1873, in Newborn, Ga. Died July 31, 1890, Covington, Ga. Buried in Covington, Ga. Issue: 2 sons and 6 daughters.

V. Frances Malinda[9]—Born December 23, 1847, Ebenezer, Ga. Living 1924, Conyers, Ga. Married George W. Gleaton, June 30, 1875, Conyers, Ga. Issue: 1. John S[10]. Married Willie Hutton. 2. Stephen[10]. 3. Lucy[10]. 4. Sally Fanny[10].

VI. Martha Antoinette[9]—Born January 10, 1853, Conyers, Ga. Died June 12, 1863, Conyers, Ga.

VII. Mary Matilda Stansell[9]—Born April 27, 1856, Conyers, Ga. Married Walter Eudox McCalla, July 23, 1878, Conyers, Ga. Died April 30, 1895, Decatur, Ga., and was buried there. No children.

VIII. Thomas Dilworth[9]—Born April 7, 1857, Conyers, Ga. Merchant and Realtor. Living 1924, Atlanta, Ga. Married Ida J. Kiser, October 15, 1879, Atlanta, Ga. Issue: 1. Nellie Kiser[10]. Married Ewing Dean, of Atlanta, Ga. 2. Mary Cliff[10].

IX. Jackson Benjamin Levi[9]—Born August 27, 1858, Conyers, Ga. Died April 28, 1881. Never married.

X. Jefferson Davis[9]—Born June 14, 1868, Conyers, Ga. Manufacturer and banker. Living, 1924, Louisville, Ky. Married Abby Churchill Ballard, June 1, 1899, Louisville, Ky., daughter of Charles Thurston and Mina (Breaux) Ballard, Louisville, Ky. Issue: 1. Abby Ballard[10]. 2. Jefferson Davis, Jr.[10].

I-9. JOHN ARCHIBALD BELLAH STEWART

Son of John Lewis[8] and Julis Ann Hollingsworth[8] Stewart. (Of Joseph[7], Joseph[6], Abraham[5], George[4], Abraham[3], Thomas[2], Valentine[1].) Born December 2, 1840, Ebenezer, Rockdale Co., Ga. Died June 2, 1891, Covington, Ga. Buried Conyers, Ga. Merchant. In the Confederate Army. Married April 4, 1867, Kitty Tennessee King, daughter of Joseph and Catharine Anne King, of Atlanta, Ga.

Issue

I. Joseph King[10]—Born February 17, 1870. Died July 21, 1913. Married September, 1896, Corinne Bickel, of Louisville, Ky. Manufacturer and capitalist, at Louisville, Ky. Issue: Helen[11]—Married Leslie McCord, III, of Pulaski. Tenn.

II. Julia Hollingsworth[10]—Born April 28, 1872. Living 1924, Shreveport, La. Married Covington, Ga., July 21, 1892, Rev. Jasper Keith Smith, son of William F. C. and Effie (McNair) Smith, of Conyers, Ga. Pastor of First Presbyterian Church, Shreveport, La. Issue: 1. Jasper Stewart[11]—Married Lois Gibson. 2. Marion King[11]—Married Gladys Backenstoe. 3. Walter Grances[11]. 4. Catharine Anne[11]—Married Robert E. Edgar. 5. Julia Anne[11]. 6. Jasper Keith, Jr.[11]. 7. Ralph Archibald[11]. 8. Robert McNair[11].

III. Eudox McCalla[10]—Died young.

IV. Mary[10]—Born July 3, 1878. Living 1924. Married Beverly Wall, of Augusta, Ga. Issue: 1. Margaret[11]. 2. Beverly C.[11]. 3. Joseph[11].

I-9. JOSEPH ALEXANDER STEWART.

Son of John Lewis and Julia Ann[s] (Hollingsworth) Stewart. Born October 17, 1845, at Ebenezer, Ga. Died July 31, 1890 at Covington, Ga. Married January 30, 1873, in Newbern, Ga., Carrie Julia Robinson, born February 19, 1852. Living Atlanta, Ga., 1924. Daughter of James Hardwick and Martha (Webb) Robinson. Joseph Alexander was the grandson of Alexander and Sarah (Stripling) Stewart, and the great-grandson of Alexander and Elizabeth (Barron) Stewart.

ISSUE

I. James Hardwick Robinson[10]. Unmarried. Atlanta, Ga.

II. Joseph Adger[10]—Married Anna Briggs Carter, Louisville, Ky.

III. Estelle[10]—Married George Kearsley Selden, of Atlanta, Ga.

IV. Mary Daisy[10]—Married Walter F. Roberts, of Utica, N. Y.

V. Emma Lucille[10]—Died young. Buried Conyers, Ga.

VI. Ann Eloise[10]—Married James P. Champion, of Albany, Ga.

VII. Francis Josephine[10]—Married Dr. Hugh I. Battey, of Atlanta, Ga.

VIII. Anita[10]—Married R. Blair Armstrong, of Atlanta, Ga.

J-10. JOSEPH ADGER STEWART

Manufacturer, Louisville, Ky., 1924. Son of Joseph Alexander[s] and Carrie Julia Robinson Stewart. Married Anna Briggs Carter, April 26, 1899, daughter of John Allen and Albana (Carson) Carter, of Louisville, Ky.

ISSUE

I. John Carter[11].   III. Joseph Alexander[11].
II. Joseph Adger, Jr[11].   IV. Jéan Hollingsworth[11].

H-8. LETITIA (HOLLINGSWORTH) STEWART

Daughter of Joseph[7] and Elizabeth Ann Jane Carr (Rogers) Hollingsworth (of Joseph[6], Abraham[5], George[4], Abraham[3], Thomas[2], Valentine[1]).
Born Laurens Co., S. C., about 1820. Moved to Georgia, 1825, with
parents. Died ...... Coosa Co., Ala. Married about 1838, Rev.
Benjamin Stewart, son of Alexander and Sarah Striplin Stewart.

ISSUE

I. William Addison[8]—Born August 22, 1839. Married Mary Swope.
    Issue: 1. Mark E[10]. 2. Benjamin Silvester[10]. 3. Charlie A[10].
    4. Largus W[10]. 5. Edgar L[10]. 6. Mary Salona[10]. 7. Ethel[10].
II. Martha Frances[8]—Born August 16, 1842. Died January 1, 1899.
III. Joseph A.—Born May 25, 1845. Married Emily Martin.
    Issue: 1. Lizzie[10]. 2. Frances[10]. 3. Benjamin D[10]. 4. Mary
    Eliza[10]. 5. Sula[10]. 6. Oscar[10].
IV. Sarah Elizabeth[8]—Born April 2, 1848. Married W. H. Tant.
    Issue: 1. James B[10]. 2. John William[10]. 3. Nettie[10]. 4. Leoma[10].
    5. Joseph M[10]. 6. Mattie Rae[10]. 7. Thomas D[10]. 8. Hardin
    Stewart[10].
V. John J[8].—Born September 3, 1850. Died June 9, 1917. Married
    Ella Kimbrough. Issue: 1. Lettie[10]. 2. John B[10]. 3. Eliza-
    beth[10]. 4. William[10]. 5. Joseph A[10]. 6. Levi[10].
VI. Julia A[8].—Born April 14, 1853. Died July 29, 1855.
VII. Mary Ann[8]—Born July 13, 1859. Married G. B. Culberson.
    Issue: 1. Walter J[10]. 2. Alma[10]. 3. Benjamin D[10]. 4. Edna[10].
    5. Mary[10].
VIII. Benjamin Thomas[8]—Born July 26, 1863. Died December 23,
    1892.

G-7. JOHN HOLLINGSWORTH

(Joseph[6], Abraham[5], George[4], Abraham[3], Thomas[2], Valentine[1]). Son
of Joseph[6] and Rosannah (Nichols) Hollingsworth. Born Laurens Co.,
S. C., November 4, 1794. Died in Georgia, 1876. Married Rebecca
Bailey, in Laurens Co., S. C., October 9, 1817. She was born in South
Carolina, April 10, 1799. Died in Georgia, August 29, 1866. Both
buried at Smyrna, Rockdale Co., Ga.

ISSUE

I. Emily⁴—Born in South Carolina, September 5, 1818. Died in Texas, 1902. Married 1837, Littleton Talley. Issue: 9 children.

II. William H.⁸—Born in South Carolina, December 24, 1822. Died in Georgia, April 13, 1837.

III. James Milton⁸—Born in South Carolina, December 24, 1822. Died October 29, 1899. Married Martha⁸ Hollingsworth, daughter of Moses⁷ Hollingsworth. Issue: 11 children.

IV. Wesley⁸—Born in South Carolina, March 27, 1825. Married Amanda Coon. Both buried Polk Co., Ga. No issue.

V. Charlotte⁸—Born in South Carolina, March 31, 1828. Died about 1897, in Tennessee. Married Pressley Abney, at First Camp Meeting held at Smyrna. Issue: John Abney⁹, of San Francisco, and 2 daughters.

VI. Martha⁸—Born in South Carolina, March 18, 1831. Moved to Georgia when two years old. Living 1917, Newton Co., Ga. Married October 5, 1848, Wm. Jackson Knight. Issue: 8 sons and 5 daughters. Living with son, J. J. Knight⁹, R.F.D. No. 2, McDonough, Ga. Has father's family bible.

VII. John Newton⁸—Born Newton Co., Ga., September 7, 1833. Soldier in Confederate Army. Died November 11, 1862, at Knoxville, Tenn., of pneumonia. Buried at Smyrna. Married Letty Stowers, 1852. Issue: 1 son, Thomas⁹, and 1 daughter, Sallie M. Stowers⁹.

VIII. Rebecca Jane⁸—Born Newton Co., Ga., February 14, 1836. Never married. Living 1918, with sister, Mrs. Martha Hollingsworth Knight.

H-8. JAMES MILTON HOLLINGSWORTH

Son of John⁷. (Joseph⁶, Abraham⁵, George⁴, Abraham³, Thomas², Valentine¹). Born in Laurens Co., S. C., December 24, 1822. Moved to Newton Co., Ga., with his father, in 1831. Married Martha Hollingsworth (who was born in Laurens Co., S. C., December 21, 1828) at Smyrna Camp Meeting, October 23, 1845. (Charlotte Hollingsworth and Jeff Abney were married at the same time and place). James Milton Hollingsworth died October 29, 1889.

Martha Hollingsworth, wife of James Milton, was the daughter of Elizabeth Rodgers Hollingsworth and Moses Hollingsworth.

Issue

I. Rebecca E[9].—Born September 19, 1846. Married Joe Granade. December 1866. Living in Rockdale ˙Co., Ga., in 1924., Issue: Marshall Walter Granade[10].

II. John Newton[9]—Born May 25, 1848. Died July 9, 1850.

III. Moses Jefferson[9]—Born May 30, 1850. Married Annie Hamilton. 3 children died in infancy. Died May 7, 1884.

IV. Mary Ann[9]—Born April 30, 1854. Married E. Jasper Argo, October 12, 1871. Living at Decatur, Ga., 1924. Issue: 1. Charlie[10]. 2. Martha[10]. 3. Susannah[10]. 4. William Milton[10]. Died in infancy. 5. Mary Euna[10]. Unmarried. 6. James Thomas[10]. 7. Joseph Madison[10]. 8. John Weyman[10].

V. William Madison[9]—Born April 4, 1856. Died July 17, 1887. Married Angie Boyd. Issue: 1. John Milton[10]. 2. Charlie[10]. 3. Lillie[10].

VI. Nancy Jane[9]—Born September 7, 1857. Died in infancy.

VII. Samuel Levi[9]—Born September 14, 1858, Newton Co., Ga. Married Mary Leila Marbut, December 21, 1876. Died Augusta, Ga., March 13, 1910. Issue: 1. Adah Viola[10]—Born November 17, 1877. Married Chas. W. Bowen, January 22, 1900. Living in Augusta, Ga., 1924. Issue: a. Charles W., Jr[11]. b. Dudley H[11]. c. Moselle[11]. 2. P. Virgil Hollingsworth[10]—Born May 10, 1879. Married Mattie Lou Greene, December 6, 1905. Living at Augusta, Ga., 1924. Issue: P. Virgil, Jr[11]. Born September 16, 1906. Issue: Martha Ann[12]. 3. Libbie Estelle[10]—Born February 5, 1881. Married W. W. Zealy, December 11, 1902. Living in Augusta, Ga., in 1924. Issue: a. Mary[11]. b. Martha[11]. c. W. W. Jr[11]. d. Sarah[11]. e. Samuel Hollingsworth[11]. 4. Winfred[10]—Died in infancy. 5. Otis Weyman[10]—Died in infancy. 6. Grady Dewitt[10]—Unmarried. Living in Cleveland, Ohio, 1920. 7. Lois[10]—Died in infancy. 8. Earl Crisp[10]—Married Margaret Marks, March 21, 1916. Living in Augusta, Ga., 1924. Issue: a. Margaret[11]. b. Mary Jane[11]. c. Earl, Jr[11]. 9. Willie Bryan[10]—Died May 19, 1901.

VIII. Susannah E[9].—Born March 19, 1861. Married W. Y. Nelms, 1877. Living in Fulton Co., Ga., in 1924. Issue: 1. Elizabeth[10]. 2. Elpheus[10]. 3. William[10]. 4. Milton[10]. 5. Izora[10]. 6. Lillie May[10]. 7. Perron[10]. 8. Bowman[10]. 9. Samuel Levi[10].

IX. James Milton, Jr².—Born May 25, 1863. Married Ida Granade.
Died April 14, 1888. Issue: Mamie¹⁰. Unmarried.
X. Joseph Andrew H⁹.—Born October 1, 1865. Died January 27,
1887.
XI. Hezekiah Lewis⁹—Born October 1, 1868. Died April 1, 1898.
Unmarried.

G-7. WILLIAM ("BILLIE") HOLLINGSWORTH

(Joseph⁶, Abraham⁵, George⁴, Abraham³, Thomas², Valentine¹). Son of
Joseph⁶ and Rosannah (Nichols) Hollingsworth. Born Laurens Co.,
S. C., March 3, 1799. Died March 28, 1883. Married January 11,
1826, Parmelia McDowell, born June 20, 1808.

ISSUE

I. Martha Frances⁸—Born June 25, 1827. Died July 31, 1842.
Unmarried.
II. John Wesley⁸—Born November 23, 1829. Married Mary J.
Marbutt.
III. Robert Henry⁸—Born November 25, 1832. Married Sarah Mar-
butt. Died December 27, 1910.
IV. James Franklin⁸—Born October 21, 1835. Married Addie Os-
born.
V. Thomas Jefferson⁸—Born November 15, 1838. Died September
2, 1910. Married Frances Reagan.
VI. Mary Jane⁸—Born October 5, 1841. Married A. J. Ogletree.
Died January 12, 1903.
VII. Parmelia Ann⁸—Born August 3, 1844. Married Geo. W. Warren.

H-8. JAMES FRANKLIN HOLLINGSWORTH

(William⁷, Joseph⁶, Abraham⁵, George⁴, Abraham³, Thomas², Valen-
tine¹.) Son of William⁷. Born Rockdale Co., Ga., October 21, 1835.
Died Atlanta, Ga., March 9, 1914. Married March 1, 1860, Sarah
Adeline Ozburn, who was born Clayton Co., Ga., December 14, 1836.
Died Atlanta, Ga., February 11, 1899. Contractor and builder.

ISSUE

I. Lizzie Catharine[9]—Born Rockdale Co., Ga., January 4, 1861. Living 1924, Atlanta, Ga. Married November 14, 1882, Atlanta, Ga., George Titus Lewis, born West Troy, N. Y., March 29, 1852. Issue: 1. William Thompson[10]—Born Atlanta, Ga., July 17, 1884. Died June 13, 1885. 2. Sarah Eliza[10]—Born August 28, 1885. Died June 3, 1886. 3. Bertha Lucinda[10]—Born November 12, 1887. Living 1924, Detroit, Mich. Married C. H. Adams. 4. George Titus[10]—Born December 30, 1888. Living 1924, Decatur, Ga. 5. Erma Lizzie[10]—Born August 31, 1890. Died Atlanta, Ga., February 10, 1915. Married E. H. Thomas. 6. Stephen John[10]—Born September 6, 1892. Living 1924, Atlanta, Ga. 7. Julian Hollingsworth[10]—Born October 6, 1894. Living 1924, Birmingham, Ala. 8. Eunice[10]—Born October 1, 1899. Died October 4, 1899.

II. Martha Frances[9]—Born March 26, 1862. Living, 1924, Atlanta, Ga. Married June 21, 1881, David Graves Hall, of Atlanta, Ga., who was born November 1, 1858. Died September 18, 1902. Issue: 1. Charlotte[10]—Born Atlanta, Ga., July 12, 1882. Living 1924. Married T. H. McCrea.

III. Charles McMurry[9]—Born December 15, 1865. Living 1924, Dalton, Ga. Manufacturer. Married June 14, 1893, Marie Amina Latimer, at Marietta, Ga. Issue: 1. Marie Amina[10]—Born Atlanta, Ga., May 28, 1894. Living 1924, Lancaster, Pa. Married Myron William Jones. 2. Joseph Latimer[10]—Born May 11, 1897. Second Lieut., Departmental. Died Silver City, N. M., October 21, 1921. 3. Helen[10]—Born December 16, 1900. Living 1924, Dalton, Ga. 4. Adelle Septima[10]—Born December 10, 1907. Living 1924.

IV. William Franklin[9]—Born March 22, 1867. Living 1924, Atlanta, Ga. Minister and Educator. Married February 17, 1904, Julia Crabtree Castex, of Goldsboro, N. C. Issue: 1. Louis Castex[10]—Born November 21, 1904. Living 1924, Atlanta, Ga. Student. 2. James Franklin[10]—Born July 22, 1906. Living 1924. Student.

V. Alonzo Judson[9]—Born December 26, 1869. Living 1924, Atlanta, Ga. Married February 22, 1913, Frankie Clark Sweets, at Atlanta, Ga. Issue: 1. Francis Adeline[10]—Born August 28, 1916. 2. Margaret Ellen[10]—Born June 2, 1919.

VI. James Victor⁹—Born December 5, 1872, Conyers, Ga. Living 1924, Atlanta, Ga. Married first at Los Angeles, Cal., February 15, 1899, Carolyn Toby Folger, who was born at Charlestown, Mass., November 7, 1872. Died October 20, 1921, Atlanta, Ga. He then married March 31, 1923, Ivah Belle Emmett. Issue: 1. Victor Folger¹⁰—Born July 29, 1901. Living 1924, Atlanta, Ga. 2. Winslow Francis¹⁰—Born November 23, 1904. Living 1924, Atlanta, Ga.

VII. Arthur⁹—Born March 1, 1877. Died in infancy.

VIII. Beulah Gertrude⁹—Born April 5, 1878, Conyers, Ga. Living, 1924, Atlanta, Ga. Married, April 8, 1903, Reginald Herbert Knapp, of Atlanta, Ga., who was born March 25, 1876. Died May 5, 1921. Issue: 1. Adeline¹⁰—Born July 27, 1904. Died March 28, 1906. 2. Beulah Hollingsworth¹⁰—Born October 27, 1905. Living 1924, Atlanta, Ga. 3. Reginald Herbert¹⁰—Born August 6, 1907. Living 1924, Atlanta, Ga.

G–7. MOSES HOLLINGSWORTH

(Joseph⁶, Abraham⁵, George⁴, Abraham³, Thomas², Valentine¹). Son of Joseph⁶ and Rosannah (Nichols) Hollingsworth. Born Laurens Co., S. C., February 1, 1801. Died November 15, 1862. Married September 26, 1821, Elizabeth Rogers. She was born January 28, 1801, and died July 4, 1875.

Issue

I. Henry Milton⁸—Born August 3, 1822. Died October 28, 1822.

II. Newton⁸—Born September 28, 1823. Died .... Married December 21, 1843, Jane Stewart.

III. Susannah⁸—Born October 23, 1825. Died ...... Married September 21, 1843, Samuel Knight.

IV. Martha⁸—Born December 21, 1827. Died July 13, 1892. Married October 20, 1845, James Milton Hollingsworth (Cousin).

V. William⁸—Born February 14, 1830. Died April 17, 1862, in the the Confederate Army, Ashland, Va.

VI. Rosanna⁸—Born January 16, 1832. Died ...... Married December 14, 1854, John Plunkett.

VII. Letty⁸—Born January 9, 1834. Died August 9, 1835.

VIII. James⁸—Born March 23, 1836. Died .... Married May 19 1864, Martha W. Warren.

IX. John⁸—Born February 21, 1838. Died July 22, 1838.

X. Joseph⁸—Born April 23, 1839. Died July 22, 1862, at Camp Wade, C. S. A., Richmond, Va.

XI. Nancy⁸—Born April 20, 1842. Died .... Married May 7, 1863, J. B. Almand.

Other records from Bible of Moses Hollingsworth:

W. A. Rogers—Died January 6, 1837

Jane Caldwell—Died January 7, 1835.

James Hollingsworth—Died March 2, 1831.

Nancy Rogers—Died June, 1846.

George Hollingsworth—Died August 2, 1846. Age 36.

Nancy R. Rogers—Died January 13, 1853.

Rosannah Nichols Hollingsworth—Died March 10, 1839.

Joseph Hollingsworth—Died April, 1844.

G–7. AARON HOLLINGSWORTH

(Joseph⁶, Abraham⁵, George⁴, Abraham³, Thomas², Valentine¹). Son of Joseph⁶ and Rosannah (Nichols) Hollingsworth. Born Laurens Co., Co., S. C., February 23, 1803. Died January 29, 1887. Married February 10, 1829, to Ruth Rogers, who was born August 6, 1809, and died August 31, 1886.

Issue

I. George W.⁸—Born November 12, 1829. Married Malinda Knight.

II. James M.⁸—Born June 1, 1831. Died September 5, 1833.

III. Nancy⁸—Born October 23, 1832.   Married James M. Butler.

IV. Joseph⁸—Born August 10, 1834. Married Jane Knight.

V. William⁸—Born October 15, 1836. Died June 6, 1864, Lynchburg, Va., C. S. A. Married Mary Ann Johnson.

VI. Rosannah Jane⁸—Born April 22, 1838. Married Samuel G. Young.

VII. Robert⁸—Born October 30, 1840. Married Nancy P. Leftwich.

VIII. Mary⁸—Born November 12, 1842. Died 1908. Married Wm. H. Brisendine.

IX. Josiah⁸—Born April 5, 1845. Died April 19, 1845.

X. Aaron⁸—Born June 11, 1846. Died February 10, 1870. Married Sallie Leftwich.

XI. Moses⁸—Born April 25, 1848.. Died June 9, 1853.

Aaron Hollingsworth also reared his niece, Maretina E. Hollingsworth⁸—Born December 10, 1843. She married John M. Leftwich.

G–7. MARY (HOLLINGSWORTH) ROGERS

Daughter of Joseph⁴ and Rosannah (Nichols) Hollingsworth. Born Laurens Co., S. C., October 11, 1805. Died June 13, 1847. Married January 13, 1825, to Nathaniel Rogers. who was born August 8, 1803, and died April 20, 1882. After Mary's death Nathaniel Rogers married Nancy Johnson Hollingsworth (widow of George⁷ Hollingsworth) and they had 7 children.

Issue 1st Marriage

    I. Emiline⁸—Born September 6, 1828. Married ...... Plunkett. She was living 1917.

    II. Joseph L.⁸—Born July 23, 1830. Married ...... Stowers.

    III. Wm. Henry⁸—Born September 19, 1833.

    IV. James Milton⁸—Born June 12, 1837.

    V. Richard W.⁸—Born October, 1838. Married Mattie Disson, nee Tucker.

    VI. Rosannah⁸—Born July 22, 1840. Never married.

    VII. James Milton⁸—Born August 15, 1842.

    VIII. John Thomas⁸—Born December 26, 1843. Married Matilda Leftwich.

    IX. Mary Nathaniel⁸—Born January 14, 1846.

Issue 2nd Marriage

    X. Martha Riddle⁸—Born September 15, 1848.

    XI. Ely M⁸.—Born September 17, 1850.

    XII. Amanda Jane⁸—Born March 27, 1852.

    XIII. Sidney Wilson⁸—Born August 22, 1853.

    XIV. Nancy Caroline⁸—Born December 10, 1855.

    XV. Tracy M⁸.—Born December 12, 1857.

    XVI. Susannah C⁸.—Born December 7, 1861.

G–7. MARTHA (HOLLINGSWORTH) ROGERS

Daughter of Joseph and Rosannah (Nichols) Hollingsworth. Born September 11, 1808. Died March 30, 1888. Married December 24, 1829, George Rogers, who was born January 13, 1804, and died March 1889.

Issue

    I. Jane⁸—Born August 29, 1830. Married William Farmer. Issue: 4 children; living, 1918.

II. Martha Frances[1]—Born May 18, 1832. Married Mathew Sorrow. Issue: 13 children; 3 living 1917.
III. James Henry[1]—Born May 14, 1834. Married Katherine Wallace, Texas.
IV. Katherine[1]—Born June 3, 1836. Married Benjamin Jacob Wallace. Issue: 3 children; 1 living 1917.
V. Mary[1]—Born July 1, 1838. Died May 19, 1851.
VI. Rosannah[1]—Born June 2, 1840. Died .... Unmarried.
VII. Samuel Riddle[1]—Born July 5, 1842. Died in Civil War at Vicksburg, Miss., July 27, 1863.
VIII. Nancy Adaline[1]—Born December 5, 1844. Married Young Drewry Butler. Issue: 5 children.
IX. Susannah[1]—Born June 21, 1848. First married Daniel Murdock, and then Wm. Thomas Butler.

G–7. GEORGE HOLLINGSWORTH

(Joseph[6], Abraham[5], George[4], Abraham[3], Thomas[2], Valentine[1]). Son of Joseph[6] and Rosannah (Nichols) Hollingsworth. Born Laurens Co., S. C., October 9, 1810. Died August 21, 1846. First married about 1835, to Elizabeth Jackson, who was born March 10, 1818, and died January 11, 1844. Second wife, Nancy Johnson. After his death his widow Nancy (Johnson) Hollingsworth married Nathaniel Rogers.

Issue 1st Marriage

I. William R.[1]—Married Nesie Sims.
II. James H.[1]—Married Mary Leftwich.
III. Margaret[1]—Born 1841. Married Benjamin Butler.
IV. Marthenia[1]—Born December 10, 1843. Died November 25, 1914. Married December 13, 1866, John M. Leftwich.

Issue 2nd Marriage

V. George[1]—First married Frances Leftwich. Second wife Sammons.
VI. Annie[1]—Married William K. Sims.

H–8. JAMES HOLLINGSWORTH

(Joseph[7], Joseph[6], Abraham[5], George[4], Abraham[3], Thomas[2], Valentine[1]). Son of Joseph[7] and Elizabeth Ann Jane Carr (Rogers) Hollingsworth. Born Laurens Co., S. C., August 1, 1817. Died Mobile, Ala., Sept. 23, 1864. Married Joyce Eppison of Ebenezer, Newton Co., Ga. She was born September 22, 1820. Died Lake Village, Ark., March 7, 1888. James Hollingsworth was a brick manufacturer. Died in the Confederate Army.

Issue

I. William Adolphus[9]—Born June 30, 1840. Died at Newman, Ga., January 21, 1855.

II. Mary Elizabeth[9]—Born January 13, 1843. Died at Newman, Ga., March 8, 1851.

III. George Washington[9]—Born March 16, 1844, at Talapoosa, Ala. Served in Confederate Army. Married Amanda Smith, Horse Shoe Bend, Tallapoosa, Ala. Died .... Issue: 2 sons and 1 daughter.

IV. Joseph Andrew[9]—Born Tallapoosa Co., Ala., November 29, 1847. Living 1917, near Hollandale, Miss. First married February 29, 1876, to Nannie Carmon, who died October 22, 1894. Issue: 4 children—Born Hollandale, Miss.: 1. Clarence[10]—Born April 3, 1877. Married Mary McGraw. Issue: 5 children. 2. Glennis[10]—Born April 18, 1879. Married L. F. Gregory. Issue: 3 sons. 3. Jessie[10]—Born August 17, 1882. 4. Farrar[10]—Born December 4, 1886. Married Clarice McGraw. Issue: 4 children. Joseph Andrew then married Ella Barfield, January 31, 1905. She died October 19, 1908. Issue: 1 son. 5. Jack[10]—Born January 1, 1906.

V. James Madison[9]—Born Griffin, Ga., July 1, 1850. Never married. Living 1917, ..., La.

VI. John Lewis[9]—Born October 21, 1853, Tallapoosa, Ala. Died in Louisiana. Left large family.

VII. Levi Wilson[9]—Born October 4, 1857. Died November 11, 1874.

VIII. Robert Jasper[9]—Born Tallapoosa Co., Ala., May 10, 1860. Married Carl (?) Green. Issue: 2 sons and 2 daughters.

IX. Samuel Dixon[9]—Born Tallapoosa Co., Ala., November 11, 1863. Died ......, Lake Village, Ark. Left widow. Issue: 2 sons and 1 daughter.

H-8. ROSANNAH (HOLLINGSWORTH) SCOTT

(Joseph[7], Joseph[6], Abraham[5], George[4], Abraham[3], Thomas[2], Valentine[1].)
Daughter of Joseph[7] and Elizabeth Ann Jane (Carr Rogers) Hollingsworth. Born at Laurens, S. C., June 7, 1825. Died, Powder Springs, Ga. December 1, 1907. Married Wm. Winfield Scott, who was born Abbeville, S. C., November 7, 1818, and died Powder Springs, Ga., March 30, 1863. He was the son of Col. Samuel Scott, who was born ......, Edinburgh, Scotland. Came to America when a young man, locating in ......, Maryland. Married Jane Robinson, Pennsylvania. Moved to Virginia; afterwards to Abbeville, S. C., and Powder Springs, Ga., where he died, May 1856.

·Issue

I. Elizabeth Jane Scott[8]—Born Powder Springs, Ga., September 7, 1842. Died Atlanta, Ga., August 3, 1911. Married Thomas Franklin Maddox, December 20, 1866.

II. Samuel Joseph Scott[8]—Born Powder Springs, Ga., November 17, 1844. Living 1917, at Chickamauga, Tenn. Married December 23, 1869, Virginia Elizabeth Kemp.

III. Mary Isabella Scott[8]—Born Powder Springs, Ga., June 3, 1847. Died Atlanta, Ga., January 29, 1914. Unmarried.

IV. William Winfield Scott, Jr[8].—Born Powder Springs, Ga., January 25, 1851. Living 1918, at Smyrna, Ga.

V. Martha Thomas Scott[8]—Born Powder Springs, Ga., August 20, 1853. Died Powder Springs, Ga., January 3, 1916. Married Henry Addison Du Pre, December 28, 1879.

VI. Sarah Samanthia Scott[8]—Born Powder Springs, Ga., May 12, 1856. Living 1917, Atlanta, Ga. Unmarried.

VII. Emma Adelaide Scott[8]—Born Powder Springs, Ga., August 29, 1861. Married Eugene Alva White, in Atlanta, Ga., May 19, 1886. Living 1917, Smyrna, Ga. Issue: 1. Clarke Scott White[10]—Born Atlanta, Ga., July 21, 1887. Married Elizabeth Katherine Oxford, September 1, 1910. Issue: a. Katharine Adelaide[11]—Born July 4, 1911. b. Sara Pearl[11]—Born October 7, 1912. Living 1918, Atlanta, Ga.

H-8. JOSEPH A. HOLLINGSWORTH

(Joseph[7], Joseph[6], Abraham[5], George[4], Abraham[3], Thomas[2], Valentine[1]).
Son of Joseph[7] and Elizabeth Ann Jane Carr (Rogers) Hollingsworth. of Atlanta, Ga. Born Newton Co., Ga., July 2, 1835. Died Ensley,

Ala., July 5, 1903. Married January 10, 1861, to Lucy H. Mosely of Heard Co., Ga. He was a contractor.

ISSUE

I. Mary Elizabeth[9]—Born May 4, 1864. Married W. B. Bradbury. Living at 66 Arkwright Place, Atlanta, Ga., 1918. Issue.
II. William Henry[9]—Born December 5, 1867. Married Darthalow Griggs. Living 1918 at ...... St., Birmingham, Ala. No issue.
III. Joseph B[9].—Born August 31, 1870. Died April 5, 1888. Unmarried.
IV. James Edwin[9]—Born December 1, 1872, DeKalb Co., Ga. Married Katherine McKewen, of Atlanta, Ga. Living 1918, at Memphis, Tenn.; of the firm of J. E. Hollingsworth & Co., General Contractors. Issue: 1. Joseph Edwin[10]—Born Oct. 17, 1896, Shreveport, La. 2. Thelma Elizabeth[10]—Born August 26, 1900, Ensley, Ala. 3. Edna Earle[10]—Born December 9, 1904, Birmingham, Ala. Joseph Edwin[10]— With U. S. Army in France, 1918, 166th Ambulance Co., 42nd Div., 117th Sanitary Train.
V. Julian P.[9]—Born August 29, 1873.
VI. Robert Emmett[9]—Born September 1, 1877. Died when 6 months of age.
VII. Charles Armstrong[9]—Born February 29, 1881. Died July 8, 1883.

C-3. ZEBULON HOLLINGSWORTH

(Henry[2], Valentine[1]). Son of Henry[2] and Elizabeth Atkinson—Born 1696. Died in Cecil Co., Md., August 8, 1763, in his 67th year. First married April 18, 1727, Ann Maulden, daughter of Col. Francis Maulden, of Cecil Co., Md. (a son of Benjamin and Miss Mackall.) She died November, 1740. Married second wife, Mary Jacobs, July 25, 1741.

He was a large land owner, also a Magistrate and President of the Cecil County Court, Md.; a prominent member of St. Mary Ann's Church, one of the Vestrymen in 1743, also largely engaged in the manufacture of flour, with his son Levi, who afterwards removed to Philadelphia. He was kind and hospitable, a lover of toddy and good eating. He was the father of 11 sons and 2 daughters. He died in 1763, and was buried in the old graveyard on the Elk River, near his residence.

ISSUE 1ST MARRIAGE

I. Elizabeth—Born February 6, 1728. Married ...... Veazey.

II. Stephen—Born May 13, 1730. Unmarried.

III. Jesse—Born March 12, 1732. Married Sinai Ricketts. Died
September 30, 1810. More of him later.

IV. Zebulon—Born May 17, 1735, Cecil County. Died March 24,
1812. More of him later.

V Henry—Born September 17, 1737, Cecil County. Died September 29, 1803. More of him later.

VI. Levi—Born November 29, 1739. Died March 24, 1824. More
of him later.

ISSUE 2ND MARRIAGE

VII. Jacob—Born July 30, 1742. Died March 1, 1803.

VIII. Lydia—Born March 13, 1744. Died September 4, 1812.

IX. Thomas—Born August 2, 1747. Died September 5, 1815.

X. Stephen—Born February 28, 1749. Died December 10, 1822.

XI. John—Born May 12, 1752. Died September 30, 1808.

XII. David—Born August 12, 1754. Died July 18, 1775.

XIII. Samuel—Born January 17, 1757. Died May 9, 1830.

D-4. JESSE HOLLINGSWORTH

(Zebulon³, Henry², Valentine¹). Second son of Zebulon³ and Ann
(Maulden) Hollingsworth. Born in Cecil Co., Md., March 12, 1732.
Married about 1758, to Sinai Ricketts, daughter of Thomas and Mary
(Savency) Ricketts and grand-daughter of Florent Savency. She was
born May 22, 1737. Died December 4, 1786. He then married Rachel
L. Parkins, widow, maiden name Goodwin. She died in 1819; had one
son, who died in infancy. Her son, Thomas Parkins, by former marriage, died of yellow fever, 1797. Jesse died September 30, 1810, at
Woodville, Baltimore Co., the residence of his daughter, Mary (Mrs.
Yellott), in the 79th year of his age. His funeral took place October 1st,
from the Methodist Church on Light Street, Baltimore, Md. He was a
Captain of a company of Volunteers from Cecil County 1757. They
marched to the relief of Fort Cumberland. He came to Baltimore from
Cecil Co., Md., 1772, and purchased property on Fell's Point, and
1766 moved to Bank Street. He was a merchant of energy and enterprise, filling many important positions in the City and State.

ISSUE

    I. Mary[5]—Born August 18, 1760. Married Captain Jeremiah Yellot.

    II. Zebulon[5]—Born September 14, 1762. Married Elizabeth Ireland. He died August 7, 1824. More of Zebulon later.

    III. Horatio[5]—Born July, 1764. Died young.

    IV. George[5]—Born January 27, 1767. Died young.

    V. Ann[5]—Born February 9, 1766. Married Rev. Henry Willis· More of Ann later.

    VI. John[5]—Born August 10, 1771. Married Rachel Wilkins.

    VII. Francis[5]—Born August 1, 1773. Married Mary Yellott, 1801. More of Frances later.

FLORENT SOVENCY

He was a Huguenot, driven with his two sisters from their native country, by the revocation of the Edict of Nantes. The family was rich. He brought considerable wealth to America. He purchased real estate in Delaware and built the St. George's Mills. The sisters resided in London and often sent valuable presents. He married—second wife— Ann Price. His granddaughter, Sinai Ricketts, married Jesse Hollingsworth[4].

ISSUE 1ST MARRIAGE

    I. Mary—Married John Thomas Ap Ricketts, a Welch lawyer.

ISSUE 2ND MARRIAGE

    II. Caleb—Unmarried.

    III. Grace—Married Col. John Evans, near Elkton, Md.

    IV. Polly—Married Jonathan Booth.

    V. Sinai—Married Jesse Hollingsworth[4].

F-6. WILLIS HOLLINGSWORTH

(Francis[5], Jesse[4], Zebulon[3], Henry[2], Valentine[1]). Son of Francis[5] and Mary (Yellott) Hollingsworth—Born in Baltimore, December 31, 1816. Died September 15, 1853. Married Caroline A. Austin, in St. Louis, April 14, 1842.

ISSUE

I. Eliza E.[7]—Born March 20, 1843. Died August 20, 1843.
II. Mary[7]—Born July 17, 1845. Died August 27, 1853.
III. Clara A.[7]—Born August 18, 1847.
IV. Elizabeth A.[7]—Born March 9, 1851. Married Edmond O. Parker, January 1, 1874.
V. Willis C.[7]—Born April 14, 1854.
VI. Edward A.[7]—Born April 14, 1854.

D-4. ZEBULON HOLLINGSWORTH

(Zebulon[3], Henry[2], Valentine[1]). Of Cecil Co., Md., third son of Zebulon[3] and Ann (Maulden) Hollingsworth—Born 1735. Died 1812. Married Mary Evans of Cecil Co., Md., June 22, 1764.

Zebulon[4] Hollingsworth inherited the property at Elk Landing, Cecil Co., Pa.

ISSUE

I. Levi[5]—Born June 25, 1765. Died September, 1822. Married Ann Dorsey. More of Levi later.
II. Peggy[5]—Born December 27, 1766. Died September 4, 1833. Married William Couch.
III. Robert[5]—Born October 4, 1768. Died April 29, 1845. More of Robert later.
IV. William[5]—Born October 25, 1770. Died young.
V. James[5]—Born December 28, 1772. Died young.
VI. John[5]—Born November 18, 1774. Died June 18, 1840.
VII. William[5]—Born April 23, 1780. Died June 13, 1844. Married Mary Evans. She died March 19, 1871. More of William later.

E-5. LEVI HOLLINGSWORTH

Of Baltimore, son of the second Zebulon[4] Hollingsworth and his wife, Mary Evans of Cecil Co., Md. Levi was born in Cecil County, in 1765. Died in Baltimore, in 1822. Married Ann Dorsey.

ISSUE

I. Ann[6]—Married Parks Winchester.
II. Mary[6]—Unmarried.

III. Louisa[6]—Married Hon. William Pinkney Whyte, and had 3 children. Issue: 1. William Hollingsworth Whyte.[7] 2. Joseph
Whyte.[7] 3. E. Clymer Whyte[7].

Hon. Wm. Pinckney Whyte, attorney-at-law. Governor of Maryland, from 1872 to 1875. U. S. Senator from Maryland, 1875 to 1881.
Mayor of Baltimore, 1882 and 1883.

E-5. JUDGE ZEBULON HOLLINGSWORTH

(Jesse[4], Zebulon[3], Henry[2], Valentine[1]). Son of Jesse[4] and Sinai (Ricketts) Hollingsworth—Born September 14, 1762. Died August 7, 1824.
Married Elizabeth, daughter of Edward Ireland of Baltimore, in 1790.
She died in Baltimore, July 19, 1840. Was appointed U. S. District
Attorney, October 1792. Elected to the first City Council of Baltimore, 3d Ward, 1797. Associate Judge of the Baltimore County Court-
from 1806 to 1817. The first Agricultural Society in the U. S. A. was
formed in Baltimore, Md., March 3, 1786, of which Harry Dorsey Gough
was President and Zebulon Hollingsworth[5] was Secretary.

Issue

I. Mary[6]—Born December 30, 1791. Married Alexander Boyd.
Died December 27, 1866. More of Mary later.
II. Edward[6]—Born 1795. Married Deborah Moale. He died
October 23, 1871. Changed his name to Ireland, the name
of his maternal grandfather. More of Edward later.
III. Horatio[6]—Born about 1796. Married Emily Ridgely. He died
in Philadelphia. More of Horatio later.
IV. George[6]—Born 1798. Died young.
V. Jesse[6]—Born March 19, 1800. Died April 8, 1872. Married
Sophia Baker, daughter of Wm. Baker of Baltimore. More
of Jesse later.
VI. John[6]—Born 1802. Married Mary Ann Keene. He died 1841.
More of John later.
VII. Ann[6]—Born 1804 or '05. Married John Colhoon. Issue.
VIII. Susan[6]—Born 1809. Married James W. Welling. He died
August 13, 1862, in his 59th year. She died July 20, 1850;
age 41 years.

EDWARD IRELAND

Of Baltimore, Md., and a native of Barbadoes. Born December 2, 1736. Died July 17, 1816, age 79 years, 7 months and 15 days. Married Mary Cheeseman, born October 28, 1746. Died March 30, 1805, age 58 years, 6 months and 2 days. His daughter, Elizabeth, married Judge Zebulon Hollingsworth[5].

ISSUE

I. Ann Phillips—Born May 5, 1770. Died June 30, 1788.

II. Mary—Born May 11, 1772. Died January 9, 1792.

III. Elizabeth—Born April 22, 1774. Baptized May 29, by Rev. Wharton, at Barbadoes. She married Judge Zebulon[5] Hollingsworth, of Baltimore, 1790. She died July 19, 1840. He then married Susan Cheeseman, a sister of his first wife. All of his family are interred in St. Paul's Church Yard, Baltimore, Md.

F-6. MARY I. (HOLLINGSWORTH) BOYD

Zebulon[5], Jesse[4], Zebulon[3], Henry[2], Valentine[1].) Daughter of Judge Zebulon[5] and Elizabeth (Ireland) Hollingsworth, of Baltimore, born December 30, 1791. Died December 27, 1866, nearly 75 years old. Married May 13, 1813, Alexander H. Boyd, of Baltimore, Md. Born November 22, 1782. Died December 11, 1827.

ISSUE

I. Elizabeth Boyd[7]—Born about 1814. Married Charles Findlay. Issue: 1. Ellen Findlay[8]. 2. Henry D'A. Findlay[8]—Died July 26, 1877, in his 26th year. 3. Elizabeth Findlay[8]. 4. Charles Findlay[8]—Died young. 5. Mary Findlay[8].

II. Mary P. Boyd[7]—Lived in Baltimore.

III. Ellen Boyd[7]—Married William Findlay. No issue.

F-6. EDWARD (HOLLINGSWORTH)[6] IRELAND

(Zebulon[5], Jesse[4], Zebulon[3], Henry[2], Valentine[1].) Son of Zebulon[5] and Elizabeth (Ireland) Hollingsworth of Baltimore. Born January 22, 1795. Died in Baltimore, Md., October 23, 1871. Took the name of his maternal grandfather, Ireland. He married Deborah Moale, daughter of Thomas Moale, of Baltimore Co., Md. Born in 1798. Died September 17, 1883. Edward[6] was a farmer in Baltimore County, afterwards in Carroll County, and later removed with his family to Baltimore City.

Issue

I. Deborah[7]—Died young.
II. Edward[7]—Married Elizabeth Colhoon. Issue.
III. Mary[7]—Married Lewis Allen. Issue.
IV. Henrietta[7]—Died young.
 V. Alice[7]—Married Rev. A. H. Zimmerman. Issue.

F-6. HORATIO HOLLINGSWORTH

(Zebulon[5], Jesse[4], Zebulon[3], Henry[2], Valentine[1].) Son of Judge Zebulon[5] and Elizabeth (Ireland) Hollingsworth, of Baltimore. Born about 1796. He married Emily Ridgely. She died December 24, 1863. Residence, Baltimore County. He died in Philadelphia, Pa.

Issue

I. Matilda Elizabeth[7]—Married John H. Carroll. Issue: Gen.
      John N. Carroll[8].
II. Emily[7]—Died in 1844.
III. Henry[7]—Died.
IV. John McHenry[7]—Superintendent at Mt. Vernon, Va. Residence,
      Georgetown. Married Virginia Nichols, November 21, 1865.
 V. Francis[7]—Married Martha J. Bower. She died in Missouri. He
      died in Paris, Mo., April 14, 1853. Issue: A daughter, Emma[8], married Judge Broddus.
VI. Edward I.[7]—Died in Mexico, December 5, 1847.
VII. Thomas M.[7]—Died.
VIII. Caroline[7]—Living.
IX. Hester Francis[7]—Married. Died.

H-8. GENERAL JOHN N. CARROLL

Of "The Caves," Baltimore County, son of John H. and Matilda Elizabeth (Hollingsworth) Carroll, married Mary, daughter of Dr. John Hanson Thomas, of Baltimore. Issue: 2 sons.

F-6. JESSE HOLLINGSWORTH

(Zebulon⁵, Jesse⁴, Zebulon³, Henry², Valentine,¹). Son of Judge Zebulon⁵ and Elizabeth (Ireland) Hollingsworth—Born in Baltimore, March 19, 1800. Married June 15, 1826, to Sophia Baker, daughter of William Baker, of Baltimore. Residence in Carroll Co., Md., from 1820 to 1867. Died in the City of Baltimore, No. 62 McCulloh Street, April 8, 1872, in his 73rd year, leaving a widow and three children.

Issue

I. Zebulon⁷—Born August 28, 1827. Died April 3, 1861. Married September 17, 1855, Catharine F. Beam, of Baltimore County. Issue: William⁸ (son of Zebulon) was adopted by his uncle, H. J. Baker of New York, who changed his name to William H. Baker. He married Miss Cornell of New York. Issue: 2 children.

II. Anna B.⁷—Died April 10, 1870.

III. William B.⁷—Living in Baltimore, in 1884. Publisher of the HOLLINGSWORTH RECORD, 1884.

IV. Jesse⁷—Died August 21, 1845.

V. George H.⁷—Died February 13, 1863.

VI. Richard J.⁷—Living in Baltimore, in 1884. Married Josephine H. Coleman, May 28, 1878. Issue: 2 sons, 1 daughter; elder son died.

VII. Sophia L.⁷—Married Rev. Thomas J. Wyatt. She died November 1, 1864. Issue: 1. Wm. E⁸. 2. Sophie I⁸.

VIII. Jane⁷—Married John D. Smith, of Virginia. She died in 1877. 2 children died in 1876.

IX. Mary⁷—Died August 1, 1863.

F-6. JOHN HOLLINGSWORTH

(Zebulon⁵, Jesse⁴, Zebulon³, Henry², Valentine¹.) Son of Zebulon⁵ and Elizabeth (Ireland) Hollingsworth, of Baltimore, Md. Born in Baltimore, in 1802. Died at his residence, Finksburg, Carroll Co., Md., May 14, 1841. Married Ann Keene, of Baltimore.

Issue

I. Robert C⁷.—Died in California.

II. Susan W⁷.

III. Sallie G⁷.

IV. John H⁷.—Married Mattie E. Price. More of John later.
V. Mary R⁷.—Married Charles Duval.
VI. Annie⁷.
VII. Jessie⁷.

G-7. JOHN H. HOLLINGSWORTH

(John⁶, Zebulon⁵, Jesse⁴ Zebulon³, Henry², Valentine.¹) Son of John⁶ and Mary Ann (Keene) Hollingsworth, of Finksburg, Md. Married Mattie E. Price, of Baltimore County, daughter of John E. Price.

ISSUE

I. Mary R⁸.—Married Benjamin C. Ireland, June 10, 1879.
II. John H. K⁸.
III. Edward Z⁸.
IV. Cardiff S⁸.
V. Mattie E⁸.
VI. Annie⁸.
VII. Jessie⁸.
VII. Samuel⁸.
VIII. Susan W⁸.

E-5. ANN (HOLLINGSWORTH) WILLIS

Daughter of Jesse⁴ and Ann (Mauldin) Hollingsworth—Born February 9, 1766. Married Rev. Henry Willis.

ISSUE

I. Francis Willis⁶.
II. Jesse H. Willis⁶—Married Ann Winchester.
III. William Willis⁶—Married Mary McClure.
IV. Mary Willis⁶—Married Samuel C. Owings.
V. Henry Willis⁶—Married Sarah Hambleton.
VI. Jeremiah Willis⁶.

E-5. FRANCIS HOLLINGSWORTH

(Jesse⁴, Zebulon³, Henry², Valentine¹.) Son of Jesse⁴ and Sinai (Ricketts) Hollingsworth. Born in Baltimore, August 1, 1773. Died February 14, 1826. Married December 24, 1801, Mary, daughter of John Yellott. She was born November 1, 1783. Died August 31, 1864.

ISSUE   266246

I. Parkin[4]—Born November 7, 1802. Married Martha Kelso, in
1827. He died in 1837.

II. Ann[6]—Born February 4, 1804. Married Charles Warfield, in
1832.

III. Hannah[6]—Born September 13, 1805. Married Dr. Jesse L.
Warfield, in 1825.

IV. Francina[6], 1st—Born February 22, 1807. Died June, 1807.

V. Francina[6], 2nd—Born April 15, 1808. Living in 1884.

VI. Mary[6]—Born January 2, 1810. Died November 30, 1864.

VII. Elizabeth Y[6].—Born October 15, 1813. Married Jeremiah Y.
Armstrong, in 1837.

VIII. Willis[6]—Born December 31, 1816. Married Caroline A. Austin,
in 1842. More of Willis later.

John Yellott, the father of Mrs. Francis[5] Hollingsworth, emigrated
with his family from England, in 1791.

E–5. ROBERT HOLLINGSWORTH

(Zebulon[4], Zebulon[3], Henry[2], Valentine[1].)   Son of Zebulon[4] and Mary
(Evans) Hollingsworth, of Cecil Co., Md.   Born October 4, 1768. Died
April 24, 1845. Married Jane Talandier, in 1826. She died in May,
1830.

ISSUE

I. Samuel[6]—Born March 9, 1827. More of him later.

F–6. REV. SAMUEL HOLLINGSWORTH

(Robert[5], Zebulon[4], Zebulon[3], Henry[2], Valentine[1].)   Of Greenfield, Mass.
Son of Robert[5] and Jane (Talandier) Hollingsworth, of Cecil Co., Md.
Born March 9, 1827. Married September 13, 1849, Margaret Sarah
Forbes. She died November 27, 1879, at Hamilton, Bermuda.

ISSUE

I. Margaret[7]—Born August 2, 1853.

II. Emily[7]—Born August 5, 1858.

E-5. ROBERT HOLLINGSWORTH

(George⁴, Abraham³, Thomas², Valentine¹.) Of Winchester, Va. Son of George⁴ and Hannah (McCoy) Hollingsworth. Born 1744, in Frederick Co., Va. Died about 1799. Married Susanna Rice. His family moved to Simpsonville, Shelby Co., Ky. Susanna died in Kentucky. Buried in family graveyard at Simpsonville, Ky. Grave marked. Will dated July 15, 1792. Probated January 7, 1800, in Frederick Co., Va. He purchased land in Frederick Co., Va., November 19, 1767. Owner of 2,666 2-3 acres of land on Highland Creek, and 533 1-3 acres on Otter Creek (Military land).

Issue

I. George⁶—Born in 1770. Married Mary Gaunt, 1799, Frederick Co., Va.

II. Joseph⁶—Born 1773, Frederick Co., Va.

III. Lewis⁶—Born 1775. Married Abigail Parkins, 1814, Frederick Co., Va. More of Lewis later.

IV. Ruth⁶—Born 1776. Died in 1797, Frederick Co., Va.

V. Robert, Jr⁶.—Born 1779, Frederick Co., Va.

VI. Esther⁶—Born 1780. Married John Young, 1803. Died 1854.

VII. Abraham⁶—Born 1782. Married Nancy Connell. Left two daughters. Lived at West Union, Ohio.

VIII. Isaac⁶—Born 1784. Married .... Issue: 1. John⁷—Died. Left 3 children. 2. Susan⁷—Died. Left 7 children. 3. Robert⁷—Lived at Uniontown, Ky. More of Isaac later.

IX. John⁶—Born 1786. Married Sallie B. Green, 1827. A son, William R⁷. Lived in Iowa. More of John later.

X. Elizabeth⁶—Born 1787. Married ..... McFadden.

XI. James⁶—Born 1789. First married Susan Pleasant Russell. More of James later.

XII. Hannah⁶—Born 1791. Died in 1833. Buried at Simpsonville, Ky.

XIII. Susannah⁶—Born 1793. Married James Russell. More of Susannah later.

XIV. Edmund⁶—Born 1796. Married Melinda Ayres. Issue: 3 children. More of Edmund later.

F-6. JAMES HOLLINGSWORTH

(Robert[6], George[5], Abraham[4], Thomas[3], Valentine[1].) Of Simpsonville, Ky. Son of Robert[5] and Susanna (Rice) Hollingsworth, of Winchester, Va. Born October 21, 1789. Died December 5, 1869. He first married, about 1816, Susan Pleasant Russell, who died March 22, 1842. He then married Martha Mount Weakley, November 27, 1843.

ISSUE 1ST MARRIAGE

I. John P[7].—Born October 28, 1818. Died November 30, 1836. Buried Simpsonville, Ky.

II. Mary E[7].—Born May 24, 1820. Died July 5, 1900. Married Wm. Crapster. Issue: 1. Addie[8]. 2. Mary Frances[8]. 3. Jennie[8]. 4. Lizzie[8]. 5. John[8]. 6. Will[8]. 7. Susan[8].

III. William E[7].—Born June 2, 1822. Died March 14, 1892. Married September 16, 1851, Eugenia B. Davenport, of Crab Orchard, Ky. She died December 25, 1906. Colonel of 139th Indiana Regiment during the Civil War, 1861–66. Issue: 10 children. More of William E. later.

IV. Harriett R[7].—Born July 4, 1824. Died June 21, 1896. Married December 24, 1839, Wm. Barbour, of Lagrange, Ky. Issue: 6 children. More of Harriett later.

V. Thomas Jefferson[7]—Born July 17, 1826. Died April 25, 1888. Married 1861, Sarah Lewis, of Evansville, Ind., who was born at Evansville, February 1, 1834. Died June 18, 1917. Issue: 1. Lewis[8]—Born August 10, 1865. Died April 24, 1873. 2. Sadie Lewis[8]—Born November 13, 1867. Married November 30, 1892, Ben. G. Thompson, of Evansville, Ind. Lived there 1917. 3. Mamie[8]—Born November 19, 1869. Married June 30, 1895, Henry P. Conwick. Lived 1917, at Evansville, Ind.

VI. Susan H[7].—Born November 19, 1828. Lived 1917, at 2230 E St., Granite City, Ill. Married August 30, 1846, Horace B. Oliver, of Simpsonville, Ky., son of Horace and Elizabeth Oliver. Issue: 6 children. More of Susan H. later.

ISSUE 2ND MARRIAGE

VII. Bushrod[7]—Born August 21, 1844. Living 1918, at Danville, Ky. Married February 6, 1868, Sue Housworth. He died 1913. Issue: 1. Frank[8]—Married Ora Morgan. Issue: Lorine[9], Katherine[9], Frank Morgan[9]. 2. Stanley[8]—Married Vinnie Conley. No issue.

VIII. Melinda⁷—Born September 15, 1846. Died October 20, 1868. Married December 15, 1867, George Howell. Issue: Hattie Frances⁸—Born October 10, 1868. Married Wiley Wellman. Living 1917, 100 Roberta Ave., Louisville, Ky.

IX. Louisa⁷—Born February 15, 1849. Died November 20, 1878. Married Thomas Lyons. Issue: Loulie Lyons⁸—Born November 10, 1870. Married Miller Fields.

X. Ann Eliza⁷—Born March 7, 1852. Living 1918, at Simpsonville, Ky. Married November 6, 1873, to Thomas Elston. He died July 26, 1917. Issue: 1. Ferdinand⁸—Born July 29, 1874. 2. Margaret Louise⁸—Born November 22, 1876. 3. Malcolm⁸—Born October 10, 1878. 4. Hattie⁸—Born September 6, 1880. Died October 10, 1883. 5. Frances Belle⁸—Born November 25, 1882. 6. Patty May⁸—Born October 19, 1891.

XI. James Robert⁷—Born July 29, 1854. Died June 2, 1917. Married Mary Coddington. Issue: Leon⁸.

F-6. EDMUND HOLLINGSWORTH

(Robert⁵, George⁴, Abraham³, Thomas², Valentine¹.) Of Danville, Ky. Son of Robert⁵ and Susanna (Rice) Hollingsworth. Born 1793. Married Melinda Ayres.

Issue

I. Samuel⁷—Born 1833. Left home. Never heard from.
II. Dorothea J.⁷—Born 1837.
III. Eliza⁷—Born 1839.

E-5. WILLIAM HOLLINGSWORTH

(Zebulon⁴, Zebulon³, Henry², Valentine¹.) Son of second Zebulon⁴ and Mary (Evans) Hollingsworth. Born April 23, 1780. Died in Cecil County, June 13, 1844. Married Mary Evans, of Cecil Co., Md. She died March 19, 1871, in her 68th year. William was a State Senator from Cecil County in the Maryland Legislature, in 1812.

Issue

I. Dr. Robert⁵—Unmarried.
II. Isabella⁵—Married R. Covington Mackall.
III. Mary⁵—Unmarried.
IV. Margaret⁵—Married Dr. John H. Jamar.

D-4. COLONEL HENRY HOLLINGSWORTH

(Zebulon[3], Henry[2], Valentine[1].) Fourth son of Zebulon[3] and Ann (Maulden) Hollingsworth. All of Cecil Co., Md.—Born September 17, 1737. Died September 29, 1803. First married Sarah Husbands, in 1769. She died in 1775. Married second wife, Jane Evans, in 1778. Died September 29, 1850.

ISSUE 1ST MARRIAGE

I. Polly[5]—Born 1771. First married John Gilpin, September 28, 1797; then Frisby Henderson, 1819. Issue: First marriage (of Polly and John Gilpin): 1. John[6]—Deceased. Leaving children. 2. Henry H[6].—Deceased. Leaving 9 children. Eldest, Wm. R.[7] 3. Joseph[6]—Unmarried. 4. Mary[6]—Living at Elkton. 5. William H[6].—Living in Baltimore. Married.

II. William[5]—Born 1773. Married Ann Black. No issue.

ISSUE 2ND MARRIAGE

III. Hannah[5]—Born 1783. Married James Partridge.

IV. Betsy[5]—Born 1785. Died unmarried.

V. Nancy[5]—Born 1787. Married Rev. John Tally. Died. No issue.

VI. Henry[5]—Born 1790. Died unmarried.

Col. Henry Hollingsworth[4] was an enterprising and patriotic citizen. He was Lieutenant-Colonel of the Elk Battalion, in 1776. He served during the campaign under Washington, and was desperately wounded in the throat by a musket ball. In 1776 he contracted to furnish a lot of gun barrels and bayonets for the use of the army. In 1778 he was appointed one of the superintendents for the purchase of flour, cattle, and supplies for the army, and was frequently engaged by the Governors of Maryland and other States, and by the officers of the army, during the war.

E-5. ISAAC HOLLINGSWORTH ("BIG ISAAC")

(George[4], Abraham[3], Thomas[2], Valentine[1].) Son of George[4] and Hannah (McCoy) Hollingsworth. Born in 1737. Died 1809. Married Susanna, daughter of John Wright.

The family moved from Frederick Co., Va., to Bush River Meeting, Newberry Co., S. C., and in 1805, to Miami Co., Ohio. They died and were buried in West Branch Meeting Grave Yard. Susanna Hollingsworth and her sister, Charity Cook, daughters of John Wright, were ministers of the Friends Society. Isaac Hollingsworth⁵ was a man of great physical courage, over six feet high and of stalwart form, and of wonderful strength. Of all of the Newberry (S. C.) immigrants, none was equal to the Hollingsworths in physical strength, and none excelled them in courage. Being of peaceful nature and of superior prowess, quarrels were not sought by them.

Issue

    I. William⁶—Born .... Married Rebecca Ramsey.
   II. Joel⁶—Born December 29, 1773. Married Annie B. Connell. Died 1863.
 III. Isaac⁶—Born .... Died young.
 IV. John⁶—Born .... Married Mary Ramsey.
   V. Kesiah⁶—Born .... Married Robert Pierson.
 VI. Ruth⁶—Born .... Married John Pierson.
VII. Rachel⁶—Born .... Married Richard Henderson.
VIII. Sarah⁶—Born .... Married 1807, Samuel or Joseph Stanton.
 IX. Susanna⁶—Born .... Married Elisha Jones.

F-6. JOEL HOLLINGSWORTH

(Isaac⁵, George⁴, Abraham³, Thomas², Valentine¹.) Son of Isaac⁵ and Susanna (Wright) Hollingsworth. Born December 29, 1778. Died in 1847. Married Annie B. Connell. She died in 1863.

Issue

    I. Rachel⁷—Married John Coppie.
   II. Sophia⁷—Married James Lundy.
 III. Susanna⁷—Married John Pemberton.
 IV. Joseph⁷—First married Margaret Coat; then married Lydia .....
   V. Rhoda⁷—Married Aaron Vandyke.
 VI. Absalom⁷—Born 1812. First married Annie Pemberton; then married Druella Small.
 VII. Cyrus⁷.
VIII. Ruth⁷—Married Barney Bushby.
 IX. Isaac⁷—First married Elizabeth Miller; then married Phoebe H. Johnson, and finally Penina Cosand.
   X. Leodica⁷—Married Joseph McCoy.
 XI. Yates⁷—Married Nancy Mott.
XII. Annie B⁷.—Married Dudley Miller.

G–7. ISAAC HOLLINGSWORTH

(Joel[5], Isaac[5], George[4], Abraham[3], Thomas[2], Valentine[1].) Son of Joel[5] and Annie B. (Connell) Hollingsworth. First married Elizabeth Miller. He then married Phoebe H. Johnson. No issue. He finally married Penina Cosand.

ISSUE 1ST MARRIAGE

- I. Mary[6]—Born 1844.
- II. Harvey M. C[6].—Born 1849.
- III. John W[6].—Born 1851.

ISSUE 3RD MARRIAGE

- IV. Benj. C[6].—Born 1859.
- V. Samuel L[6].—Born 1861.
- VI. Lindley M[6].—Born 1863.
- VII. Clarkson[6]—Born 1865.
- VIII. Hanna M[6].—Born 1868.
- IX. Calvin W[6].—Born 1871.

E–5. JOSEPH HOLLINGSWORTH

(George[4], Abraham[3], Thomas[2], Valentine[1].) Son of George[4] and Hannah (McCoy) Hollingsworth and brother of Abraham[5] of Laurens, S. C. Born in 1735. First married, about 1761, ... Frost. He then married Margaret Hammer, nee Wright. Went to Bush River, S. C., in 1768.

ISSUE 1ST MARRIAGE

- I. Jonathan[6]—Married Mary Ramsey, 1786.
- II. David[6]—Married Catherine Nickle. Issue: 5 children.

ISSUE 2ND MARRIAGE

- III. Abraham[6]—Born 1769. First married Eunice Steddom. He then married Sarah Pidgeon, 1817.
- IV. Isaac[6]—First married Hannah Crem. Married again ....
- V. Jacob[6]—Married Martha Henderson.
- VI. John[6]—Married ......
- VII. Joseph[6]—Married Hannah Hawkins.
- VIII. Zebulon[6]—Married ....
- IX. Ezekiel[6]—First married Jane Hollingsworth. Married again.....

X. Charity[6]—Married Miles Kelley.
XI. William[6]—Born January 18, 1785. Married Margaret Cook, who
was born November 18, 1794, and died March 26, 1850. William died September 24, 1855.
XII. Susanna[6]—Married Eli Hudson.

F-6. JONATHAN HOLLINGSWORTH

(Joseph[5], George[4], Abraham[3], Thomas[2], Valentine[1].) Son of Joseph[5]
and ...... (Frost) Hollingsworth. Born in Virginia, 1763. Died
1851. Married Mary Ramsey, 1786. Born in Georgia, 1767. She
died 1851; age 84 years and 6 months.

ISSUE

I. Isaiah[7]—Born 1788. Died 1873. Married Patience Smith, 1811.
Born, 1794. Died, 1877.
II. Sally[7].
III. Miriam[7].
IV. Rebecca[7].
V. Ebert[7].
VI. Abijah[7].

D-4. LEVI HOLLINGSWORTH

(Zebulon[3], Henry[2], Valentine[1].) Of Philadelphia, Pa. Son of Zebulon[3]
and Ann (Mauldin) Hollingsworth, of Maryland. Born in Cecil Co.,
Md., November 29, 1739. Died in Philadelphia, March 24, 1824.
Married Hannah Paschall, March 10, 1768.

ISSUE

I. Stephen Paschall[5]—Born March 11, 1769. Died September 23,
1769.
II. Lydia[5]—Born July 19, 1770. Died January 23, 1788. Drowned
in Darby Creek, Delaware Co., Pa.
III. Paschall[5]—Born February 23, 1773. Died May 17, 1852. Married Mary Wilson. More of Paschall later.
IV. Margaret[5]—Born August 16, 1774.
V. Mary[5] (or Molly)—Born April 19, 1776. Died June 22, 1820.
Married Israel W. Morris. More of Mary later.
VI. Sarah[5]—Born September 17, 1779. Died September 15, 1780.
VII. Henry[5]—Born February 6, 1781. Died January 18, 1854. Married Sarah Humphreys. More of Henry later.
VIII. Stephen[5]—Born March 18, 1782. Died July 15, 1782.

Levi[4] was the fifth, and youngest, son of Zebulon[3]. He was a man of energy, industry, and decision of character. The family considered him the most perfect of the name. At the age of eighteen, he was captain of a sloop and delivered large quantities of flour, and sold it in Philadelphia. Afterwards, in partnership with his father, both entered largely into business. He removed from Cecil Co., Md., to Philadelphia, Pa., and continued in business until the Revolutionary War. He was elected Captain of the First City Troop, in 1774. In 1775 he was sent to Canada to pay the Army with specie. The Troop served under Washington until the close of the war, when he was honorably discharged.

E-5. MARY OR MOLLY (HOLLINGSWORTH) MORRIS

(Levi[4], Zebulon[3], Henry[2], Valentine[1].) Daughter of Levi[4] and Hannah Paschall Hollingsworth. Born April 19, 1776. Died June 22, 1820. Married ...... Israel W. Morris, of Philadelphia, Pa., youngest son of Samuel Morris (known as Fighting Sam or Christian Sam) who was Captain of the Philadelphia First Troop of Cavalry and General Washington's bodyguard during the Revolutionary War.

Issue

I. Stephen Paschall[6]—He first married Rachel Johnson. No issue. He then married Mary Ann Cope. No issue.

II. Henry[6]—Born .... Died ....., 1882. Married Caroline Old. Issue: 1. Ellen[7]. 2. Stephen[7]. 3. Henry G[7]. 4. Emily[7].

III. Dr. Caspar[6]—Born ...... Died March 17, 1884. Married a second cousin, Ann Cheston, granddaughter of Col. Samuel Hollingsworth, of Baltinore, Md. Half-brother of Levi Hollingsworth. Issue: 1. Dr. Cheston[7]—Living, 1918, 1514 Spruce St., Philadelphia, Pa. 2. Israel W[7]. 3. Mary H[7]. 4. Galloway[7].

IV. Levi[6]—Married Naomi McClanahan. Issue: 1. Sally[7]. 2. Catharine[7]. 3. Emma[7].

V. Hannah[6]—Never married.

VI. Jane[6]—Never married.

VII. Israel[6]—Married ...... Longstreth. Issue: 1. Theodore H[7]. 2. Frederick W[7]. 3. William H[7]. 4. Anna[7].

VIII. Wistar[6]—Married ...... Harris. Issue: 1 daughter.

E-5. HENRY HOLLINGSWORTH

(Levi[4], Zebulon[3], Henry[2], Valentine[1].) Of Philadelphia. Son of Levi[4] and Hannah Paschall Hollingsworth. Born February 6, 1781. Died January 18, 1854. Married Sarah, daughter of Joshua Humphreys, of Philadelphia, Pa.

ISSUE

I. Levi[6]—Died unmarried.
II. Hannah[6]—Married Dr. Thomas Stewardson. More of Hannah later.
III. Mary[6]—Married Dr. Joseph Carson. More of Mary later.
IV. Ann[6]—Died unmarried.
V. Rebecca[6]—Married Gen. Humphreys, U. S. A.
VI. Clement[6]—Died at 19 years of age.

F-6. HANNAH (HOLLINGSWORTH) STEWARDSON

Of Philadelphia, Pa. Daughter of Henry[5] (Son of Levi[4], Zebulon[3], Henry[2], Valentine[1]) and Sarah (Humphreys) Hollingsworth. Married Dr. Thomas Stewardson.

ISSUE

I. Harry Stewardson[7].
II. Anna Stewardson[7].
III. Caroline Stewardson[7]—Married Captain Henry H. Humphreys, U. S. A.
IV. Mary Stewardson[7].
V. Langdon C. Stewardson[7]—First married Miss Bull. She died. No issue. He then married Miss Smith.

F-6. MARY (HOLLINGSWORTH) CARSON

Daughter of Henry[5] (Son of Levi[4], Zebulon[3], Henry[2], Valentine[1]) and Sarah (Humphreys) Hollingsworth. Married Dr. Joseph Carson. Died June, 1868.

ISSUE

I. Hampton L[7].   III. Susan[7].
II. Annie[7].

E-5. PASCHALL HOLLINGSWORTH

(Levi[4], Zebulon[3], Henry[2], Valentine[1].) Of Philadelphia. Son of Levi[4] and Hannah (Paschall) Hollingsworth. Born February 23, 1773. Died May 17, 1852. Married Mary Wilson, daughter of Hon. James Wilson, of Pennsylvania, Judge of the U. S. Supreme Court.

ISSUE

I. Emily[6].

D-4. JACOB HOLLINGSWORTH

(Zebulon[3], Henry[2], Valentine[1].) Son of Zebulon, and his second wife Mary (Jacobs) Hollingsworth. Born July 30, 1742. Died March 1, 1803. He married January 25, 1770, Ruth M. Adams of Christiana, Del. Their residence was "Head of Elk," Cecil Co., Md. They died without issue.

D-4. LYDIA (HOLLINGSWORTH) WALLIS

Daughter of Zebulon[3] (son of Henry[2], Valentine[1]) and Mary (Jacobs) Hollingsworth. Married J. Wallis.

5

ISSUE

I. Molly[5]—Married ...... Lathy. Issue: Henry[6].
II. Samuel[5]—Married ...... Cowden. Issue: Cowden[6].
III. Hannah[5]—Married ...... Miller. Issue: Susan[6].
IV. Cassandra[5]—Married ...... Smith.
V. Sarah[5]—Married Hugh Brady.

D-4. JOHN HOLLINGSWORTH

(Zebulon[3], Henry[2], Valentine[1].) Son of Zebulon[3] and Mary (Jacobs) Hollingsworth. Born, May 12, 1752. Died September 30, 1808. Married Mary Fisher.

ISSUE

I. Mary[5]—Died unmarried.
II. Susan[5]—Married Charles Lloyd, of Muncy, Pa.

D-4. STEPHEN HOLLINGSWORTH

(Zebulon[3], Henry[2], Valentine[1].) Son of Zebulon[3] and Mary (Jacobs) Hollingsworth. Born February 28, 1749. Died December 10, 1822. Unmarried.

D–4. THOMAS HOLLINGSWORTH

(Zebulon[3], Henry[2], Valentine[1].) Son of Zebulon[3] and Mary (Jacobs) Hollingsworth. Born in Cecil Co., Md., August 2, 1747. Died at Baltimore, Md., September 5, 1815. Buried, St. Paul's Church Yard, Baltimore, Md. Married Ann Adams, Christiana, Del.

ISSUE

I. Zebulon[5].
II. Jacob[5].
III. Thomas[5].
IV. Lydia[5]—Died in 1865.
V. Ann M[5].—Married John B. Morris, of Baltimore, Md., 1847.

E–5. SAMUEL HOLLINGSWORTH

(Samuel[4], Zebulon[3], Henry[2], Valentine[1].) Of Elkton, Cecil Co., Md. Son of Col. Samuel[4] and Sarah (Adams) Hollingsworth. Born February 22, 1794. Died May 20, 1855. He married Ellen Maria Moale, October 16, 1816.

ISSUE

I. Samuel[6]—Born about 1818.
II. Ellin[6]—Married R. Alick Wright. Issue: 3 children.
III. Thomas B[6].—Married Mary G. Sharp, daughter of Dr. S. Sharp, U. S. A. Issue: Henry S.[7]
IV. William G[6].—Married Rosa Glenn, of Baltimore, Md. Issue: 1. William Glenn[7]. 2. Ellin M. Glenn[7].
V. Flora[6]—Married Wm. Ward Henderson. No issue. Other children died in infancy. No names given.

E–5. ELIZABETH (HOLLINGSWORTH) RIDGELY

(Samuel[4], Zebulon[3], Henry[2], Valentine[1].) Daughter of Col. Samuel[4] and Sarah (Adams) Hollingsworth, of Baltimore, Md. Married General Charles S. Ridgely, of Elkridge, Md.

ISSUE

I. John[6].
II. Samuel[6].
III. Juliana[6].
IV. James[6].

V. Charles S[4].
VI. Randolph[4]—Died in Mexico.
VII. Sallie[4]—Married ...... Graison.
VIII. Joseph[4].
IX. Margaret[4].
X. Ann[4].
XI. Andrew S[4].—Married Miss Johnson.

E-5. ANN M. (HOLLINGSWORTH) MORRIS

Daughter of Thomas[4] (Son of Zebulon[3], Henry[2], Valentine[1]) and Ann (Adams) Hollingsworth. Married John B. Morris, of Baltimore, Md.

ISSUE

I. James[5].
II. Thomas Hollingsworth[5]—Married Mary, daughter of the Hon. Reverdy Johnson, of Maryland. He died in 1872.
III. John B[5].—Married Louise K. Vandyke.
IV. Lydia[5]—Married Frank Key Howard.
V. Nancy[5]—Married Hon. Henry Winter Davis. Born August 16, 1817. Died December 30, 1865. Issue: 2 daughters.

D-4. COL. SAMUEL HOLLINGSWORTH

(Zebulon[3], Henry[2], Valentine[1].) Youngest son of Zebulon[3] and his second wife, Mary (Jacobs) Hollingsworth. Born in Cecil Co., Md., January 17, 1757. Died in Baltimore, May 9, 1830. Age 73 years. Buried in St. Paul's Church Yard, Baltimore. He married Sarah Adams, of Christiana, Del., in 1782.

He was placed in a counting room in Philadelphia about the commencement of the Revolutionary War. Soon after he entered the army as a volunteer and was in the Battles of Trenton and Princeton. After the campaign he removed to Baltimore. He was a partner with his brother Thomas. They were leading merchants, wealthy and highly respected, and contributed largely to the commercial advancement of the city.

ISSUE

I. Jacob[5]—Born 1790. Married Nancy Gooding. He died 1869. More of Jacob later.
II. Samuel[5]—Born 1794. Married Ellen M. Moale. He died 1855.

III. Sarah⁵—Married Prof. William Gibson, of Philadelphia, Pa.
IV. Elizabeth⁵—Married Gen. Charles Sterett Ridgely.
V. Mary Ann⁵—Married James Cheston.
VI. Juliana⁵.
    Other children died young. No names given.

E-5. COL. JACOB HOLLINGSWORTH

(Samuel⁴, Zebulon³, Henry², Valentine¹.) Of Hagerstown, Md. Son of
Samuel⁴ and Sarah (Adams) Hollingsworth. Born August 6, 1790.
Died in 1869. Married Anne G. Gooding, of England, about 1812,
adopted daughter of Captain Jeremiah Yellott, of Baltimore. She died
in 1870.

Issue

  I. J. Yellott⁶—Born 1813. Married Francis V. Walker, of Louisiana.
 II. Samuel⁶—Born 1814. Married Elenora M. Walker, of Louisiana.
III. George Howard⁶—Died at Cambridge, Md., in 1878.
 IV. Mary Y⁶.—Married William Gibson, Chestnut Hill, Baltimore
     Co., Md. Issue: William H. Gibson⁷.
  V. Lydia⁶—First married James Kennedy, of Hagerstown, Md. She
     then married Rev. William G. Jackson.
 VI. Sallie A⁶.—Married Edward Watts, of Carlisle, Pa.
VII. Elizabeth R⁶.—Married Judge George French, of Hagerstown,
     Md.
VIII. Jacob⁶—Unmarried. Living at Beauvoir, Miss.
 IX. Thomas⁶—Unmarried. Living at Beauvoir, Miss.
  X. William G⁶.—Unmarried. Died in California.
 XI. Rebecca G⁶.—Married Col. Henry M. Lazelle, West Point. Is-
     sue: 1. Jacob Lazelle⁷. 2. Horace Lazelle⁷.

F-6. J. YELLOTT HOLLINGSWORTH

(Jacob⁵, Samuel⁴, Zebulon³, Henry², Valentine¹.) Of Beauvoir, Harrison Co., Miss. Son of Jacob⁵, of Hagerstown, Md., and Anne G.
(Gooding) Hollingsworth. Born in 1813. Married Frances V. Walker,
of Louisiana.

Issue

  I. Mary Y⁷.—Married Edw. Peckham, of England, in 1872. Died
     1875. Issue: 1 son.
 II. J. Howard⁷—Died in infancy.
III. Nannie G⁷.—Married Charles R. Dahlgren, of Mississippi.

IV. G. Yellott[7]—Married Olivia Semple, of Mississippi.

V. S. Dorsey[7]—Died in Natchez, in 1864.

VI. F. V. B[7].—Born 1861.

F-6. SAMUEL HOLLINGSWORTH

(Jacob[6], Samuel[4], Zebulon[3], Henry[2], Valentine[1].) Son of Jacob[6] and Anne G. (Gooding) Hollingsworth. Born in 1814. Married Elenora M. Walker, of Louisiana.

Issue

I. Wina F[7].—Born 1846. Married W. B. Logan, New Orleans, La. in 1876.

II. J. Cheston[7] and Elenora[7]—Died in infancy.

III. William Walker[7]—Unmarried.

IV. Sallie R[7].—Unmarried.

V. Robert Lee[7]—Born 1861. Unmarried.

E-5. SARAH (HOLLINGSWORTH) GIBSON

Daughter of Samuel[4] (son of Zebulon[3], Henry[2], Valentine[1]) and Sarah (Adams) Hollingsworth. Married William Gibson, of Philadelphia, Pa.

Issue

I. Eyre[6].

II. Thomas[6].

III. William[6].

IV. Sallie[6]—Married Dr. Reese.

V. Mary[6].

VI. Charles[6].

E-5. MARY ANN (HOLLINGSWORTH) CHESTON

Daughter of Col. Samuel[4] (son of Zebulon[3], Henry[2], Valentine[1]) and Sarah (Adams) Hollingsworth. Born about 1783. She married, in 1803, James Cheston, Jr., born in 1779. He was the son of James, Sr., and Ann (Galloway) Cheston. James, Sr., was born in 1747, the son of Dr. Daniel and Francina A. (Frisby) Cheston. Ann Galloway Cheston, mother of James Cheston, Jr., was the daughter of James and Ann Galloway.

ISSUE

I. Dr. James[4]—Born 1804. He first married Mary Thomas. He then married Cornelia Thomas, and finally, Sallie Scott Murray.
II. Galloway[4]—Married Margaret Carey. He died March 9, 1881.
III. Samuel[4]—Died 1875.
IV. Ann[4]—Married Dr. Casper Morris, of Philadelphia, Pa.
V. Mary[4]—Married Dr. James H. Murray.
VI. Fannie[4]—Married Dr. James H. Murray.

C-3. THOMAS HOLLINGSWORTH

(Thomas[2], Valentine[1].) Son of Thomas Hollingsworth[2] of Rockland Manor, and his second wife, Grace Cook. Born December 23, 1698. Died September 1, 1753. He was buried in William Farquhar's burying place, Pipe Creek, Md. He married Judith Lampley, daughter of Nathaniel and Susan (Bezar) Lampley, December 28, 1723. She was born in 1700. Died in 1766.

ISSUE

I. Susanna[4]—Born February 13, 1724. Died 1754.
II. Grace[4]—Born December 27, 1726. Died 1729.
III. Thomas[4]—Born and died in 1727.
IV. Thomas[4]—Born December 13, 1729. Died March 1, 1799. Married Jane Smith, November 20, 1754.
V. Isaac[4]—Born June 13, 1731. Died 1795. Married Hannah Scott, in 1769. She died in 1810. More of Isaac later.
VI. Nathaniel[4]—Born August 29, 1733. Died 1754.
VII. Rachel[4]—Born August 29, 1733.
VIII. Emmor[4] or Amor[4]—Born May 29, 1739. Died 1826.   Married Mary Chandler, in 1766. More of Emmor later.
IX. Christopher[4]—Born March 15, 1742. Married Elizabeth Chandler, in 1765. More of Christopher later.
X. Judith[4]—Born May 14, 1744. Married John Pyle, in 1765.

D-4. THOMAS HOLLINGSWORTH

(Thomas[3], Thomas[2], Valentine[1].) Son of second Thomas[3] and Judith (Lampley) Hollingsworth. Born December 13, 1729. He died March 1, 1799. Married Jane Smith, in 1754. She died May 6, 1825.

I. Nathaniel⁶—Born August 4, 1755. Married Abigail Green, October 22, 1783. More of Nathaniel later.

II. Thomas⁶—Born October 31, 1756. Married Susanna Jackson, 1798. He died in 1834.

III. John⁶—Born October 31, 1756. Married Jemima Blackhouse, 1781. Thomas and John were twins. More of John later.

IV. Susanna⁶—Born September 12, 1758. Married Robert Burnet.

V. Mary⁶—Born August 29, 1760. Married George Chandler of Ohio.

VI. Err⁶—Born June 26, 1762. Married Phebe Mercer, in 1795. More of Err later.

VII. Levi⁶—Born April 22, 1764. Married Mary Harry, in 1789. More of Levi later.

VIII. Judith⁶—Born July 21, 1767. Died 1769.

IX. Aaron⁶—Born June 4, 1769. Died 1778.

X. Jane⁶—Born September 9, 1771. Died 1833.

XI. Joshua⁶—Born February 24, 1774. Married Hannah Harvey. 1798. More of Joshua later.

XII. David⁶—Born July 3, 1777.

F-6. ROBERT HOLLINGSWORTH

(Abraham⁵, George⁴, Abraham³, Thomas², Valentine¹.) Son of Abraham⁵ and Margaret (Wright) Hollingsworth. Born November 22, 1767. Married Jennie Hamilton, about 1790 or '91. Lived near Cross Hill, S. C. Both buried at Liberty Springs Church, Laurens Co., S. C. Robert died prior to November 1, 1826. Book F, page 49, Laurens, S. C., Probate Court records "Wm. Ligon granted administration to the estate of Robert Hollingsworth, deceased. Berry Lick and John McWilliams, sureties, November 1, 1826." Also, Ibid page 146 "Robert Hollingsworth, about 20 years, Susan Hollingsworth, about 18 years, and Unice Hollingsworth, about 15 years, make request that Wm. Ligon be appointed their guardian, January 2, 1828."

I. Abraham⁷—Born November 30, 1792. Married, lived, and died near Cross Hill, S. C.; had large family.

II. Elizabeth⁷—Born December 20, 1794.

III. Marian⁷—Born June 11, 1797.

IV. Isaiah[7]—Born September 28, 1799. Married Miss Chandler.
Settled at Stockbridge, Ga. Issue, large family.

V. Abigail[7]—Born June 7, 1802. Married 1826, to James Davis.
Lived in Laurens Co., S. C. He was born in 1802. Died
1870. More of Abigail later.

VI. Jane[7]—Born June 1, 1805. Married ......

VII. Robert[7]—Born November 11, 1807. Married, lived, and died in
Decatur, Ga. No children.

VIII. Susannah[7]—Born March 15, 1810. Married ...... McWilliams.
Settled near Atlanta, Ga. Several children.

IX. Eunice[7]—Born March 14, 1813. Married Edward Martin.
Lived in Laurens Co., S. C. Died about 1840, leaving one
son and one daughter. Son died in early boyhood. The
daughter, Margaret Caroline[8], married Wm. Aiken Martin, of
Charleston, S. C. Died a few years ago. Buried in Magnolia
Cemetery, Charleston, S. C. Their only daughter, Mrs. Wm.
Dunkin, lived, in 1918, at 59 Meeting St., Charleston, S. C.

G-7. ABIGAIL (HOLLINGSWORTH) DAVIS

Daughter of Robert[6] (Son of Abraham[5], George[4], Abraham[3], Thomas[2]
Valentine[1]) and Jennie Hamilton Hollingsworth. Born near Cross
Hill, S. C., June 2, 1802. Died December 16, 1870. Married June...,
1826, to James Davis, of Laurens Co., S. C. Born January 1, 1800.
Died June 18, 1878. He was the son of John and ...... Davis, of
Salisbury, Md.

Issue

I. Jane Hamilton[8]—Born May 6, 1829. Married L. P. Davenport,
of Waterloo, S. C. Died December 10, 1886. Buried at Gate-
ville, Texas. Issue: 1. Burket[9]. 2. Susie[9]. 3. Martin[9]. Living,
1918, at Laurens, S. C.

II. John J[8].—Born October 18, 1832. Died December 24, 1872.
Never married. Was a prominent and successful lawyer.

III. Dr. Frank[8]—Born May 5, 1836. Died October 24, 1908. For
many years a successful physician in Shreveport, La. Married
Miss White, of Shreveport, La. Issue: 2 children. Both
died in infancy.

IV. Susan Byrd[8]—Born July 30, 1852. Living, 1917. Married
J. J. Pluss, March 5, 1874, a banker of Laurens, S. C. He
died February 27, 1916. No issue.

G–7. ABRAHAM HOLLINGSWORTH

(Robert⁸, Abraham⁵, George⁴, Abraham³, Thomas², Valentine¹.) Of
Laurens Co., S. C. Son of Robert⁶ and Jennie Hamilton Hollingsworth.
Born November 30, 1792. Died January 9, 1873. Buried Liberty
Springs Church, Laurens Co., S. C. First married January 9, 1817, to
Elizabeth Hitt. Born September 3, 1801, and died September 11, 1826.
He then married, November 4, 1828, Fannie Hitt, a cousin, who was
born February 13, 1799 and who died December 9, 1864.

Issue 1st Marriage

I. Maryan⁸—Born May 30, 1818. Married Richard Owens.
II. Henry⁸—Born February 17, 1820. Died September 23, 1826.
III. Elizabeth⁸—Born April 28, 1822. Married Aaron Wells.
IV. Susannah⁸—Born December 25, 1823. Married David Whiteford.
V. John R⁸.—Born January 24, 1826. Died August 28, 1828.

Issue 2nd Marriage

VI. Robert⁸—Born October 22, 1829. Died October 2, 1838.
VII. Sallie⁸—Born September 23, 1831. Married, in 1867, to James
    Hefferman. Lived at Ninety Six, S. C.
VIII. Abraham⁸—Born December 19, 1833. Killed at the Battle of
    South Mountain, Md., September 4, 1862. Never married.
    In S. C. Batallion, Company B, Confederate Army.
IX. John⁸—Born September 25, 1835. First married Carrie Good-
    man. Issue: 5 children. Died April 11, 1907 at Cross Hill,
    S. C. In 3rd S. C. Regiment, Company F. Then married
    Sallie Cook Coleman. Issue: 2 children.
X. Frances⁸—Born December 1, 1837. First married Col. Tandy
    Walker, Veteran of 2 wars. Issue: Robert Walker⁹, She
    then married M. L. Bullock, who died in 1916. She died in
    Laurens Co., S. C., November ......, 1917.
XI. Robert T⁸.—Born April 18, 1841. First married Ada Jones.
    Issue: 5 children. He then married Mary Dennis. Living
    in 1917, near Cross Hill, S. C. Issue: 5 children. Robert had
    the family Bible in his possession, in 1917. In Confederate
    Army, 3rd S. C. Battalion, Co. B.

H-8. ROBERT T. HOLLINGSWORTH

(Abraham[7], Robert[6], Abraham[5], George[4], Abraham[3], George[2], Valentine[1].)
Of Cross Hill, S. C. Son of Abraham[7] and Fannie (Hitt) Hollingsworth.
Born Laurens Co., S. C., April 18, 1841. In Confederate Army 4 years.
First married Ada Jones, in 1875. He then married Mary Dennis,
February 14, 1888. Living 1917, Cross Hill, S. C. Was a farmer,
living in the house in which he was born.

Issue 1st Marriage

I. Abraham Augustus[8]—Born February 22, 1876. Died July 16,
1877.

II. Robert Eugene[8]—Born September 1, 1877. Living, unmarried,
1918, at Chappels, S. C.

III. William G[8].—Born March 19, 1879. Living, unmarried, 1918,
at Chappels, S. C.

IV. John Bonner[8]—Born July 20, 1881. Living, unmarried, 1918,
at Chappels, S. C.

V. Ada Bell[8]—Born January 7, 1884. Married Wm. G. Stove, May
3, 1905. Issue: 1 daughter. Born August 33, 1911. Living,
1918, at 9 Bradley Ave., Atlanta, Ga.

Issue 2nd Marriage

VI. Herman D[8].—Born June 14, 1889. Living, 1918, unmarried,
Chappels, S. C.

VII. Bernard Young[8]—Born May 15, 1891. Living, 1918, unmarried,
Cross Hill, S. C.

VIII. Frances Susannah[8]—Born March 8, 1894. Died October 31,
1909.

IX. James T[8].—Born October 21, 1895—Address 1917: Co. 9, Coast
Artillery, Moultrieville, S. C.

X. Idalia[8]—Born November 26, 1897. Living, 1918, Cross Hill,
S. C.

D-4. ISAAC HOLLINGSWORTH

(Abraham[3], Thomas[2], Valentine[1].) Son of Abraham[3] and Ann (Robinson) Hollingsworth. Born Fabruary 22, 1722. Died September 10,
1759. Married, in 1748, to Rachel Parkins, daughter of Isaac Parkins.
She was born May 3, 1724. Died September 10, 1805. Both were
buried at Fairfax, Va.

Isaac Hollingsworth[4] became a minister when about 21 years of age, and lived near Hopewell Monthly Meeting, Va., until 1757, when he moved to Fairfax, Va. A Memorial of him, printed in 1787, says: "He died 9th month 10th, 1759, age 37 years."

ISSUE

I. Abraham[5]—Born May 9, 1749.

II. Ann[5]—Born December 6, 1751. Married John Neill.

III. Lydia[5]—Born October 27, 1752. Married John Hough, April 9, 1772.

IV. Jonah[5]—Born February 24, 1754. Married Hannah Miller, January 15, 1778.

V. Phebe[5]—Born March 20, 1757. Married Isaac Steer, April 21, 1779.

VI. Mary[5]—Born December 3, 1758. Married Davis Lupton, June 12, 1777. Issue: Jonah[6].

E-5. JONAH HOLLINGSWORTH

(Isaac[4], Abraham[3], Thomas[2], Valentine[1].) Of Winchester, Va. Son of Isaac[4] and Rachel (Parkins) Hollingsworth. Born February 24, 1754, near Winchester, Va. Died 1801. Married Hannah Miller, of Maryland, January 15, 1778. Born September 27, 1755. Died 1836.

ISSUE

I. Isaac[6]—Born October 14, 1778. Died November 25, 1829. Married.

II. Solomon[6]—Born December 5, 1779. Died June 5, 1820. Married Sarah Brown.

III. Sarah[6]—Born September 9, 1781. Died 1862.

IV. Rachel[6]—Born January 26, 1783. Died . . . . . .

V. Samuel[6]—Born August 31, 1784. Married Susanna B. Richardson, in 1811. More of Samuel later.

VI. Joseph[6]—Born March 17, 1786. Married Rhoda Whitacre.

VII. Jonah[6]—Born December 18, 1787. Married Catherine Calvert.

VIII. David[6]—Born December 24, 1789. Died September 29, 1859. Married Eleanor Hollingsworth, in 1833. More of David later.

IX. Betsey[6]—Born November 27, 1791. Living in 1884.

X. Ruth[6]—Born October 19, 1793.

XI. Mary[6]—Born January 21, 1795. Died July 18, 1855.

XII. Hannah[6]—Born January 21, 1795. Married Jesse Wood.

XIII. Abraham[6]—September 3, 1797. Died May 23, 1857.

F-6. SAMUEL HOLLINGSWORTH

(Jonah[5], Isaac[4], Abraham[3], Thomas[2], Valentine[1].) Of Winchester, Va. Son of Jonah[5] and Hannah (Miller) Hollingsworth. Born August 31, 1784. Married December 23, 1811, Susanna B. Richardson, of Frederick Co., Va. Born November 18, 1791.

ISSUE

I. Jonah William[7]—Born 1813. Married Eliza West. Issue: 1. Milton West[8]. 2. Susan West[8].

II. Samuel R[7].—Born 1814. Married ...... Died November 6, 1843.

III. Hannah Rebecca[7]—Born 1816. First married Oliver Whitacre. She then married William Hampton.

IV. Sarah Ann[7]—Born 1819. Married John Hoover.

V. Charles Buck[7]—Born 1821. Married R. Richardson.

VI. Mary E[7].—Born 1823. Married William West.

VII. America[7]—Born 1825. Married Joseph R. Bowman.

VIII. Frances Amelia[7]—Born 1828. Married Wesley Shirley.

G-7. JONAH WILLIAM HOLLINGSWORTH

(Samuel[6], Jonah[5], Isaac[4], Abraham[3], Thomas[2], Valentine[1].) Son of Samuel[6] and Susanna B. (Richardson) Hollingsworth. Born in Frederick Co., Va., January 10, 1813. Married, in 1840, to Eliza West, of Ohio.

ISSUE

I. Martha A[8].—Born 1842. Married William Milliken, 1861.

II. Rebecca S[8].—Born 1844. Married William Dixon, 1862. Born in Ohio.

III. Joseph M[8].—Born 1845.

IV. Mary E[8].—Born 1847.

V. William A[8].—Born 1849.

VI. Lewis N[8].—Born 1851. Married Sarah Hudson, 1872. Issue: 1 child.

VII. Rhoda I[8].—Born 1853. Married Thomas A. Knox, in 1879.

VIII. Jonah H[8].—Born 1855.

IX. John J[8].—Born 1857.

X. Luela[8]—Born 1860.

G-7. CHARLES BUCK HOLLINGSWORTH

(Samuel[6], Jonah[5], Isaac[4], Abraham[3], Thomas[2], Valentine[1].) Son of Samuel[6] and Susanna B. (Richardson) Hollingsworth. Born 1821, Shenandoah Co., Va. Died .... Married .... Susan R. Richardson, of Ohio.

Issue

I. Joseph R[7].—Born 1847.
II. Samuel C[7].—Born 1849. Died 1870.
III. Anna[7]—Born 1852. Married 1878, Frank Hoffman. Issue: J. Clyde[9] Hoffman, lawyer, Indianapolis, Ind.
IV. Charles B[7].—Born 1854. Married 1878, Mary ....
V. Walter S[7].—Born 1856. Died 1861.
VI. William M[7].—Born 1858. Died 1861.
VII. Lilly Bell[7]—Born 1860. Died 1872.
VIII. Marquis J[7].—Born 1862.
IX. Allen Scott[7]—Born 1864.
X. Orville Frank[7]—Born 1868. Died 1878.

F-6. DAVID HOLLINGSWORTH

(Jonah[5], Isaac[4], Abraham[3], Thomas[2], Valentine[1].) Of Winchester. Son of Jonah[5] and Hannah (Miller) Hollingsworth. Born December 24, 1789. Died September 29, 1859. He lived in the Stone House, built by his grandfather, Isaac Hollingsworth[4], near Winchester, in 1754. He married Eleanor Hollingsworth, in 1833.

Issue

I. Jonah Isaac[7].   II. Mary E[7].
III. Annie V[7].

The above three sisters never married. They were living at the old homestead near Winchester as late as 1894, with their Aunt Betsy.

G-7. DE WITT CLINTON RUSSELL

Son of James Lillburn and Susanna [6](Hollingsworth) Russell. (Susanna[6] was the daughter of Robert[5] and Susanna Rice Hollingsworth, of Winchester, Va.) Born September 7, 1828. Died April 18, 1903 at Troy, Mo. Married June 5, 1855, to Sarah Catherine Ellis, of Simpsonville, Ky.

ISSUE

I. William Henry[8]—Born in Troy, Mo., September 28, 1856. Married October 14, 1884, Emma Miller. Issue: 1. Ethel Dixon[9]—Married Harvey Cruch. 2. Hazel E[9].—Married Charles H. Davis. 3. Della L[9].—Married Charles A. Pauly. 4. Cecil[9]—Married Emma A. Bruene. 5. Beatrice Middleton[9]—Married Fred von Gruenegen.

II. Charles Smith[8]—Born October 12, 1858. Died September 21, 1859.

III. Ira Leon[8]—Born April 14, 1860. Living 1918, Troy, Mo. First married, September 30, 1891, Louise L. Browning. He later married Kathleen Tuphohn, of Sheffield, England. Issue, 1st marriage: 1. ...... Died in infancy. 2. Florence Mary[9]—Married Clarence Kercheval. 3. Edmund William[9]. 4. Edgar Dee[9]. 5. Leon Helmkampf[9]. 6. Henry Lindle[9].

IV. Elizabeth Quarles[8]—Born December 24, 1861. Living 1918, ... Married, April 27, 1882, to John H. Thurman. Issue: 1. Dee Russell[9]—Married Mary Campbell. 2. Virginia Evelyn[9]—Married Wm. J. Cunningham. 3. Susanna May[9]—Married Eugene Wells. 4. Sarah Catherine[9]—Married Edward F. Wolf. 5. Joseph Lindley[9]—Married Anna L. Burgomaster. 6. Mary Garrett[9]—Born March 24, 1891. Died May 1, 1892. 7. John Quarles[9]—Born June 2, 1892. 8. Effie Rowena[9]—Married Wm. Oscar Allison. 9. Daisy Mabel[9]—Born December 6, 1895. Died March 21, 1902. 10. Thos. U. Frink[9]. 11. Jas. Jackson[9].

V. Florence Hughes[8]—Born May 14, 1864. Died May 17, 1865.

VI. Annie Smith[8]—Born November 3, 1865. Died October 2, 1868.

VII. Nellie[8]—Born November 9, 1869. Living, 1918, Troy, Mo. Married November 14, 1894, Oscar Downing Bradley. Issue: Clinton Augustine[9].

VIII. Ernest Norton[8]—Born November 29, 1872. Died July 18, 1873.

G–7. HONORA HUGHES RUSSELL SMITH

Daughter of James Lillburn and Susanna[6] (Hollingsworth) Russell, of Simpsonville, Ky. Born June 11, 1822. Died .... Married September 26, 1839, William Smith of ......, Ky.

Issue

I. George Thomas[8]—Born May 30, 1841. Died August 23, 1914. Married Irene H. Parker. Issue: 1. Florence Coleman[9]. 2. Eva Coleman[9]. 3. Leland Frazier[9].

II. Louisiana Coleman[8]—Born December 27, 1842. Died July 23, 1865.

III. John Robert[8]—Born October 5, 1846. Died March 21, 1847.

IV. James Lillburn[8]—Born August 19, 1848. Died April 30, 1864.

V. Henry Clinton[8]—Born October 30, 1850. Living 1918. Married May 31, 1888, to Kate Florence Snyder. Issue: Helen Clyde[9]—Married John Steele.

VI. Robert Marcellus[8]—Born September 25, 1852. Living 1918, La Grange, Ky. First married Emily Beard. Then married, August 29, 1900, Margaret Hays. Issue: 1. Emily Honora[9]. 2. Robert Whitman[9]. 3. Henry Ralston[9].

VII. Josiah Wheeler[8]—Born September 25, 1852. Died September 25, 1852.

VIII. Persifor Frazer[8]—Born July 9, 1858. Died January 16, 1859.

IX. Amelia Preston[8]—Born August 25, 1862. Living 1918, Pendleton, Ky. Married June 20, 1903, Louis Montague Ballard.

X. Harry Rodman[8]—Born October 10, 1867. Died April 15, 1899. Married October 3, 1891, Emma C. Bowers.

G-7. JOHN RICHARD RUSSELL

Son of James Lillburn and Susanna[6] Hollingsworth Russell, of Simpsonville, Ky. Born July 2, 1820. Died November 11, 1877. First married, January 1839, America Dorsey. He then married .... No issue. He married third, October 5, 1858, Virginia Mason.

Issue 1st Marriage

I. Richard[8].

II. Patsey[8].

III. Carbin[8]—Lives in Anchorage, Ky.

IV. Fannie[8]—Married Harry Goose, of Louisville, Ky.

Issue 3rd Marriage

V. Wm. Randolph[8]—Born September 13, 1859. Living 1918. First married, March 14, 1883, Lillie F. Cottle. He then married, November 1, 1899, Emma F. Gordon. Issue, 1st marriage: 1. Hallie Eugenia[9]—Married Henry F. Harbricht.

2. Frederick William[s]—Born May 24, 1886. 3. Mina Lewis[s]—
September 9, 1888. 4. Virginia[s]—Born August 30, 1890.
5. Jessie Buchanan[s]—Married Wm. H. Hutt.

VI. John Matthews[s]—Born January 31, 1867. Living 1918. Married May 8, 1894, Agnes McCormick. Issue: 1. Lou Ellen[s].
2. Robert[s]. 3. McCormick[s]. 4. Dorcas[s]. 5. Leland[s].

G–7. SARAH COLEMAN (RUSSELL) YOUNG

Daughter of James Lillburn and Susanna[s] Hollingsworth Russell, of
Simpsonville, Ky. Born July 1, 1818. Died May 6, 1907. Married
October 27, 1835, Judge William Young, of ......, Ky. He was born
March 24, 1803. Died March 23, 1886.

Issue

I. James Randolph[s]—Born November 4, 1836. Married October
10, 1867, Alice M. Shores. Issue: 1. Wm. Henry[s]—Born
February 11, 1869. Died September 30, 1870. 2. Annie L[s].—
Married James M. Brooks, of Camden, Ark. 3. Eugene Randolph[s]—Married Virginia Beatty. 4. Inez[s]—Born July 13,
1881. Died April 20, 1884. 5. T. Harold R[s].—Married Agnes
Donaldson Williams.

II. Richard Samuel[s]—Born October 7, 1838. Died September 14,
1897. Married November 1, 1865, Mary E. McHaney.
Issue: 1. Wm. Randolph[s]—Married Mildred A. Ellis, of Troy,
Mo. 2. Annie Cornelia[s]—Married Wm. J. McBurney, of St.
Louis, Mo. 3. Jas. McHarvey[s]—Married Norah Greamba, of
Denver, Colo. 4. Louisiana Smith[s]—Married Geo. Nagle
Martin, of St. Louis, Mo. 5. and 6. Both died in infancy.

III. William Henry[s]—Born December 25, 1842.

IV. Ariana Belle[s]—Born July 7, 1849. Living 1918. Married November 3, 1869, Elbert E. Hickok, of New York. Issue:
1. Howard Russell[s]—Married Anna E. Whitehead, of New
York. 2. Alma Young[s]—Married Dwight Aultman. 3. Elbert
Eugene[s]—Born August 21, 1875. 4. Elizabeth McLellan[s]—
Married Greyson B. McNair. 5. Clyde Vernon[s]—Born October
25, 1885. Died September 16, 1890.

V. Susan F. E[s].—Born July 24, 1855. Living 1918. Married December 19, 1872, D. Marcus McLellan, of .... Issue:
1. William Russell[s]—Born July 7, 1874. 2. Elbert Eugene[s]—
Born December 29, 1880. 3. Richard Young[s]—Married Nan
J. Larkin.

F-6. SUSANNA (HOLLINGSWORTH) RUSSELL

Daughter of Robert[5] (son of George[4], Abraham[3], Thomas[2], Valentine[1].) and Susanna Rice Hollingsworth. Born November 16, 1793. Died June 28, 1871. Married Fabruary 3, 1814, James Lillburn Russell, of Simpsonville, Ky., son of Lieut. John and Hannah Storr Russell, of Richmond, Va.

ISSUE

I. Patsy Storr[7]—Born January 29, 1815. Died ......, 1830.

II. Randolph Railey[7]—Born September 20, 1816. Died April, 1864, Danville, Va., a Confederate prisoner.

III. Sarah Coleman[7]—Born July 1, 1818. Died May 6, 1907. Married October 27, 1835, Judge William Young. Issue: 5 children. More of Sarah Coleman later.

IV. John Richard[7]—Born July 2, 1820. Died November 11, 1877, Troy, Mo. Married 3 times. Issue: 6 children. More of John Richard later.

V. Honora Hughes[7]—Born June 11, 1822. Married September 26, 1839, William Smith. Issue: 10 children. More of Honora Hughes later.

VI. Patrick Henry[7]—Born May 18, 1824. Died February 10, 1906, Sacramento, Cal. Married June 20, 1850, Harriet A. Williams. Issue: 1. Sallie Cornelia[8]. 2. Lara Clark[8]. 3. Elsie[8]. 4. Susan Augusta[8]. 5. Harry A[8].

VII. Robert Bell[7]—Born June 13, 1826. Died June 10, 1852, in New Mexico, near Fort Kearney, en route to California.

VIII. DeWitt Clinton[7]—Born September 7, 1828. Died April 18, 1903, at Troy, Mo. Married June 5, 1855, Sarah Catherine Ellis, of Simpsonville, Ky. Issue: 8 children. More of De Witt Clinton later.

IX. Patsey Storr[7]—Born October 14, 1831. Married November 9, 1858, James Hughes, of Simpsonville, Ky.

X. William Edmund[7]—Born February 20, 1834. Died May 13, 1865, in Nelson Co., Ky., when returning home from the Confederate Army.

G-7. SUSAN H. (HOLLINGSWORTH) OLIVER

Daughter of James[6] (Robert[5], George[4]. Abraham[3], Thomas[2], Valentine[1].) and Susan P. Russell Hollingsworth, of Simpsonville, Ky. Born November 19, 1828. Living, 1917, 2230 E St., Granite City, Ill. Married, August 30, 1846, Horace B. Oliver, of Simpsonville, Ky. Son of Horace and Elizabeth Oliver.

ISSUE

I. George Edwin[8]—Born August 23, 1847. Married Abbie Stead-
man, of Evansville, Ind., May 9, 1872. No issue. She died
February 8, 1875. He then married Elizabeth Smith, January 1, 1884. Issue: 1. Mabel Hollingsworth[9], who married
Dr. L. V. Brady, October, 1913. Issue: Grace Allen[10].

II. Taylor F[8].—Born July 30, 1849. Married Lillian E. Daniels,
September 3, 1872. Issue: 1. Muir Hollingsworth[9]. 2. Mary
Belle[9]. Muir Hollingsworth married Effie Able. Issue: 4
children. Mary Belle married Dr. Ralph Hunt, of Syla-
cauga, Ala. Issue: Ralph[10].

III. Belle Russell[8]—Born May 21, 1851. Married Rev. Wm. Edmund Waller, of Simpsonville, Ky., January 30, 1877. Issue:
1. Edwin Dudley[9]. 2. Willia[9]. Edwin D. Waller—Born
November 17, 1877, married Naomi Caldwell, of Fulton, Ky.
Issue: a. George Dudley[10]. b. Helen Belle[10]. c. Henry Douglas[10]. d. William Edmund[10]. Willia Waller—Born February
24, 1879, married George Wilson, of St. Louis, Mo. Issue:
Donald Wolf Wilson[10].

IV. Addie Barbour[8]—Born December 26, 1853. Married Geo. K.
Cowherd, January 11, 1887. Issue: 1. Horace Oliver Waller[9]. 2. Frank Fosdick[9]. 3. Charles Lamb[9]. Horace O. W.
married Agnes Lehman, of Nakomis, Ill., September 7, 1912.
Issue: Jaquelyn[10]—Born July 19, 1915. Frank Fosdick—
Born September 26, 1891, married Margaret Mellon, September 15, 1916. Charles Lamb—Born September 18, 1894.

V. Horace B[8].—Born March 31, 1858. Died June 2, 1878.

VI. Henry F[8].—Born June 5, 1860. Married Rosa Sherwood, October
1888. Issue: 1. Pierson Sherwood[9]—Born October ..., 1890.
2. Wallace Hollingsworth[9]—Born February ......, 1892.
Married Margaret Pierce, of ......, Tenn., 1916. Issue:
Rosemary[10]—Born May 5, 1917. 3. Lois[9]—Born July 25, 1898.
4. Henry Hughes[9]—Born October ......, 1902.

G-7. WILLIAM E. HOLLINGSWORTH

(James[6], Robert[5], George[4], Abraham[3], Thomas[2], Valentine,[1].) Son
of James[6] and Susan Pleasant (Russell) Hollingsworth. Born June 2,
1822, at Simpsonville, Ky. Died March 14, 1892. Married September
16, 1851, Eugenia B. Davenport, of Crab Orchard, Ky., who died December 25, 1906. He was Colonel 139th Indiana Regiment during the
Civil War, 1861-66. Lived at Evansville, Ind.

I. Leila[s]—Died September 17, 1900.

II. Edwin M[s].—Married Emma Q. Wannell, at Jeffersonville, Ind., June 20, 1882. No issue. Living 1917, at Inglefield, Cal.

III. John[s]—Married Mary T. Baird, of Louisville, Ky., July 3, 1888. Issue: 1. Wm. T[s].,—Born May 10, 1891. Living 1918, in Chicago. Maintains commercial artist's studio.

IV. Lyman D[s].—Married Elizabeth Huffman, of Lancaster, Ky., March 27, 1889. Issue: 1. Lyman D[s]., Jr.. 2. Robert Y[s]. Living 1917, in Paducah, Ky.

V. Henry[s]—Born November 21, 1859. Died March 6, 1868.

VI. Hallie Barbour[s].

VII. Laura Davenport[s].

VIII. Belle[s]—Living 1917, in Chicago.

IX. Richard Davenport[s]—Born .... Married Nell Mitchell, of Louisville, Ky., August 17, 1899. Died April 8, 1903, at St. Louis. No Issue.

X. W. Nisbett[s]—Born .... Married Charlotte K. Sauer, of Evansville, April 17, 1898. Was 1st Lieutenant, Co. M, I. N. G., 139th Inf., Spanish-American War. Issue: 1 son, who died in infancy. Living 1918, at 602 Linwood Ave., Evansville, Ind.

G–7. MARY E. (HOLLINGSWORTH) CRAPSTER

Daughter of James[s] and Susan P. Russell Hollingsworth, of Simpsonville, Ky. Born May 24, 1820. Died July 5, 1900. Married about 1837, to Wm. H. Crapster, son of Peter and Elizabeth Hobbs Crapster, of Jefferson Co., Ky., formerly of the Eastern shore of Maryland. They came to Kentucky, about 1820.

I. Susan[s]—Born 1837. Died 1840.

II. Adelaide[s]—Born November 22, 1840. Living 1918, at Louisville, Ky. Married Lewis J. Wagner, of Akron, Ohio. Issue: 1. Mary Louise[s]—Born August 11, 1869, Akron, Ohio. Married G. G. Sharrard, of Louisville, Ky. Issue: Charles F[10]. 2. Ella Wheeler[s]—Born 1871. Died 1879.

III. Mary Frances[s]—Born February 3, 1844. Living 1918, Louisville, Ky. Married to Rufus S. Frazier, of Shelby Co., Ky. No issue.

IV. Jane Shaw[8]—Born 1846. Died 1912. Married to Henry Cannon, of Georgetown, Ky. Issue: W. H. Cannon[9], who married Nancy Jones, of Millersburg, Ky. Issue: Ann. Elizabeth[10].

V. John Samuel[8]—Born 1848. Died 1872.

VI. Elizabeth[8]—Born 1850. Died 1915.

VII. Wm. Henry[8]—Born 1853. Living 1918, LaGrange, Ky. Married 1887, Frances Wright. Issue: 1. Robert Norman[9]—Born 1890, in France 1918. 2. Mary Elizabeth[9].

G-7. HARRIET R. (HOLLINGSWORTH) BARBOUR

Daughter of James[6] and Susan P. Russell Hollingsworth. Born July 4, 1824. Died June 21, 1896. Married December 24, 1839, William Barbour, of LaGrange, Ky. Farmer.

Issue

I. Mary Susan[8]—Born June 1, 1841. Died August 9, 1900. Married February 27, 1862, T. J. Hurley, of Louisville, Ky. Issue: 1. William[9]—Born September 4, 1863. Married Mattie Caseldine. 2. Horace O[9].—Born January 17, 1870. Married Louise Parker. 3. Hallie[9]—Born January 15, 1874. Married Ed. E. Rowland.

II. William[8]—Born May 30, 1844. Died September 12, 1915. Married November 19, 1868, Mattie Wheeler, of Thornton, Ind. Issue: Fanny Barbour[9]. Married John Sonntag, of Evansville, Ind.

III. Fanny[8]—Born June 15, 1847. Living 1918, at Pendleton, Ky. Married Thomas Coleman, of Pendleton, Henry Co., Ky. No issue.

IV. Frank[8]—Born July 28, 1850. Died February 12, 1905. Married Little Hudspeth, of Evansville, Ind. No issue.

V. Thomas[8]—Born September 25, 1853. Died July 1, 1903. Married, Henry McMillen, of Knoxville, Tenn., June 16, 1910.

VI. Retta[8]—Born May 5, 1857. Living 1918. Married T. J. Howe, of Louisville, Ky.

F-6. LEWIS HOLLINGSWORTH

(Robert[5], George[4], Abraham[3], Thomas[2], Valentine[1].) Son of Robert[5] and Susanna (Rice) Hollingsworth. Born April 8, 1775. Married January 10, 1814, Abigail Parkins, daughter of Isaac and Abigail Parkins. She was born February 9, 1784.

ISSUE

I. Robert J[7].—Born November 10, 1814. Lived in Loudon Co.,
Va.

II. Mary Susanna[7]—Born September 6, 1816. Lived in Loudon Co.,
Va.

III. Edward[7]—Born October 11, 1817. Lived in Loudon Co., Va.

IV. Elizabeth P[7].—Born January 10, 1822. Lived in Loudon Co.,
Va.

V. Charles L[7].—Born April 20, 1825. Living 1878, in Loudon Co.,
Va.

VI. Lydia J[7].—Born November 27, 1826. Died October 20, 1879.

G-7. ROBERT J. HOLLINGSWORTH

(Lewis[6], Robert[5], George[4], Abraham[3], Thomas[2], Valentine[1].) Son of
of Lewis[6] and Abigail (Parkins) Hollingsworth. Born November 10,
1814, in Frederick Co., Va. Married Miss R. J. Stone, September 10,
1847. She was born November 16, 1818.

ISSUE

I. Sallie A[8].—Born in 1848.

II. Lewis D[8].—Born 1850.

III. Ella E[8].—Born 1852. Married ......, in Loudon Co., Va.

IV. Abigail[8]—Born 1856. Went to Texas.

F-6. ISAAC HOLLINGSWORTH

(Robert[5], George[4], Abraham[3], Thomas[2], Valentine[1].) Of Uniontown,
Ky. Son of Robert[5] and Susanna (Rice) Hollingsworth. Born February 20, 1784. Died in 1863.

ISSUE

I. John[7]—Died in Illinois. Issue: 2 sons, 1 daughter.

II. Susan[7]—Married ...... Lambert. Issue: 4 sons and 3 daughters; born in Kentucky.

III. Robert[7]—Lived in Uniontown, Ky.

F-6. JOHN HOLLINGSWORTH

(Robert[6], George[4], Abraham[3], Thomas[2], Valentine[1].) Son of Robert[5] and Susanna (Rice) Hollingsworth. Born Fabruary 1, 1786. Died October 29, 1857. First married Sarah B. Green, November 29, 1827. He then married Amelia Roper, in 1836.

ISSUE 1ST MARRIAGE

I. Sarah E[7].—Born October 1, 1828. Married William Bradley.
II. Susan R[7].—Born October 18, 1830. Died young.

ISSUE 2ND MARRIAGE

III. William R[7].—Born January 17, 1840, in Maysville, Ky. Married May 24, 1867, Annie S. Thornloe. No issue.
IV. Mary L[7].—Died young.

G-7. ABSALOM HOLLINGSWORTH

(Joel[6], Isaac[5], George[4], Abraham[3], Thomas[2], Valentine[1].) Son of Joel[6] and Annie B. (Connell) Hollingsworth. Born December 6, 1812. Married Annie Pemberton, 1834. She died 1870.

ISSUE

I. Barclay[8]—Born 1836. Married Phœbe A. Jones. Issue: 3 children.
II. Mary[8]—Born 1838. Married Isaiah Glaze.
III. Joel[8]—Born 1841. Died 1867.
IV. Eunice[8]—Born 1843   Married John B. Pancoast.
V. Robert[8]—Born 1845.
VI. Annie B[8].—Born 1848. Died 1852.
VII. Susanna[8]—Born 1850. Died 1852.
VIII. John[8]—Born 1852. Died 1752.
IX. Samuel[8]—Born 1854.
X. Martha[8]—Born 1857.
XI. Leodica[8]—Born 1860. Married William Jay, Leavenworth. Kan. Jay then married Drucilla Small. No issue.

G-7. ISAIAH HOLLINGSWORTH

(Jonathan⁶, Joseph⁵, George⁴, Abraham³, Thomas², Valentine¹.) Son
of Jonathan⁶ and Mary (Ramsey) Hollingsworth. · Born in 1788. Died
in 1873. Married Patience Smith in 1811.

ISSUE

    I. Annie⁸—Born 1812.
   II. Joseph⁸—Born 1814.
  III. ......⁸—Born 1816.
  IV. Samuel⁸—Born 1816.
   V. Jonathan⁸—Born 1818.
  VI. Mary⁸—Born 1819.
 VII. Hannah⁸—Born 1822.
VIII. Caroline⁸—Born 1824.
  IX. Sally⁸—Born 1826.
   X. Newton⁸—Born 1827.
  XI. Smith⁸—Born 1830.
 XII. Eber⁸—Born 1832.

H-8. NEWTON HOLLINGSWORTH

(Isaiah⁷, Jonathan⁶, Joseph⁵, George⁴, Abraham³, Thomas², Valentine¹.)
Son of Isaiah⁷ and Patience (Smith) Hollingsworth. Born 1827. First
married Lavinia Moore, 1851. She died 1855. He then married
Jemima Beemer, 1858.

ISSUE 1ST MARRIAGE

   2 daughters. Died young.

ISSUE 2ND MARRIAGE

 I. Elkton⁹—Born 1860. Married Mary A. Beck, 1880.
II. Elmer E⁹.—Born 1864.

G-7. JOSEPH HOLLINGSWORTH

(Abraham⁶, Joseph⁵, George⁴, Abraham³, Thomas², Valentine¹.) Son of
Abraham⁶ and Eunice (Steddom) Hollingsworth. Born May 25, 1802,
at Newberry. S. C. Moved to Lebanon, Ohio, 1804. Married Sarah
Sallie Furness, of Montgomery Co., Ohio, 1833. Joseph died in Warren
Co., Ohio, July 30, 1883.

Issue

I. William[8]—Born January 17, 1834.   Died January 12, 1863.
II. Elwood[8]—Born 1836.   Married Angelina Packet, 1862.
III. Alice[8]—Born 1838.   Married Henry Jay.   She died 1875.
IV. Abraham[8]—Born 1840.   Married Celeste Mote, 1861.
V. Margaret Ann[8]—Born 1842.   Married Frank Sherwood, 1865. She died 1867.
VI. Joseph Furness[8]—Born 1845.   Married Susannah Pemberton, 1865.
VII. Jabez[8]—Born 1847.   Unmarried.
VIII. Eunice[8]—Born 1849.   Married Isaac Stubbs, 1876.
IX. Mary[8]—Born 1852.   Died 1852.

H–8. ELWOOD HOLLINGSWORTH

(Joseph[7], Abraham[6], Joseph[5], George[4], Abraham[3], Thomas[2], Valentine[1].)
Son of Joseph[7] and Sarah (Furness) Hollingsworth.   Of Lebanon, Ohio.
Born 1836.   Married Angelina Packet, 1862.

Issue

I. Alpha[9].
II. Douglas[9].
III. Emma[9].
IV. Nathan[9].
V. Omer[9].
VI. Addie M[9].

H–8. ABRAHAM HOLLINGSWORTH

(Joseph[7], Abraham[6], Joseph[5], George[4], Abraham[3], Thomas[2], Valentine[1].)
Son of Joseph[7].   Born 1840.   Married Celestia Mote, 1861.

I. Albert[9].
II. Charles[9].
III. Wm. Francis[9].
IV. Clarence[9].
V. Wildie[9].
VI. Maurice[9].
VII. Joseph[9].

H–8. JOSEPH FURNESS HOLLINGSWORTH

(Joseph[7], Abraham[6], Joseph[5], George[4], Abraham[3], Thomas[2], Valentine[1].)
Son of Joseph[7] and Sarah (Furness) Hollingsworth.   Born 1845.   Married 1865, Susanna H. Pemberton.

Issue

I. Idella[9].
II. Clifford[9].
III. Mary[9].
IV. Eber[9].

F-6. DAVID HOLLINGSWORTH

(Joseph⁵, George⁴, Abraham³, Thomas², Valentine¹.) Son of Joseph⁵ and ...... (Frost) Hollingsworth. First married Catharine Nichel. Name of second wife unknown. No issue.

Issue 1st Marriage

I. Thomas⁷—Born 1803. Died 1862. Married Joanna Johnson, 1823.

II. Joseph⁷.   IV. William⁷.
III. Jonathan⁷.   V. Martha⁷.

G-7. THOMAS HOLLINGSWORTH

(David⁶, Joseph⁵, George⁴, Abraham³, Thomas², Valentine¹.) Son of David⁶ and Catharine (Nichel) Hollingsworth. Born 1803. Died 1862. Married Joanna Johnson, 1823.

Issue

I. Milton⁸—Married Susan M. Wallis.
II. Martha⁸.
III. Thomas E⁸.
IV. Christopher⁸.
V. David⁸.
VI. Franklin⁸.
VII. Seth⁸.
VIII. Albert⁸.

H-8. MILTON HOLLINGSWORTH

(Thomas⁷, David⁶, Joseph⁵, George⁴, Abraham³, Thomas², Valentine¹.) Son of Thomas⁷ and Joanna (Johnson) Hollingsworth. Married Susan M. Wallis, 1847.

Issue

I. Joanna⁹—Born 1848.
II. Clarence⁹—Born 1850.
III. Ona⁹—Born 1856.
IV. Arabel L⁹.—Born 1858.
V. Martha⁹—Born 1860.
VI. M. Franklin⁹—Born 1862.
VII. Elwood C⁹.—Born 1865.
VIII. Joseph F⁹.—Born 1867.
IX. Milton⁹—Born 1869.

F-6. WILLIAM HOLLINGSWORTH

(Joseph⁵, George⁴, Abraham³, Thomas², Valentine¹.) Son of Joseph⁵
and his second wife, Margaret (Hammer) Hollingsworth. Born January 18, 1785, in Ohio. Died September 24, 1855. Married Mary
Cook, about 1811. Born November 18, 1794. Died March 28, 1850.

ISSUE

- I. Sarah⁷—Born November 18, 1812. Deceased.
- II. Susanna⁷—Born November 9, 1813. Married John Holeman,
    1838. She died 1841.
- III. John⁷—Born April 14, 1816. Married Sarah L. Haworth, 1840,
    More of John later.
- IV. Elihu⁷—Born April 20, 1818. First married Ann M. Haworth.
    1844. She died 1861. He then married Hannah Coffin,
    1866. More of Elihu later.
- V. Midian⁷—Born January 12, 1820. Died 1846.
- VI. Asenath⁷—Born November 20, 1821. Died 1836.
- VII. Olive⁷—Born November 22, 1823. Died 1858. Married Alfred
    Kelly, 1854.
- VIII. Milton⁷—Born November 14, 1825. Married Elizabeth Binford,
    1857. Issue: 4 children. More of Milton later.
- IX. Hannah⁷—Born November 19, 1827. Married Wm. E. Hawkins,
    1845.
- X. Eli⁷—Born October 6, 1830. Married Eliza Butler, 1874. Issue:
    2 children.
- XI. Josephus⁷—Born May 19, 1834. Married Dorcas D. Hunt,
    1866. Issue: 3 children.
- XII. Addison⁷—Born February 9, 1837. Married Harriett O'Neal,
    1858. Issue: 4 children; one named Annie E⁸.

G-7. JOHN HOLLINGSWORTH

(William⁶, Joseph⁵, George⁴, Agraham³, Thomas², Valentine¹.) Son of
William⁶ and Mary (Cook) Hollingsworth. Born April 14, 1816. Died
.... Married Sarah L. Haworth, 1840.

- I. Marietta⁸—Born 1840. Married Martin Hayward, 1860.
- II. Pleasant⁸—Born 1843. Died young.
- III. Caroline⁸—Born 1845. Died young.
- IV. Thomas⁸—Born 1846. Died young.

V. Clinton*—Born 1848. Died young.
VI. Calvin*—Born 1850.
VII. William P*.—Born 1853.
VIII. James C*.—Born 1855.

G-7. ELIHU HOLLINGSWORTH

(William*, Joseph*, George*, Abraham*, Thomas*, Valentine*.) Son of William* and Mary (Cook) Hollingsworth. Born April 20, 1818. First married Ann M. Haworth, 1844. She died in 1861. He then married Hannah Coffin, in 1866.

Issue 1st Marriage

I. Joel*—Born 1845. Died young.
II. Jerome*—Born 1849. Married Ida E. Weaver, 1878. Issue: 2 children.
III. Mary E*.—Born 1849. Married J. Walker Hays, 1876.
IV. Cassius*—Born 1854. Died young.
V. Emma*—Born 1859. Married Fremont Baugh.

Issue 2nd Marriage

VI. Frankie*—Born 1871.
VII. Ernest C*.—Born 1872.
VIII. Albert E*.—Born 1874.

G-7. MILTON HOLLINGSWORTH

(William*, Joseph*, George*, Abraham*, Thomas*, Valentine*.) Son of William* and Mary (Cook) Hollingsworth. Born Hamilton, Butler Co., Ohio, November 14, 1825. Died Los Angeles, Cal., March 28, 1907. Married October 26, 1857, Elizabeth Binford. Lived at Farmer's Institute, Ind., to 1872; at Stuart, Guthrie Co., Iowa, to 1895, and at Los Angeles, Cal., to 1907. Farmer.

Issue

I. Joseph Edwin*—Born Farmer's Institute, Ind., June 7, 1859. Living at Hemet, Riverside Co., Cal. Married June 21, 1888, Martha Ellen Woody. Issue: 1. Milton*—Born August 19, 1889. Living in Los Angeles, Cal., 1918. Married February 18, 1914, to Marguerite Bernice Flulks. Issue: Milton, Jr*.—Born November 17, 1914. 2. Daniel Woody*—Born July 11, 1895, Harrison, Neb. In U. S. Navy, 1917–1918. 3. James Edwin*—Born December 8, 1899, Harrison, Neb. 4. John Binford*—Born August 19, 1908, Salem, Ore.

II. William Irving⁶—Born Farmer's Institute, Ind., April 30, 1862.
Living 1917, Los Angeles, Cal. Married October 26, 1903,
Harriet G. Hord, daughter of Mason and Elmira Hord.
Issue: 1. William Irving, Jr⁹.—Born Los Angeles, Cal., De-
cember 4, 1906. 2. Flora Elizabeth⁹—Born Los Angeles, Cal.,
February 23, 1909.

III. Margaret Binford⁶—Born Farmer's Institute, Ind., April 3, 1864.
Died November 20, 1865.

IV. Clarence Binford⁶—Born Farmer's Institute, Ind., November 3,
1867. Living 1917, Los Angeles, Cal. Married March 23,
1891, to Laura May Doane. Issue: Daisy Ruth⁹—Born Bo-
darc, Sioux Co., Neb., September 6, 1893.

F–6. ABRAHAM HOLLINGSWORTH

(Joseph⁵, George⁴, Abraham³, Thomas², Valentine¹.) Son of Joseph⁵
and Margaret (Hammer) Hollingsworth. Born April 3, 1769. Lived
in Newberry, S. C., until 1804. Died at Lebanon, Ohio, 1855. First
married Eunice Steddom, about 1798. He then married Sarah Pidgeon,
Warren Co., Ohio, 1817.

ISSUE 1ST MARRIAGE

I. Martha⁷—Born 1800. Married Jacob Freestone, Ohio.
II. Joseph⁷—Born 1802. Married Sarah Furness, Ohio, 1833.
III. Henry⁷—Born 1804. Married Hannah Zetmier, Ohio. Issue:
1. Elizabeth⁸. 2. Deborah⁸. 3. Anna⁸.
IV. Anna⁷—Born 1806. Married Robert Furness, Ohio.
V. John⁷—Unmarried.
VI. Jabez⁷—Unmarried.

ISSUE 2ND MARRIAGE

VII. Elizabeth⁷—Unmarried.
VIII. Samuel⁷—Married Sarah Jones. Issue: Theodore⁸.
IX. Margaret⁷—Unmarried.
X. Isaac⁷—First married Elizabeth Hunt. He then married Sarah
Bowrenger.
XI. Zebulon⁷—Married Martha .... Issue: 1. Frank⁸. 2. Sarah⁸.
3. Abigail⁸.
XII. Mary⁷—Unmarried.
XIII. Eunice⁷—Married William Hunt.

F-6. JAMES HOLLINGSWORTH

(John⁵, George⁴, Abraham³, Thomas², Valentine¹.) Son of John⁵ and
Rachel (Wright) Hollingsworth. Born 1790. Died 1864. Married
Esther Cadwalader, 1818.

Issue

    I. Elias⁷—Born 1820. Married Lydia Sherwood, 1842. Issue: 6
        children. He then married Rachel A. Adams, 1868. Issue: 2
        children. More of Elias later.
    II. Mahlon⁷—Born 1822. Married Mary Whiteacre, 1843. More
        of Mahlon later.
    III. Zimri⁷—Born 1824. Married Sarah Bond, 1845.
    IV. Jane⁷—Married Clarkson Hiatt.
    V. Martha⁷—Married Amos Hiatt.
    VI. Rachel⁷—Married Dayton Townsend.
    VII. Abner⁷—Unmarried.
    VIII. Seth⁷—Born 1835. Married Mrs. Lucinda Colerazier, 1870.
    IX. Nathan⁷.
    X. Emily⁷—Born 1839. Married John Townsend, 1861.
    XI. Rhoda⁷—Born 1846. Unmarried.

G-7. ELIAS HOLLINGSWORTH

(James⁶, John⁵, George⁴, Abraham³, Thomas², Valentine¹.) Son of
James⁶ and Esther (Cadwalader) Hollingsworth. Born near Morrow,
Warren Co., Ohio, 1820. Died Richmond, Indiana, 1905. First mar-
ried Lydia Sherwood, Warren Co., Ohio, 1842. He then married
Rachel A. Adams, 1869. She died at Richmond, Ind., 1905.

Issue 1st Marriage

    I. Thomas⁸—Born October 7, 1843. Died October 10, 1864, Camp
        Denison, Ohio (Civil War). Was in Company "A," 79th
        Ohio Regiment.
    II. John⁸—Born October 14, 1845. Died March 30, 1865, Camp
        Denison, Ohio (Civil War). Was in Co. "A," 79th Ohio
        Regiment.
    III. Ann⁸—Born November 8, 1847. Died .... Married Frank
        Strate. Issue: 1. Rosa⁹. 2. Clifford⁹. 3. Harry⁹.

IV. Rev. James[2]—Born October 28, 1849. Married Laura A. Skill-
ings. Living 1917, Blanchester, Ohio. Issue: 1. Ordella[3]—
Born October 2, 1876, at Rowley, Mass. 2. Clyde Eben[3]—
Born November 21, 1880, at Cleveland, Ohio. 3. Ralph Waldo[3]
—Born February 6, 1884, at Hillsboro, Ohio. 4. Esther[3]—
Born April 11, 1889, at Hillsboro, Ohio. 5. James Sherwood[3],
Jr.—Born January 14, 1897. Died March 7, 1913.
V. Franklin Sherwood[2]—Born October 15, 1853. Married Jennie
C. Vance, 1879. Living 1917. Issue: 1. Virginia[3]—Born
November 19, 1881. 2. Ray Sherwood[3]—Born March 12,
1885. Living 1918, at 347 Cincinnati Ave., San Antonio, Tex.
VI. Henry[2]—Born June 7, 1863. Died November 13, 1863.

Issue 2nd Marriage

VII. Homer Lee[2]—Born October 3, 1875. Living at Richmond, Ind.
VIII. Geneva[2]—Born September 29, 1879. Died January 21, 1885.

G–7. MAHLON HOLLINGSWORTH

(James[6], John[5], George[4], Abraham[3], Thomas[2]; Valentine[1].) Son of
James[6] and Esther (Cadwalader) Hollingsworth. Born 1822. Married
Mary Whitacre, 1843.

Issue

I. Edward[8]—Born 1843. Married Amanda Hunt, 1862. Issue: 4
children. More of Edward later.
II. James[8]—Born 1845. Married Isadore Jenkins, 1868. Issue: 3
children. More of James later.
III. Rebecca[8]—Born 1846. Died 1851.
IV. Charles M[8].—Born 1848.
V. Rachel[8]—Born 1849. Married Aaron W. Mead, 1871.
VI. Aquilla[8]—Born 1851. Married Pamela Gibson, 1872. More of
Aquilla later.
VII. Esther[8]—Born 1854. Married Joshua Secrist, 1873.
VIII. Harriett[8]—Born 1860. Died 1865.

H–8. EDWARD HOLLINGSWORTH

(Mahlon[7], James[6], John[5], George[4], Abraham[3], Thomas[2], Valentine[1].)
Son of Mahlon[7] and Mary (Whitacre) Hollingsworth. Born 1843.
Married Amanda Hunt, 1862.

ISSUE

I. Frederick[8]—Born 1864.
II. Mary[9]—Born 1865.
III. Nellie[9]—Born 1867.
IV. Lavella[9]—Born 1868.

H-8. JAMES HOLLINGSWORTH

(Mahlon[7], James[6], John[5], George[4], Abraham[3], Thomas[2], Valentine[1].)
Son of Mahlon[7] and Mary (Whitacre) Hollingsworth. Married Isadore
Jenkins, 1868.

ISSUE

I. Alice[9]—Born 1870.
II. Frank I[9].—Born 1872.
III. Harriett[9]—Born 1874.

F-6. JOSEPH HOLLINGSWORTH

(Joseph[5], George[4], Abraham[3], Thomas[2], Valentine[1].) Of Iowa. Son of
Joseph[5] and Margaret (Wright) Hammer Hollingsworth. Born about
1776. Married Hannah Hawkins.

ISSUE

I. Amos[7].
II. Martha[7].
III. William[7].
IV. Benjamin[7].
V. Joseph[7].
VI. Seth[7].
VII. Mary Ann[7].
VIII. James[7].

E-5. JOHN HOLLINGSWORTH

(George[4], Abraham[3], Thomas[2], Valentine[1].) Son of George[4] and second
wife, Jane (Elwell) Hollingsworth. Brother of Abraham Hollingsworth[5],
Laurens, S. C. Born in Frederick Co., Va., in 1764. Died in Ohio,
1807. Married Rachel Wright, 1788.

ISSUE

I. James[6]—Born 1790. Died 1864. Married Esther Cadwalader,
1818. More of James later.
II. Henry[6]—Born 1791. Died 1873. First married Ada Skinner,
1816. Second, Leah Littleton, 1829. Third, Maria Sachel,
1833. Fourth, Eliza Aberly, 1854. Fifth, Phebe Beecher,
1856. More of Henry later.

III. Jane⁶—Born 1793. Married John Cammack.
IV. Charity⁶—Born 1795. Married Jonathan Cox.
V. John⁶—Born 1797. Married Mary Vestal. More of John later.
VI. Nathan⁶—Born 1799. Married Elizabeth Vestal. More of Nathan later.
VII. George⁶—Born 1801. Married Jane Henry. More of George later.
VIII. Hannah⁶—Born 1803. ·Married Samuel Cammack.
IX. Joseph⁶—Born 1805. First married Rachel Vestal. He·then married Adaline Bell. More of Joseph later.

F-6. HENRY HOLLINGSWORTH

(John⁵, George⁴, Abraham³, Thomas², Valentine¹.) Son of John⁵ and Rachel Wright Hollingsworth. Born ......, 1791. Died 1873. First married Ada Skinner, 1816. Second, Leah Littleton, 1829. Third, Maria Sachel, 1833. Fourth, Eliza Aberly, 1854. Fifth, Phoebe Beecher, 1856.

Issue 1st Marriage

I. Harriett⁷—Born 1817.
II. Sarah Ann⁷—Born 1819. Married Absalom Glasscock, 1844.
III. Richard⁷—Born 1821. Married Rebecca Hastings. More of Re-chard later.
IV. Lawson⁷—Born 1823. Married Lucinda Maudlin. More of Lawson later.
V. Mary Jane⁷—Born 1825. First married Michael Crook, 1845. She then married Samuel R. Jepson, 1877.

Issue 2nd Marriage

VI. Littleton⁷—Born 1830.
VII. Jonah⁷—Born 1832.

Issue 3rd Marriage

VIII. Warner L⁷.—Born 1835.
IX. Ruth Anna⁷—Born 1836. Died 1853.
X. Martha Ellen⁷—Born 1838. Married Wm. McIntyre.
XI. James L⁷.—Born 1840. Died 1859.

G–7. RICHARD HOLLINGSWORTH

(Henry[6], John[5], George[4], Abraham[3], Thomas[2], Valentine[1].) Son of Henry[6] and Ada (Skinner) Hollingsworth. Born 1821. Married Rebecca Hastings, 1842.

ISSUE

I. Margaret[8]—Born 1843. Married Thomas Sweetman, 1859.
II. William[8]—Born 1845. First married Rosa Townsend, 1863. He then married Effie Hutz, 1872.
III. Julianna[8]—Born 1847. Married Wm. H. Allen, 1863.
IV. Albert W[8].—Born 1849. Married Monta Jayne, 1871.
V. Perry S[8].—Born 1853. Married Mary Cote, 1871.

H–8. AQUILLA HOLLINGSWORTH

(Mahlon[7], James[6], John[5], George[4], Abraham[3], Thomas[2], Valentine[1].) Son of Mahlon[7] and Mary (Whitacre) Hollingsworth. Born 1851. Married Pamelia Gibson, 1872.

ISSUE

I. Clarence[8]—Born 1874.

H–8. WILLIAM HOLLINGSWORTH

(Richard[7], Henry[6], John[5], George[4], Abraham[3], Thomas[2], Valentine[1].) Son of Richard[7] (Hastings) Hollingsworth and Rebecca. Born 1845. He first married Rosa Townsend, 1863. He then married Effie Hutz, 1872.

ISSUE 1ST MARRIAGE

I. Charles[9]—Born 1864.
II. Edward[9]—Born 1865.
III. Ernest[9].
IV. Perry[9].

ISSUE 2ND MARRIAGE

V. James[9].
VI. William[9].

G–7. ZIMRI HOLLINGSWORTH

(James[6], John[5], George[4], Abraham[3], Thomas[2], Valentine[1].) Son of James[6] and Esther (Cadwalader) Hollingsworth. Born 1824. Married Sarah Bond, 1845.

ISSUE

I. Allen[8]—Born 1851.
II. Annie[8]—Born 1860.
III. Mary[8]—Born 1863. Married......Shrock.

G-7. LAWSON D. HOLLINGSWORTH

(Henry[6], John[5], George[4], Abraham[3], Thomas[2], Valentine[1].) Son of Henry[6] and Ada Skinner Hollingsworth. Born June 14, 1823. Married Lucinda Maudlin. Died January 30, 1902, at Pasadena, Cal.

Issue

I. Preston[8]—Born January, 1846. Died February 20, 1879, at Pasadena, Cal. Married Ellen Jepson. Issue: 1. Edward[9]. 2. Clarence[9].

II. Henry Thomas[8]—Born June 11, 1849. Married Mary Catherine Banbury. Issue: 1. Everett Thomas[9]—Born August 6, 1879. Married Mabel Dalton. 2. Loren Duncan[9]—Born September 26, 1882. Married Rose Cook. 3. Richard Henry[9]—Born December 27, 1884. Married Valma M. Ward.

III. Arthur Stewart[8]—Born March 28, 1851. First married March 14, 1872, Mary Embree. He then married Melvina C. Crothers. He finally married, September 7, 1908, Lucy Russell Pinkerton. Issue, 1st marriage: 1. Jessie Lillian[9]—Born January 29, 1873. Married W. H. Nuss. 2. Lawson Leroy[9]— Born November 12, 1874. 3. Frank Duane[9]—Born November 10, 1876. Married Emma Cross, May 25, 1913. Issue: Duane Cross[10]—Living Pasadena, Cal., 1918.

IV. Ellen (Nellie)[8]—Born ...... 30, 1855. Married August 4, 1875, William Vore. Issue: 1. Jessie Raymond[9]—Born April 4, 1876. Married September 5, 1902, Ethel Horner. 2. Fred H[9].—Born December 10, 1877. Married June 14, 1904, Anna Barnes.

V. Jane[8]—Born .... Married ...... Giddings. Issue: 1. Lawson[9]. 2. Levi[9]. 3. Joseph[9]. 4. Blanche[9]. 5. Paul[9]. 6. June[9].

F-6. NATHAN HOLLINGSWORTH

(John[5], George[4], Abraham[3], Thomas[2], Valentine[1].) Son of John[5] and Rachel (Wright) Hollingsworth. Born January 20, 1799, South Carolina. Died February 23, 1875. Married Elizabeth Vestal, February 27, 1822. She was born December 25, 1802 and died July 10, 1878.

Issue

I. Jemima[7]—Born 1823. Married James M. Strong.

II. John H[7].—Born 1824. Married Sarah A. Wolf. Their son, Omar[8], married Alice Westcott. Issue: Mary E[9].

III. Samuel V[7].—Born 1827. Died October 1828.
IV. Jane H[7].—Born 1830. Married David Meredith. No issue.
V. Charles[7]—Born 1833. Married Caroline Fulgram. Issue: Iola[8].
VI. Narcissa[7]—Born 1838. Unmarried.
VII. Rachel[7]—Born 1842. Married Leroy Noble. Issue: 4 children.
VIII. Hannah[7]—Born 1847. Died 1847.

E-5. HENRY HOLLINGSWORTH

(George[4], Abraham[3], Thomas[2], Valentine[1].) Son of George[4] and second wife, Jane (Elwell) Hollingsworth, and half-brother of Abraham[5], Laurens, S. C. Born 1760. Married Sarah Cook, 1782.

ISSUE

I. Eli[6]—Born 1783. First married Rachel Neill. Died 1807. He then married Rebecca Newman, 1809.
II. Isaac[6]—Born 1785. Married Jane Coppic. Issue: 11 children.
III. Charity[6]—Born 1787. Married ...... Coppic.
IV. Jane[6]—Born 1789. Married......Vernon.
V. Susanna[6]—Born 1791. Married......Coppic.
VI. Rachel[6]—Born 1793. Married ......Coppic.
VII. Mary Ann[6]—Born 1795. Married Valentine Pegg.

F-6. JOSEPH HOLLINGSWORTH

(George[5], George[4], Abraham[3], Thomas[2], Valentine[1].) Son of George[4] and Jane (Elwell) Hollingsworth. Born 1777. Died 1848. Married Sallie Cox, 1797. Joseph was a half-brother of Abraham[5].

ISSUE

I. Mary[7]—Born 1799. Married Seth Rodabaugh.
II. George[7]—Born 1801. Married Jane Davison. Died 1860.
III. Lydia[7]—Born 1803. Married Aaron Gullifer. Died 1871.
IV. Jonathan[7]—Born 1805. First married Susan Bodkin. He then married Catherine Allright. More of Jonathan later.
V. Ira[7]—Born 1808. Married Deborah Bennett. Died 1874.
VI. Asa[7]—Born 1810. Married Susan Bennett. Died 1872, Kansas.
VII. Jeremiah[7]—Born 1812. Married Elixabeth Pollard. Died 1876, Iowa.
VIII. Eliza[7]—Born 1817. Married Austin Guthrie, Indiana.
IX. Kuhn[7]—Born 1819. Married Lydia Asborn, Iowa. More of Kuhn later.
X. Dan[7]—Born 1821. Married Emily Pollard, Indiana. More of Dan later[8].

F-6. JOSEPH HOLLINGSWORTH

(John[5], George[4], Abraham[3], Thomas[2], Valentine[1].) Son of John[5] and Rachel (Wright) Hollingsworth. Born August 22, 1805, South Carolina. First married Rachel Vestal, 1827. She died 1858. He then married Adaline Bell, 1858.

Issue 1st Marriage

    I. Erwin[7]—Married Susan Morris. Issue: 1. Munroe[8]. 2. Celestia[8]. 3. Raymond[8]. 4. Jerome[8]. 5. Charles[8]. 6. Walter[8]. 7. Jesse[8]. 8. Susan W[8].

    II. Addison[7]—Born 1830. Died February 4, 1880. Married Sarah A. Camp, 1851. Issue: 4 children. More of Addison later.

    III. Lewis[7]—Died in infancy.

    IV. Enoch[7]—Born 1835. Married Mary A. Morris, 1857. Issue: 8 children. More of Enoch later.

    V. Allen[7]—Married Martha Bell. Issue: 1. Courtney[8]. 2. Ralph[8]. 3. Alice[8]. 4. Bessie[8]. 5. Grace[8].

    VI. Nelson[7]—Married Martha Furtherington. Issue: 3 children. More of Nelson later.

    VII. Williard[7]—First married Clarinda Blake. He then married Adaline Bell, 1858. Issue, first marriage: 1. Clarence[8]. 2. Everetta[8]. 3. Frederick[8].

Issue 2nd Marriage

    VIII. Jane Elizabeth[7]—Born 1860. Died 1862, Indiana.

    IX. Brady W[7].—Born 1862.

    X. Joseph[7]—Born 1865. Died December 26, 1879, near Oquasha, Ill.

G-7. ADDISON HOLLINGSWORTH

(Joseph[6], John[5], George[4], Abraham[3], Thomas[2], Valentine[1].) Of Kansas. Son of Joseph[6] and first wife, Rachel Vestal. Born in 1830. Died February 4, 1880. Married Sarah A. Camp, 1851.

Issue

    I. George E[8].—Born 1851.

    II. Theodore C[8].—Born 1852.

    III. Lydia J[8].—Born 1854.

    IV. Frank H[8].—Born 1857.

G-7. ENOCH HOLLINGSWORTH

(Joseph⁵, John⁴, George⁴, Abraham³, Thomas², Valentine¹.) Son of Joseph⁵ and first wife, Rachel Vestal. Born in 1835. Married Mary A. Morris, 1857.

Issue

    I. Edward M⁸.—Born 1859.
    II. Allen G⁸.—Born 1861.
    III. Joseph H⁸.—Born 1864.
    IV. Nelly J⁸.—Born 1866.
    V. Ruth A⁸.—Born 1868.
    VI. Rozetta H⁸.—Born 1872.
    VII. Clifford E⁸.—Born 1873.

G-7. NELSON HOLLINGSWORTH

(Joseph⁵, John⁴, George⁴, Abraham³, Thomas², Valentine¹.) Of Kansas. Son of Joseph⁵ and his first wife, Rachel Vestal. Born in 1841. Married Martha J. Furtherington, 1866.

Issue

    I. Effie J⁸.—Born 1867.
    II. Harry W⁸.—Born 1869.
    III. John C⁸.—Born 1871.
    IV. Edith M⁸.—Born 1874.
    V. Barton L⁸.—Born 1876.
    VI. Rachel V⁸.—Born 1878.

F-6. JOHN HOLLINGSWORTH

(John⁵, George⁴, Abraham³, Thomas², Valentine¹.) Son of John⁵ and Rachel (Wright) Hollingsworth. Born 1797. Married Mary Vestal.

Issue

    I. Elizabeth⁷.   V. Joseph⁷.
    II. Merzy⁷   VI. John⁷.
    III. Hannah⁷.   VII. Mary⁷.
    IV. Samuel⁷.   VIII. Jemima⁷.

F-6. GEORGE HOLLINGSWORTH

(John⁵, George⁴, Abraham³, Thomas², Valentine¹.) Son of John⁵ and Rachel (Wright) Hollingsworth. Born 1801. Married Jane Henry.

ISSUE

I. Hannah⁷.

F-6. ELI HOLLINGSWORTH

(Henry⁵, George⁴, Abraham³, Thomas², Valentine¹.) Son of Henry⁵ and Jane (Elwell) Hollingsworth. Born in 1783. First married Rachel Neill, who died in 1807. He then married Rebecca Newman, in 1809.

ISSUE 1ST MARRIAGE

I. William⁷—Born 1805. Died 1835.
II. Ursula⁷—Born 1807. Married ...... Sinks.

ISSUE 2ND MARRIAGE

III. Mary⁷—Born 1810.
IV. Elizabeth⁷—Born 1812.
V. Sarah⁷—Born 1814.
VI. Nathan⁷—Born 1816. Married Elizabeth Westlake.
VII. Isaac⁷—Born 1818. Married Elizabeth Ballon.
VIII. Thomas⁷—Born 1820. Married Elizabeth Yount.
IX. John⁷—Born 1824. Married Susanna Silver. Issue: 3 children.

E-5. GEORGE HOLLINGSWORTH

(George⁴, Abraham³, Thomas², Valentine¹.) Son of George⁴ and Jane (Elwell) Hollingsworth. Born 1755. Died .... Married Jane Henry.

ISSUE

I. Jeremiah⁵—Born 1775. Died unmarried.
II. Joseph⁵—Born 1777. Married Sallie Cox. More of Joseph later.
III. Ruth⁵—Born 1780. Married Thomas Madden.
IV. Jane⁵—Born 1783. Married Ezehiel Hollingsworth.
V. Mary⁵—Born 1785. Married James Crumey.
VI. Zepheniah⁵—Born 1787. Married Polly Dailey. More of Zepheniah later.
VII. John⁵—Born 1791. First married Abigail Broderick. He then married Mary Bell.
VIII. Ann⁵—Born 1795. Married John Cassiday.

F-6. ZEPHENIAH HOLLINGSWORTH

(George[5], George[4], Abraham[3], Thomas[2], Valentine[1].) Son of George[5] and Jane (Henry) Hollingsworth. Born 1787. Married Polly Dailey.

ISSUE

    I. George[7]—Born 1812. Died 1852.
   II. Elias[7]—Born 1813. Married Nancy Larrabee. Died 1854.
 III. Josiah[7]—Born 1815. Married Ruth Todd.
 IV. Jane[7]—Born 1817. Married John Herbert.

      Jacob M. Hollingsworth[9], son of Joseph B[8]., of Indiana. Issue: Everett S.[10] and Alice L[10].
      John S. Hollingsworth[8], son of Dan[7]. Issue: Nellie[9] and Fred[9].
      Austin G. Hollingsworth[8], son of Kuhn[7]. Issue: Frank[9], John[9] and Jessie A[9].
      John B. Hollingsworth[8], son of Kuhn[7], of Iowa. Issue: Emma[9]— Born 1877.

F-6. EZEKIEL HOLLINGSWORTH

(Joseph[5], George[4], Abraham[3], Thomas[2], Valentine[1].) Son of Joseph[5] and ...... (Frost) Hollingsworth. Born...... Died at Rickland, Keokuk Co., Iowa. Married Jane Hollingsworth.

ISSUE

     I. Zebulon[7]—Born .... Died 1879.
    II. Jeremiah[7]—Married Catherine Amos.
   III. Miles[7]—Married Mrs. Dunn.
   IV. Mahondra[7]—Married Nancy Wolf.
     V. Mary[7].
   VI. Cynthia[7].
  VII. John[7].
 VIII. William[7].
   IX. Lydia[7].
    X. Elias[7]. }Twins.
   XI. Eliza[7].
  XII. Ruth[7].

G–7. ZEBULON HOLLINGSWORTH

(Ezekiel[6], Joseph[5], George[4], Abraham[3], Thomas[2], Valentine[1].) Son of Ezekiel[4] and Jane (Hollingsworth) Hollingsworth. Born .... Died January 21, 1878. Married Eliza Karr, April 15, 1834.

Issue

    I. Elbert[8]—Born February 12, 1835.
   II. Rebecca Jane[8]—Born September 13, 1836.
  III. Katherine[8]—Born January 6, 1839.
  IV. Amanda[8]—Born January 31, 1844.
   V. Mahondra[8]—Born November 16, 1847.

G–7. GEORGE HOLLINGSWORTH

(Joseph[6], George[5], George[4], Abraham[3], Thomas[2], Valnentine[1].) Son of Joseph[4] and Sallie (Cox) Hollingsworth. Born 1801. Died 1860. Married Jane Davison, 1820.

Issue

    I. Davison[8]—Born 1822. Married Elizabeth Pugh. More of Davison later.
   II. Susanna[8]—Born 1824. Married J. Guion.
  III. Sarah[8]—Born 1826. Married ......
  IV. Nero[8]—Born 1829. Married Lucinda Pugh. More of Nero later.
   V. Rachel[8]—Born 1831.
  VI. Jeremiah[8]—Born 1834. First married Elizabeth Guion. He then married Elizabeth Churchill. More of Jeremiah later.
 VII. Mary J[8].—Born 1836. Married Robert Suindle.
VIII. Jonathan[8]—Born 1839. Married Christine Guion.
  IX. Sylvanius[8]—Born 1843. Married Elizabeth Turley. More of Sylvanius later.
   X. Ada[8]—Born 1848. Married Christopher Cady.
  XI. Addison[8]—Born 1852. Died ......

G–7. JONATHAN HOLLINGSWORTH

(Joseph[6], George[5], George[4], Abraham[3], Thomas[2], Valentine[1].) Son of Joseph[4] and Sallie (Cox) Hollingsworth. Born 1805. First married Susan Bodkin. He then married Katherine Allright.

ISSUE 1ST MARRIAGE

I. Rachel[6]—Born 1825.
II. Sarah[8].
III. Candace[8].
IV. Mary[8].
V. Eliza[8].
VI. Nancy[8].

VII. Jane[8].
VIII. George .W[8].
IX. Henry C[8].
X. Neldo[8].
XI. Farmer[8].
XII. Elmer E[8].

ISSUE 2ND MARRIAGE

XIII. Alto[8].
XIV. Dora[8].

XV. John[8].
XVI. Oral[8].

H-8. JONATHAN HOLLINGSWORTH

(George[7], Joseph[6], George[5], George[4], Abraham[3], Thomas[2], Valentine[1].)
Of Indiana. Son of George[7] and Jane (Davison) Hollingsworth. Born
1839. Married Christine Guion, 1858.

ISSUE

I. John E[9].—Born 1859.
II. Rufus[9]—Born 1875.
III. Bertha[9]—Born 1877.

H-8. SYLVANIUS HOLLINGSWORTH

(George[7], Joseph[6], George[5], George[4], Abraham[3], Thomas[2], Valentine[1].)
Of Indiana. Son of George[7] and Jane (Davison) Hollingsworth. Born
1843. Married Elizabeth Turley about 1862.

ISSUE

I. Ulysses G[9].—Born 1864.
II. Jennie[9]—Born 1870.

Henry C Hollingsworth[8], son of Jonathan[7]. Issue: Clarence[9]
and Perry[9].
Neldo Hollingsworth[8], son of Jonathan[7]. Issue: Bertha[9].
Joseph B. Hollingsworth[8], son of Ira[7], of Indiana, son of Joseph[6].
Issue, first marriage: 1. Jacob M[9]. 2. Olive[9]. 3. Martha[9].
4. Mary A[9]. Issue, second marriage: Ida B[9].

G–7. ASA HOLLINGSWORTH

(Joseph⁶, George⁵, George⁴, Abraham³, Thomas², Valentine¹.) Of Iowa.
Son of Joseph⁶ and Sallie (Cox) Hollingsworth. Born 1810. Died
1872. Married Susannah Bennett, about 1828.

Issue

    I. Sarah⁸—Born 1829. Married Stacy Jones.
    II. Ruth⁸—Born 1831. Married Robert Kinsley.
    III. Dan⁸—Born 1833. First married Mary McDermot. He then
        married Martha . . . .
    IV. Eliza⁸—Born 1835. Married Thomas . . . .
    V. Ira⁸—Born 1838. Married Mary J. Jones.
    VI. Francis⁸—Born 1840. Married Hannah Jones.
    VII. Deborah⁸—Born 1842. Married Thompson Miller.
VIII. Newton⁸—Born 1846. Died 1863.

H–8. NERO HOLLINGSWORTH

(George⁷, Joseph⁶, George⁵, George⁴, Abraham³, Thomas², Valentine¹.)
Of Indiana. Son of George⁷ and Jane (Davison) Hollingsworth. Born
1829. Married Lucinda Pugh, about 1853.

Issue

    I. William⁹—Born 1854.
    II. George M⁹.—Born 1859.
    III. John S⁹.—Born 1865.
    IV. Mary M⁹.—Born 1868.

G–7. KUHN HOLLINGSWORTH

(Joseph⁶, George⁵, George⁴, Abraham³, Thomas², Valentine¹.) Of Iowa.
Son of Joseph⁶ and Sallie (Cox) Hollingsworth. Born 1819. Married
Lydia Osborn, 1841.

Issue

    I. Eunice⁸—Born 1842. Married Samuel Long.
    II. Austin G⁸.—Born 1845. Married Martha A. Everman.
    III. Esther A⁸.—Born 1847. Married John O. Wood.
    IV. John B⁸.—Born 1849. Married Mary P. McMurray.
    V. William F⁸.—Born 1851.
    VI. William O⁸.—Born 1853.

VII. Alva A⁸.—Born 1854.
VIII. Sarah F⁸.—Born 1857.
IX. Harvey H⁸.—Born 1860.
X. Nellie A⁸.—Born 1864.

G-7. DAN HOLLINGSWORTH

(Joseph⁶, George⁵, George⁴, Abraham³, Thomas², Valentine¹.) Of
Indiana. Son of Joseph⁶ and Sallie (Cox) Hollingsworth. Born 1821.
Married Emily Pollard, 1840.

Issue

I. Elizabeth⁸—Born 1841. Married Allen Avery.
II. Caroline⁸—Born 1846. Married Benjamin F. Abrams.
III. John S⁸.—Born 1851. Married Frances Turna.

H-8. DAVISON HOLLINGSWORTH

(George⁷, Joseph⁶, George⁵, George⁴, Abraham³, Thomas², Valentine¹.)
Son of George⁷ and Jane (Davison) Hollingsworth. Born 1822. Married Elizabeth Pugh, 1843.

Issue

I. Mary Jane⁸—Born 1844. Married Parker Brown.
II. Margaret⁸—Born 1852.
III. Marcellus⁸—Born 1854. Married Lucetta Trowbridge.
IV. Lilly M⁸.—Born 1857. Died ....
V. Julia⁸—Born 1859. Married George Avery.
VI. Marshall⁸—Born 1862.

H-8. JEREMIAH HOLLINGSWORTH

(George⁷, Joseph⁶, George⁵, George⁴, Abraham³, Thomas², Valentine¹.)
Of Indiana. Son of George⁷ and Sallie (Cox) Hollingsworth. Born
1834. First married Elizabeth Guion. He then married Elizabeth
Churchill.

Issue

I. First marriage: Jennie⁸—Born 1856.
II. Second marriage: Laurie⁸—Born 1860.

G-7. IRA HOLLINGSWORTH

(Joseph⁶, George⁵, George⁴, Abraham³, Thomas², Valentine¹.) Son of
Joseph⁶ and Sallie (Cox) Hollingsworth. Born 1808. Died 1874.
Married Deborah Bennett, 1827.

Issue

    I. Joseph⁸—Born 1828. First married Orilla Monroe. He then
        married Nancy Zink.

   II. Ruth Anna⁸—Born 1829. Married James Hame.

 III. Sarah Jane⁸—Born 1831. Married J. Hightshue.

 IV. Eliza⁸—Born 1832. Married C. Haines.

  V. Elizabeth⁸—Born 1834. Married H. Cook.

 VI. Job⁸—Born 1835. Died . . . .

VII. Francis M⁸.—Born 1837. Married C. Hightshue.

VIII. Martin L⁸.—Born 1838. Married Martha E. Dydley.

 IX. William H⁸.—Born 1840. Married M. A. Martin.

  X. Sylvania⁸—Born 1841. Married John Wright.

 XI. Lurana⁸—Born 1843. Married Elisha Endaly.

XII. Sanders⁸—Born 1844. Married Eliza Gossett.

XIII. Oliver C⁸.—Born 1847. Married Sallie Farr.

XIV. Victoria⁸—Born 1851. Married Melville Bair.

H-8. FRANCIS M. HOLLINGSWORTH

Of Indiana. Second son of Ira⁷.

Issue

  I. Albert⁹.   III. Frank⁹.

 II. Fred⁹.

     Martin L⁸., of Indiana, third son of Ira⁷. Issue: 1. Clarissa⁹,
        2. Mervin S⁹. 3. Benjamin G⁹. 4. Willis A⁹. 5. Nora M⁹.
        6. Ida G⁹.

     William H⁸., fourth son of Ira⁷. Issue: 1. Martha⁹, 2. Lillie⁹.

     Sanders⁸, fifth son of Ira⁷. Issue: 1. Allen M⁹., 2. James I⁹.

     Oliver C⁸., sixth son of Ira⁷. Issue: 1. Nellie V⁹.

G-7. ELIAS HOLLINGSWORTH

Son of Zepheniah⁶.

Issue

   I. Eliza⁸.   IV. Clark⁸.

  II. Frank⁸.   V. Zepheniah⁸.

 III. Ellis⁸.   VI. Malissa⁸.

Clark[8], son of Elias[7]. Issue: 1. Fletcher[9]. 2. Linea[9]. 3. Mattie[9].
4. Frank[9].

Frank[8], son of Elias[7]. Issue: 1. Laurie[9]. 2. William H[9]. 3. Charlie[9].

D-4. AVANANT HOLLINGSWORTH

Grandson of Abraham. Born in North Carolina, 1800. Married Mary Reno.

ISSUE

    I. Holliet[5]—Born in Illinois, 1828. Married Mary E. Cowan, 1864. Living in California. Issue: 2 daughters.

D-4. ISAAC HOLLINGSWORTH

(Thomas[3], Thomas[2], Valentine[1].) Son of Thomas[3] and Judith (Lampley) Hollingsworth. Born June 13, 1731. Died October 28, 1795. Married Hannah Scott, daughter of Timothy and Sarah Scott, of New Castle Co., Del., 1769. She was born February 22, 1744 and died May 28, 1810.

ISSUE

    I. Job[5] ⎱ Twins—Born August 24, 1770. Jesse died 1843.
   II. Jesse[5] ⎰

  III. Joseph[5] ⎱ Twins Born March 10, 1774. Joseph died July 1,
  IV. Benjamin[5] ⎰   1842. More of Joseph later.
            More of Benjamin later.

    V. Judith[5]—Born December 21, 1776. Married David Preston, 1797. More of Judith later.

  VI. Hannah[5]—Born July 2, 1781. Married Lewis Williamson.

 VII. Eli[5]—Born January 28, 1784. Married Lydia Pierce. More of Eli later.

E-5. JOB HOLLINGSWORTH

(Isaac[4], Thomas[3], Thomas[2], Valentine[1].) Son of Isaac[4] and Hannah (Scott) Hollingsworth. Born August 24, 1770. Married Ann Cann.

ISSUE

    I. Achilles[6].   III. Henry[6].

   II. Sylvester[6].   IV. Josephus[6].

    Mrs. S. Z. Hollingsworth, widow of Achilles[6], died August 19, 1878, in her 80th year. No issue.

E-5. JESSE HOLLINGSWORTH

(Isaac[4], Thomas[3], Thomas[2], Valentine[1].) Son of Isaac[4] and Hannah (Scott) Hollingsworth. Born August 24, 1770. Died 1843. Married Mary Powell.

Issue

I. Benjamin P[6].—Born 1807. More of Benjamin later.
II. Reese J[6].—Born 1809. More of Reese later.
III. Charles D[6].—Born 1811.
IV. Thomas[6]—Born 1817. More of Thomas later.
V. William P[6].—Born 1821. More of William P. later.
VI. Mary[6]—Born 1826.

F-6. BENJAMIN POWELL HOLLINGSWORTH

(Jesse[5], Isaac[4], Thomas[3], Thomas[2], Valentine[1].) Son of Jesse[5] and Mary (Powell) Hollingsworth. Born 1807. Died 1860.

Issue

I. George W[7].—Born ......, Philadelphia.
II. Henry[7]—Born .... Moved to Council Bluffs, Iowa.
III. Charles F[7].—Born ......, Philadelphia.
IV. Francis L[7].—Born .... Died ......

F-6. REESE J. HOLLINGSWORTH

(Jesse[5], Isaac[4], Thomas[3], Thomas[2], Valentine[1].) Son of Jesse[5] and Mary (Powell) Hollingsworth. Born September 14, 1809. Married Amanda M. Lasher, about 1834.

Issue

I. Kate F[7].—Born February 28, 1836.
II. William W[7].—Born March 13, 1843.

E-5. BENJAMIN HOLLINGSWORTH

(Isaac[4], Thomas[3], Thomas[2], Valentine[1].) Son of Isaac[4] and Hannah (Scott) Hollingsworth. Born March 10, 1774. Died .... Married Elizabeth Cann.

Issue

I. John R[6].—Deceased.
II. Martha[6].
III. Samuel W[6].—Lived at Wilmington, Del.
IV. Rachel C[6].—Deceased.

E-5. JOSEPH HOLLINGSWORTH

(Isaac⁴, Thomas³, Thomas², Valentine¹.) Son of Isaac⁴ and Hannah
(Scott) Hollingsworth. Born March 10, 1774. ·Died July 1, 1842.
Married Jane Cann.

Issue

I. Hannah⁶.
II. Isaac⁶.
III. Ann⁶.
IV. James⁶—Living in Chicago, 1878.

E-5. JUDITH (HOLLINGSWORTH) PRESTON

Daughter of Isaac⁴ and Hannah (Scott) Hollingsworth.   Born December 21, 1776. Married David Preston, 1797.

Issue

I. Isaac⁶.
II. Hannah⁶.
III. Deborah⁶.
IV. Edmund⁶—Married Phebe H. Hoskins.

E-5. ELI HOLLINGSWORTH

(Isaac⁴, Thomas³, Thomas², Valentine¹.) Son of Isaac⁴ and Hannah
(Scott) Hollingsworth. Born January 28, 1784. Married Lydia
Pierce. Died ....·...

Issue

I. Eliza⁶—Married John Woodward.
II. Edmund⁶—Married Ruth Ann Huston.   More of Edmund
    later.
III. George⁶—Married Louisa Woollens.   More of George later.
IV. Rachel⁶—Married Joshua Valentine.
V. Susan⁶—Married Joshua Mendenhall.
    Edmund Preston, son of David, who married Judith Hollingsworth.
Edmund married Phebe H. Hoskins.

F-6. WILLIAM P. HOLLINGSWORTH

(Jesse[5], Isaac[4], Thomas[3], Thomas[2], Valentine[1].) Of Philadelphia, Pa. Son of Jesse[5] and Mary (Powell) Hollingsworth. Born December 25, 1821. Married Amanda Whiteman, January 18, 1853.

ISSUE

I. Tilden Harris[7]—Born October 19, 1853.
II. Claude R[7].—Born July 8, 1872. Died January 21, 1876.

F-6. THOMAS C. HOLLINGSWORTH

(Jesse[5], Issac[4], Thomas[3], Thomas[2], Valentine[1].) Son of Jesse[5] and Mary (Powell) Hollingsworth. Born 1817. Married Mary E. Thompson.

ISSUE

I. Robert D[7].—Born 1844.
II. Emma T[7].—Born 1847.
III. Helen[7]—Born 1850.
IV. Thomas C[7].—Born 1853.
V. Mary T[7].—Born 1855.
VI. Clara[7]—Born 1857.
VII. William H[7].—Born 1860. Died 1868.
VIII. Ella D[7].—Born 1863.

E-5. RACHEL HOLLINGSWORTH HARVEY

Daughter of Amor[4] and Mary (Chandler) Hollingsworth. Born 1781. First married Thomas Harvey, 1802. He died 1865. She then married Eli Harvey.

ISSUE 1ST MARRIAGE

I. Mary Ann[6]—Born 1802. Married Robert Poole.
II. William[6]—Married Esther Pierce.
III. Amor[6]—Married Martha Derrickson.

ISSUE 2ND MARRIAGE

IV. Chalkley[6]—Married Sallie Baker.
V. Elizabeth Edge[6].
VI. Lydia Edge[6].
VII. Edith[6]—Married Isaac Watkins.
VIII. Eveline[6]—Married Thomas Darlington Elwood.
IX. Lewis[6]—Married Mary Hoopes.
X. Philena[6]—Married Mordecai Lewis.
XI. Mary[6]—Married Watson Magill.

F-6. EDMUND B. HOLLINGSWORTH

(Eli[5], Isaac[4], Thomas[3], Thomas[2], Valentine[1].) Son of Eli[5] and Lydia (Pierce) Hollingsworth. Married Ruth Ann Huston.

ISSUE

I. Allen R[7].

II. William H[7].

III. George W[7].

IV. Samuel H[7].

V. James[7].

VI. Frank[7].

F-6. GEORGE W. HOLLINGSWORTH

(Eli[5], Isaac[4], Thomas[3], Thomas[2], Valentine[1].) Son of Eli[5] and Lydia (Pierce) Hollingsworth. Married Louisa Woollens.

ISSUE

I. Georgianna L[7].

II. William W[7].—Married Lena Doun.

III. Sydney P[7].

IV. Mary E[7].

V. W. Walter[7].

VI. Lydia C[7].

VII. Caroline D[7].

D-4. CHRISTOPHER HOLLINGSWORTH

(Thomas[3], Thomas[2], Valentine[1].) Son of Thomas[3] and Judith (Lampley) Hollingsworth. Born March 15, 1742. First married Elizabeth Chandler, 1765. He then married Sarah Webb, 1775.

ISSUE 1ST MARRIAGE

I. Elizabeth[5]—Born 1766. Married Eg. Webb, 1787.

ISSUE 2ND MARRIAGE

II. William[5]—Born 1776.

III. Sarah[5]—Born 1778.

IV. Christopher[5]—Born 1781.

V. Samuel[5]—Born 1784.

D-4. AMOR HOLLINGSWORTH

(Thomas[3], Thomas[2], Valentine[1].) Son of Thomas[3] and Judith (Lampley) Hollingsworth. Born May 29, 1739. Died 1826. Married Mary Chandler, 1766. She died 1821, age 79.

ISSUE

I. Isaac⁵—Born 1767. First married Cassandra Divers. He then married Ruth Stanbury. He died 1837.

II. Elijah⁵—Born 1770. Went South. Unmarried. Died 1794.

III. Joel⁵—Born 1773. Married Phebe Kirk, 1802. Died 1848.

IV. Mark⁵—Born 1777. Married Waitstill Tileston, 1804. Went to Boston. Died 1855.

V. Rachel⁵—Born 1781. Married Thomas Harvey, 1802. He died 1865.

VI. Amor⁵—Born 1785. Unmarried. Died 1838.

VII. Sarah⁵—Died 1794.

E-5. ISAAC HOLLINGSWORTH

(Amor⁴, Thomas³, Thomas², Valentine¹.) Son of Amor⁴ and Mary (Chandler) Hollingsworth, a flour merchant, in Baltimore. Born 1767. Died 1837. First married Cassandra Divers. He then married Ruth Stansbury.

ISSUE 1ST MARRIAGE

I. Mary Cassandra⁵—Married Cheyney Hoskins.

II. Jarrett⁵—Died unmarried.

ISSUE 2ND MARRIAGE

III. Elizabeth O⁵.—Married Abraham Staitzman.

IV. Oliver⁵—Lost at sea.

V. Maria Cornelia⁵—Married Dr. John F. Bull, Harford Co., Md.

E-5. JOEL HOLLINGSWORTH

(Amor⁴ Thomas³, Thomas², Valentine¹.) Son of Amor⁴ and Mary (Chandler) Hollingsworth. Born January 7, 1773. He died April 15, 1848. Married Phoebe Kirk, 1803. She was born February 20, 1781. She died in 1817. Buried at Center Meeting. He then married Ann Kirk, his sister-in-law, who died August 3, 1864, age 75.

ISSUE 1ST MARRIAGE

I. Lydia⁵—Born 1805. Married David Barry. Lived in Iowa.

II. Elijah⁵.—Born 1806. Married Anna Richards Fairlamb, 1839.

III. Caleb Kirk⁵—Born 1809. Married Elizabeth B. Miller, 1837.

IV. Sarah⁵—Born 1811. Married John Elliott. Died 1843.

V. Ferdinand⁶—Born 1814. First married Annie Hynman. He
      married second wife, Mary Ann Springer. Died 1847,
      Wilmington.

ISSUE 2ND MARRIAGE

VI. Phœbe Ann⁶—Married Thomas Woolens, 1853. Lived on the
      original land purchased from William Penn, 1699, on the
      Brandywine River, Del.

From DELAWARE REPUBLICAN, Wilmington, Del., of May, 1848.

"Died at his residence, in Christiana Hundred, on the 15th inst.,
Joel Hollingsworth, in the 76th year of his age. The deceased was one
of those few individuals whose characteristic trait was a contented dis-
position, never evincing a desire for more of this world than was suf-
ficient for the maintenance of himself and family, in a plain and com-
fortable way. He possessed a degree of cheerfulness, calculated to
render himself an agreeable and interesting companion to those with
whom he associated. His memory was of the most retentive order,
and was stored with many novel and interesting traditionary tales and
anecdotes, connected with the early settlement of the Brandywine.
His conversational powers were great, and he delighted in rendering
himself entertaining and interesting to those around him. He retained
a few acres of his forefather's estate, which he was enabled to cultivate
with his own hands to the last year of his life. He leaves a legacy of
good will and friendship to his large circle of friends and acquaintances.''

F-6. CALEB KIRK HOLLINGSWORTH

(Joel⁵, Amor⁴, Thomas³, Thomas², Valentine¹.) Son of Joel⁵ and Phœbe
(Kirk) Hollingsworth. Born 1809. Married Elizabeth B. Miller, 1837.
She died April 22, 1868, Delaware Co., Pa.

ISSUE

  I. Joel⁷—Born 1837. Lived at Media, Pa.
 II. John⁷—Born 1839. Lived at Media, Pa.
III. Ann⁷—Born 1848. Lived at Media, Pa.

F-6. FERDINAND HOLLINGSWORTH

(Joel⁵, Amor⁴, Thomas³, Thomas², Valentine¹.) Son of Joel⁵ and
Phœbe (Kirk) Hollingsworth. Born 1814. First married Annie Hynman. He then married Mary Ann Springer. Died Wilmington, 1847.

ISSUE 2ND MARRIAGE

  I. William C⁷.—Born 1852. Living at Wilmington, Del., 1884.
 II. Sallie⁷—Born 1853. Living at Wilmington, Del., 1884.

F-6. ELIJAH HOLLINGSWORTH

(Joel⁵, Amor⁴, Thomas³, Thomas², Valentine¹.) Son of Joel⁵ and Phœbe (Kirk) Hollingsworth. Born 1806. Died 1866. Married Anna Richards Fairlamb, 1839.

ISSUE

I. Susan Harlan⁷—Married Edward Siter, 1861. Issue: 3 children.
II. Ida⁷—Married Dr. Ralph M. Townsend, 1872. Issue: 1 child.
Mahlon Betts, Samuel Harlan and Elijah Hollingsworth formed a partnership, August 28, 1841. Mr. Betts retired, 1849. After Elijah Hollingsworth's death, 1866, the present company, known as the Harlan and Hollingsworth Company, was formed and incorporated, 1867.

E-5. MARK HOLLINGSWORTH

(Amor⁴, Thomas³, Thomas², Valentine¹.) Son of Amor⁴ and Mary (Chandler) Hollingsworth. Born February 19, 1777. Died February 27, 1855, age 78 years. Married Waitstill Tileston, Dorchester, Mass., October 16, 1804. She was born November 29, 1779. Died March 31, 1858.

ISSUE

I. Charles Mark⁶—Born August 7, 1805. Drowned 1809.
II. Leander Nelson⁶—Born June 13, 1807. Died February, 1827.
III. Amor⁶—Born August 11, 1808. Married Jane M. Robinson, 1834. Died 1871.
IV. Charles Mark⁶—Born July 31, 1810. Died June 11, 1824.
V. John Mark⁶—Born January 23, 1812. Married Emeline Cornell, 1834. Died 1865.
VI. George⁶—Born October 17, 1813. Married Polly Eastman, 1859.
VII. Lyman⁶—Born July 17, 1815. Married Mary W. Thayer, 1840.
VIII. Maria Harvey⁶—Born June 9, 1817. Married Emmet Cornell, 1835.
IX. Anderson⁶—Born March 6, 1819. Married Susan J. Sumner, 1844. More of Anderson later.
X. Cornelia Waitstill⁶—Born October 7, 1821. Married Lemuel W. Babcock, 1844.
XI. McLean⁶—Born October 23, 1823. Died September 15, 1825.

F-6. MARIA HARVEY HOLLINGSWORTH CORNELL

Daughter of Mark and Waitstill Hollingsworth. Born June 9, 1817. Died at Bridgewater, Mass., August 24, 1865. Married Emmet Cornell, 1835.

ISSUE

I. Cornelia Waitstill[7].

II. Mark Hollingsworth[7].

III. Julia Maria[7]—Married James M. Mitchell. Issue: 1. Harvey James[8]. 2. George Hollingsworth[8]. 3. Lillian May[8].

IV. Henry Lyman[7]. Living 1918. Married Harriet Sophia Withington. Issue: 1. Worthington[8]. 2. Josephine[8]. 3. Shirley Merritt[8]. 4. France[8]. 5. Henry Lyman, Jr[8]. 6. Marguerite Aspinwalt[8].

F-6. AMOR HOLLINGSWORTH

(Mark[5], Amor[4], Thomas[3], Thomas[2], Valentine[1].) Of Boston, Mass. Son of Mark[5] and Waitstill (Tileston) Hollingsworth. Born August 11, 1808. Married 1834, Jane M. Robinson. Died 1871.

ISSUE

I. Amor L[7].—Married Marion Davis.

II. Jennie[7]—Married Gen. Lucien H. Warren.

III. Zackary Taylor[7]—Married Mrs. Ida Hollingsworth Townsend (daughter of Elizah[6] and Anne Farlam Hollingsworth). Widow of Dr. Ralph M. Townsend, of Philadelphia. Issue: 1. Amor[8]. 2. Valentine[8]. Z. T. Hollingsworth[7], President, 1918, of Hollingsworth & Vose Co., Paper Manufacturers, 141 Milk St., Boston. His son, Valentine[8], is Treasurer of the Company.

IV. Mark[7]—Married Minnie Merrill.

F-6. JOHN MARK HOLLINGSWORTH

(Mark[5], Amor[4], Thomas[3], Thomas[2], Valentine[1].) Son of Mark[5] and Waitstill (Tileston) Hollingsworth. Born January 23, 1812, Dorchester, Mass. Died Groton, Mass., April 6, 1865. First married June 8, 1834, Emeline Cornell, daughter of Walter and Mary Batty Cornell, who was born at Cambridge, Washington Co., N. Y., November 28, 1815, and died March 5, 1853. Issue: 2 children. He then married, December 15, 1856, Anne Sarah Tileston, daughter of Edmund Pitt and Sarah

McLean Boies Tileston. She was born December 15, 1825, Dorchester, Mass., and died in Groton, Mass., May 21, 1893, having married the second time June 20, 1866, George Sumner Graves of Groton, Mass.

Issue 1st Marriage

I. George[7]—Born July 29, 1836, Braintree, Mass. Died August 8, 1859, Groton, Mass.
II. Mary Rachel[7]—Born January 11, 1839, Braintree, Mass. Died December 25, 1846, Boston, Mass.

Issue 2nd Marriage

III. Grace[7]—Born January 23, 1858. Living 1918 at Groton, Mass. Married July 15, 1884, Frank Lawrence Blood. Issue: Mark Hollingsworth[8]. Born June 30, 1894, Groton, Mass.

F-6. CORNELIA WAITSTILL (HOLLINGSWORTH) BABCOCK

Daughter of Mark[6] and Waitstill (Tileston) Hollingsworth. Born October 7, 1821. Died August 21, 1899. Married November 4, 1844, Lemuel Whiting Babcock, at Milton, Mass. He was a prosperous farmer.

Issue

I. Lemuel[7]—Born December 20, 1850, Milton, Mass. Died January 10, 1915, New York. Married, December 1, 1880, Mary Kennard, of Brookline, Mass. Lawyer of New York City. Graduate of Harvard. Issue: 1. Pauline[8]—Born November 15, 1881, Brookline, Mass. First married Henry Holt, of New York City, April 14, 1903. Issue: Barbara[9]. She then married Elwyn Poor, of New York, September 30, 1911, a cotton merchant and Harvard graduate. 2. Philip Hollingsworth[8]—Born January 31, 1887, New York. Graduate of Harvard. Occupation: Fruit farming in town of Harbord, Mass. Married February 1, 1913, to Frieda Brewer of New York City, N. Y. Issue: (a.) Constance Hollingsworth[9]. (b.) Lemuel Whiting[9].
II. Edith[7]—Born January 6, 1846. Living 1918, Groton, Mass. Unmarried.

F-6. ANDERSON HOLLINGSWORTH

(Mark[5], Amor[4], Thomas[3], Thomas[2], Valentine[1].) Son of Mark[5] and Mary Waitstill (Tileston) Hollingsworth. Born March 6, 1819. Married Susan J. Sumner, 1844.

ISSUE

    I. Sumner[7]—Born 1845.
   II. Ellis[7]—Born 1846. Died 1917. No issue.

E-5. JOSHUA HOLLINGSWORTH

(Thomas[4], Thomas[3], Thomas[2], Valentine[1].) Of Nottingham, Pa. Son of third Thomas[4] and Jane (Smith) Hollingsworth. Born February 24, 1774. Died 1830. Married Hannah Harvey, October 17, 1798. She died 1859.

ISSUE

    I. Harvey[5]—Born 1799. Died April 27, 1826.
   II. William[5]—Born 1801. Unmarried.
  III. Caleb[5]—Born 1803. Married Mary H. Kirk, June 8, 1829. He
        died June 25, 1882. More of Caleb later.
  IV. Thomas[5]—Born 1806. Died November 28, 1832.
   V. Mary[5]—Born 1810. Died May 17, 1829.
  VI. Jane[5]—Born 1817. First married Lewis Kirk, August 6, 1829.
        She then married William Kirk. She died January 17, 1872.
        Buried in Indiana; at first lived in Chester Co., Pa.

F-6. CALEB HOLLINGSWORTH

(Joshua[5], Thomas[4], Thomas[3], Thomas[2], Valentine[1].) Of West Chester, Pa. Son of Joshua[5] and Mary Harvey Hollingsworth. Married Mary H. Kirk, June 8, 1829. He died June 25, 1882.

ISSUE

    I. Joshua R[7].—Born 1830. Married Elizabeth Pool.
   II. Hannah Jane[7]—Born 1832. Married Thomas Mendenhall.
  III. Mary Emma[7]—Born 1839. Married Caleb Wright.

E-5. JOHN HOLLINGSWORTH

(Thomas[4], Thomas[3], Thomas[2], Valentine[1].) Of Louden Co., Va. Son of third Thomas[4] and Jane (Smith) J. Hollingsworth. Born October 31, 1756. Died Louden Co., Va., 1806. Married Jemima Backhouse, in Pennsylvania, 1781. She died, Belmont Co., Ohio, 1853.

ISSUE

I. Judith[5]—Born 1782. Died young.
II. Jehu[5]—Born 1784. Married Sevior McDaniel. More of Jehu later.
III. John[5]—Born 1786. Died 1843. Married Elizabeth Nichols. More of John later.
IV. Jemima[5]—Born 1790. Died 1851. Married ......Hesket.
V. Jane[5]—Born 1795. Died 1860. Married Samuel Neptune.
VI. Sarah[5]—Born 1798. Died 1875. Married Isaiah Nichols.
VII. Hannah[5]—Born 1799.

F-6. JOHN HOLLINGSWORTH

(John[5], Thomas[4], Thomas[3], Thomas[2], Valentine[1].) Of Ohio. Son of John[5] and Jemima (Backhouse) Hollingsworth. Born 1786. Died 1843. Married Elizabeth Nichols, 1820.

ISSUE

I. Adelaide[7]—Born 1821. Married Joseph McNichols.
II. Thomas N[7].—Born 1822. Married Elizabeth A. Beatty. Issue: 2 children.
III. Sampson L[7].—Born 1824. Married William Hodgin.
IV. Montrabello[7]—Born 1826. First married Elizabeth Buchanan. Issue: 3 children. He then married Mary S. Dillon. Issue: 2 children.
V. Lydia Ann[7]—Born 1828. Died 1859.
VI. Hannibal R[7].—Born 1830. Married Sarah Harris. Issue: 2 children.
VII. Dr. John B[7].—Born 1832. First married Ruth Talbot. Issue: 1 child. He then married Martha P. Embree.
VIII. William K[7].—Born 1835. Married Maria McKelvey. Issue: 6 children.
IX. Dr. George W[7].—Born 1839. Married Ellen McKelvey. Issue: 2 children.
X. Jemima E[7].—Born 1841. Married Theodore Dowdell.
XI. Henley H[7].—Born 1843. Married Zepha D. Noling. Issue: 2 children.

F-6. JEHU HOLLINGSWORTH

(John[6], Thomas[4], Thomas[3], Thomas[2], Valentine[1].) Of Louden Co., Va.
Son of John[6] and Jemima (Backhouse) Hollingsworth. Born July 18,
1784. Married Sevior McDaniel, 1807.

ISSUE

    I. Mary[7]—Born 1809. Died 1846. Married Stacy Taylor.
    II. William[7]—Born August 17, 1811. Died August 26, 1881. Mar-
        ried Deborah Vincent, 1834. More of William later.
    III. John Edward[7]—Born January 20, 1815. Died 1864. Married
        Rachel Harn, 1839. More of John Edward later.
    IV. Jemima[7]—Born February 4, 1820. Unmarried.
    V. Thomas[7]—Born November, 1822. Unmarried.
    VI. James[7]—Born November, 1824. Unmarried.

G-7. WILLIAM HOLLINGSWORTH

(Jehu[6], John[5], Thomas[4], Thomas[3], Thomas[2], Valentine[1].) Son of Jehu[6]
and Sevior (McDaniel) Hollingsworth. Born August 17, 1811. Died
August 26, 1881, St. Mary's, Ohio. Married 1834, Deborah Vincent.

ISSUE

    I. Amanda[8]—Born November 1, 1836. Died February 14, 1864.
    II. Jehu Jackson[8]—Born December 10, 1839. Living 1918, St.
        Mary's Ohio. Married Hattie Gregory. Issue: Netta M[9].
        Married . . . .
    III. Curthbur[8]—Died in infancy.
    IV. Charles L[8].—Born September 27, 1844. Died November 25,
        1890. Married Maggie Roney, June 30, 1874; 3 of following
        issue living 1918, Ogden, Utah. Issue: 1. William[9]—Born
        June 17, 1875. Died December 17, 1875. 2. Chas. R[9].—Born
        July 4, 1877. Married. 3. Howard J[9].—Born October 18,
        1879. Issue: 1 daughter. Married. 4. Fred P[9].—Born Sep-
        tember 18, 1882.

G-7. JOHN EDWARD HOLLINGSWORTH

(Jehu[6], John[5], Thomas[4], Thomas[3], Thomas[2], Valentine[1].) Son of Jehu[6]
and Sevior (McDaniel) Hollingsworth. Born January 20, 1815, at
Louden Co., Va. Died April 18, 1864, St. Mary's, Ohio. Lived at
St. Mary's, Ohio. Married January 15, 1839, Rachel Harn, daughter
of Denton and Pickett Harn, of Maryland.

Issue

I. Henrietta⁴—Born January 23, 1840. Living 1918. Married Dr. W. G. Kishler, January 30, 1908, St. Mary's, Ohio.

II. Josephus⁴—Born November 10, 1841. Died September 1, 1863.

III. William⁴—Born August 3, 1843. Died December 16, 1859.

IV. Isabella⁴—Born June 28, 1847. Died March 31, 1910. Married May 20, 1870, D. W. Jay, of St. Mary's, Ohio. Issue: 6 children; 3 living 1918. 1. C. E. Jay⁵, St. Mary's, Ohio. 2. Mrs. E. Quinby⁵, St. Mary's, Ohio. 3. C. H. Jay⁵, Columbus, Ohio.

V. John E⁴.—Born May 28, 1849. Died October 8, 1870.

VI. Thomas Elwood⁴—Born December 7, 1853. Living 1918, St. Mary's, Ohio. Married February 24, 1876, Eleanora Coney. Issue, all living 1918: 1. Harriet Belle⁵—Married J. A. Long. 2. Nora May⁵. 3. Edward Clinton⁵—404 Eighth Ave., Brooklyn, N. Y. Married Lee Morvilius. No issue. 4. Florence Coney⁵. Married Harry G. Smith. 5. Thomas Elwood, Jr⁵.—Born May 5, 1892. Address 1918: Sergeant, 305th Field Artillery, Battery E, Camp Upton, New York. He was the first New Yorker to pass the physical examination. See New York TIMES of August 1, 1917, which gave him a write-up on the first column of the front page. He was in the first quota, the first day, and surprised the Board with the remark: "Sign me up, I do not claim any exemption." May 1918, commissioned 2nd Lieutenant.

E–5. ERR HOLLINGSWORTH

(Thomas⁴, Thomas³, Thomas², Valentine¹.) Son of third Thomas⁴ and Jane (Smith) Hollingsworth. Born June 26, 1762. Died 1819. Married Phœbe Mercer, of Mill Creek Hundred, Del., 1795. Err moved to Middleton, Ohio, 1815.

Issue

I. Samuel⁴—Born 1796. Married Margaret Leech, 1824. Lived at Middleton, Columbiana Co., Ohio. Died near Pennsville, Morgan Co., 1864. Large family. More of Samuel later.

II. Elisha⁴—Born 1798. Died 1869. First married Sarah Oliphant. He then married Sarah Heald, who died 1869. More of Elisha later.

III. Mercer⁴—Born 1801. Died 1813.

IV. Sarah⁶—Born 1804. Died 1818.

V. Phœbe⁶—Born 1806. Died 1861. Married T. Llewelyn.

VI. Jane⁶—Born 1809. Married Samuel Kimball, Williams Co., Ohio.

VII. Ann⁶—Born 1812. Married Isaac Stokesbury, Columbiana Co., Ohio.

VIII. Mahlon⁶—Born 1816. Married Rachel James. Went to Iowa. Died there. More of Mahlon later.

F-6. ELISHA HOLLINGSWORTH

(Err⁵, Thomas⁴, Thomas³, Thomas², Valentine¹.) Son of Err⁵ and Phœbe (Mercer) Hollingsworth. Born in Delaware, December 15, 1798. Died at Pennsville, Ohio, 1869. He was a farmer. First married Sarah Heald, Middleton, Ohio, 1820. He married second wife, Mrs. Sarah Ann Griffith, nee Penrose. No issue.

ISSUE 1ST MARRIAGE

I. Edwin⁷—Born June 29, 1821. Married Betsey Heald, 1844 or '45. Issue: 5 children.

II. Ruth⁷—Born February, 1823. Married Abram Patton, 1841 or '42. Died one year after marriage.

III. Phœbe⁷—Born 1825. Married Harrison P. Gamble, autumn 1842. Issue: 9 children; 6 grew to adult life.

IV. Err⁷—Born May 3, 1827. First married Mary J. Harris, 1847. He married second wife, Sarah Tavender. Issue, 1st marriage: 1 daughter, died in infancy; the other 5 married and have families. Issue, 2nd marriage: 1 daughter.

V. Martha⁷—Born June 11, 1829. Married Thomas Llewellyn, January, 1841. Issue: 7 children; 2 died in infancy.

VI. William⁷—Born August 20, 1831. Married Frances Peck, December 1860, Iowa. Issue: 7 children; 5 sons and 2 daughters.

VII. Lydia⁷—Born May, 1833. Married Jacob Worthington, 1851. Issue: 5 children.

VIII. Ezra⁷—Born January 22, 1836. First married Lydia Ann Plummer. He married second wife, Mary C. Holdren, and finally Nancy Pierpont. Issue: 6 children. More of Ezra later.

IX. Anne⁷—Born February 11, 1838. Married Joseph Vaughan, December 25, 1861. Issue: 4 children. All are living, married, and have families.

X. Emmet⁷—Born October 4, 1846. Married Sarah Gilbert, November 21, 1867. Issue: 4 children.

G–7. EZRA HOLLINGSWORTH

(Elisha[6], Err[5], Thomas[4], Thomas[3], Thomas[2], Valentine[1].)   Son of Elisha, Hollingsworth, of Pennsville, Ohio.   Born Columbiana Co., Ohio. January 22, 1836.   Living 1917.   First married November 9, 1866, Lydia Ann Plummer.   Born August 31, 1839.   Died October 6, 1876. He married second wife, Mary C. Holdren, March 8, 1879.   Third wife, Nancy Pierpont.   He served 3 years in the Civil War, 33rd Infantry, Iowa Vol., Co. H.

Issue 1st Marriage

I. Mary Frances[8]—Born July 16, 1867.   Died January 28, 1896.

II. Thomas Dillon[8]—Born November 13, 1868.   Living 1917, at Akron, Ohio.   Married September 2, 1894, Artie A. Gensemer, daughter of Urias and Eunice J. Keck Gensemer, of Marshall-ville, Ohio.   Issue: 1. Edith May[9]—Born May 15, 1897. 2. Esther Ada[9]—Born Jan. 15, 1903.   3. Frances Mary[9]—Born March 16, 1908.   He graduated in medicine at the Eclectic Medical College, Cincinnati, Ohio, June 1893.   Practicing medicine at Akron, Ohio.

III. Lewis Milton[8]—Born April 2, 1871.

IV. Martha Jane[8]—Born October 20, 1872.   Died November 29, 1899.

V. Edgar Clifton[8]—Born August 6, 1875.   Married April 9, 1902, Mary Esley, daughter of Henry and Rosonna Esely, of Lou-donville, Ohio.   No issue.

Issue 2nd Marriage

VI. Adelbert E[8].—Born August 8, 1883.   Died May 9, 1903.

No issue by third marriage.

F–6. MAHLON HOLLINGSWORTH

(Err[5], Thomas[4], Thomas[3], Thomas[2], Valentine[1].)   Son of Err[5] and Phœbe (Mercer) Hollingsworth.   Born 1816.   Died in Iowa, 1864. Married Rachel W. James, 1839.

Issue

I. Err[7]—Born 1840.   Died 1843.

II. Susannah[7]—Born 1841.   Died 1877.   Married John Riley, 1858.

III. Joseph M[7].—Born 1844.   Married Mary E. Hayward, 1867. More of Joseph later.

IV. Phœbe Jane[7]—Born 1846. Married Haney A. Evans, 1868.

V. James[7]—Born 1849. Married Minnie McNamara, 1874. More of James later.

VI. William L[7].—Born 1852.

VII. Annie J[7].—Born 1854. Married Thornton R. Lincoln, 1875.

G–7. JOSEPH M. HOLLINGSWORTH

(Mahlon[6], Err[5], Thomas[4], Thomas[3], Thomas[2], Valentine[1].) Son of Mahlon[6] and Rachel W. (James) Hollingsworth. Born 1844. Married Mary E. Hayward, 1867.

ISSUE

I. Cora[8].

II. Dora[8].

III. Frank E[8].

IV. Hattie B[8].

V. Ettie M[8].

VI. Minnie[8].

G–7. JAMES HOLLINGSWORTH

(Mahlon[6], Err[5], Thomas[4], Thomas[3], Thomas[2], Valentine[1].) Son of Mahlon[6] and Rachel W. (James) Hollingsworth. Born 1849. Married Minnie McNamara, 1874.

ISSUE

I. James[8].

II. Rachel[8].

III. Mahlon[8].

G–7. THOMAS HOLLINGSWORTH

(Samuel[6], Err[5], Thomas[4], Thomas[3], Thomas[2], Valentine[1].) Son of Samuel[6] and Margaret (Leech) Hollingsworth. Born 1835. Married Elizabeth Kannal, at New Lisbon, Ohio, October 23, 1861. Died January 25, 1872.

ISSUE

I. Emmet Louis[8]—Born January 22, 1864, New Lisbon, Ohio. Living 1918, Rensselear, Ind. Married Fannie M. Allen, at Kalamazoo, Mich., December 31, 1887. Issue: 1. Cecilia Georgia[9] —Born November 22, 1888. Married Horace Chadbourne, December 31, 1915. 2. Louis Dorothea[9]—Born October 31, 1892. Married February 20, 1914, Ralph T. Upjohn. Issue: (a) Mary Louise[10]; (b) Joanne M'Liss[10]; (c) Virginia Ruth[10]. 3. Ruth Irene[9]—Born March 6, 1894. Died in infancy. 4. Gerald Emery[9]—Born June 9, 1895. 5. Emmet Louis, Jr[9].—Born October 14, 1897.

II. George Kannal[6]—Born September 26, 1868, Rensselear, Ind.
Living 1918, Chicago, Ill. Married September 28, 1889, Nora
A. Hopkins. Issue: 1. Donald H[9].—Born October 30, 1891,
Rensselear, Ind. Married Dorothy Fox, April 17, 1915, in
Chicago, Ill. Issue: Donald H., Jr[10].—Born June 9, 1916.
2. Thomas[9]—Born February 24, 1894, Rensselear, Ind.

G–7. LOUIS HOLLINGSWORTH

(Samuel[6], Err[5], Thomas[4], Thomas[3], Thomas[2], Valentine[1].) Son of
Samuel[6] and Margaret (Leech) Hollingsworth, and grandson of Err[5].
Born March 5, 1831. Married Hannah C. Fawcett, 1859. Was a
banker. Lived at Des Moines, Iowa.

Issue

I. Luella E[8].—Born 1860. Married. No issue.
II. Samuel[8] and William[8].—Born 1863. ⎫
III. Thomas I[8].—Born 1864.   ⎬ Died in infancy.
                                                 ⎭
IV. Horace S[8].—Born 1868. Married. No issue. Living 1917, 702
Maple St., Des Moines, Iowa.

F–6. SAMUEL HOLLINGSWORTH

(Err[5], Thomas[4], Thomas[3], Thomas[2], Valentine[1].) Son of Err[5] and
Phœbe (Mercer) Hollingsworth. Born August 2, 1796. Died 1864.
First married Margaret Leech, Ohio, 1824. She was born 1804. She
died 1856. He then married Martha Hall, 1860. No issue.

Issue 1st Marriage

I. Jane[7]—Born 1825. Died 1838.
II. Phœbe Ann[7]—Born 1827. Married Jonathan Edmundson, 1848.
III. Louis[7]—Born 1831. Married Hannah C. Fawcett. Lived in
Des Moines, Iowa. Was a banker. Issue: 4 children. More
of Louis later.
IV. Sarah[7]—Born 1833. Died 1854.
V. Thomas[7]—Born 1835. Married Elizabeth Kannal. Was a mer-
chant at Rensselaer, Ind. Died there January 25, 1872. Issue:
2 children. 1. Emmet Louis[8]. 2. George Kannal[8]. More of
Thomas later.

VI. Hannah[7]—Born 1838. Married Louis Cope. Lived near Fayette City, Pa. Now deceased.

VII. Mary L[7].—Born 1840. Died 1840.

VIII. William[7]—Born 1842. Died 1854.

IX. Margaret[7]—Born 1844. Married Joseph C. Vanlaw. Lived at Zanesville, Ohio. Now deceased.

X. Samuel A[7].—Born 1847. Died 1854.

XI. James E[7].—Born 1850. Died 1854.

E-5. LEVI HOLLINGSWORTH

(Thomas[4], Thomas[3], Thomas[2], Valentine[1].) Of Pennsylvania. Son of third Thomas[4] and Jane (Smith) Hollingsworth. Born April 23, 1764. Died in Ohio, June 11, 1829. He married Mary Harry, 1789. They removed to Loudon Co., Va., 1793. They removed to Belmont Co., 1804. They were of the Friends' Society.

Issue

I. Thomas[6]—Born 1790. Died 1823. Unmarried.

II. David[6]—Born 1791. Died 1855. More of David later.

III. Rachel[6]—Born 1793. Died 1795.

IV. Sarah[6]—Born 1796. Died 1867. Married Abraham Packer.

V. Hannah[6]—Born 1798. Living 1882. Married Elisha M. Ellis.

VI. Isaac[6]—Born 1801. Died 1874. Married Phœbe Kirk. Issue. More of Isaac later.

VII. Susanna[6]—Born 1803. Married Samuel B. Scoles.

VIII. Levi[6]—Born 1805, Monmouth, Ill. 3 wives. More of Levi later.

IX. Eli[6]—Born 1807, Xenia, Ind. Married Elizabeth Ellis. More of Eli later.

X. John[6].—Born 1809, Flushing, Ohio. Married Elizabeth Brock. More of John later.

XI. Mary[6]—Born 1811. Died 1811.

XII. Elihu[6]—Born 1813, Flushing, Ohio. Married Lydia A. Fisher. More of Elihu later.

F-6. LEVI HOLLINGSWORTH

(Levi[5], Thomas[4], Thomas[3], Thomas[2], Valentine[1].) Of Ohio. Son of Levi[5] and Mary (Harry) Hollingsworth. Born 1805. Married Lavinia Rodgers, 1830. He then married Eliza Allen. No issue. He finally married Elizabeth Fisher. No issue.

ISSUE 1ST MARRIAGE

I. Lydia Ann⁷—Born 1831. Married William Boyd.
II. Thomas S⁷.—Born 1834. Married Sarah Wood.
III. Mary I⁷.—Born 1836. Married Hiram J. Chesser.
IV. Samuel W⁷.—Born 1839. Married Emma H. Lyon.
V. Charles W⁷.—Born 1841. Married Lide Johnson.
VI. John Wm⁷.—Born 1844. Married Esther White.
VII. David S⁷.—Born 1847. Married Maggie Wood.
VIII. Lavinia E⁷.—Born 1850. Married G. W. Smith.

F–6. JOHN HOLLINGSWORTH

(Levi⁵, Thomas⁴, Thomas³, Thomas², Valentine¹.) Son of Levi⁵ and Mary (Harry) Hollingsworth. Born 1809. Married Elizabeth Brock. Lived at Flushing, Ohio.

ISSUE

I. George⁷.
II. Catharine⁷.
III. Jesse⁷.
IV. Martha⁷.

F–6. ELIHU HOLLINGSWORTH

(Levi⁵, Thomas⁴, Thomas³, Thomas², Valentine¹.) Son of Levi⁵ and Mary (Harry) Hollingsworth. Born 1813. Lived at Flushing, Ohio. Married Lydia A. Fisher, 1838.

ISSUE

I. Benjamin F⁷.—Born 1840. Died 1863. Unmarried.
II. Mary L⁷.—Born 1842. Married Joseph Farmer.
III. David A⁷.—Born 1844. Married Belinda McBean. Issue.
IV. Lavinia⁷—Born 1849. Married Frank Judkins.

F–6. DAVID HOLLINGSWORTH

(Levi⁵, Thomas⁴, Thomas³, Thomas², Valentine¹.) Son of Levi⁵ and Mary (Harry) Hollingsworth. Born 1791. Died 1855. First married Hannah Jones. He then married Elizabeth Crossley. No issue.

ISSUE 1ST MARRIAGE

I. Grace⁷.
II. Eliza⁷.
III. Mary⁷.
IV. Elwood⁷.
V. Levi⁷.
VI. Sarah⁷.

F-6. ISAAC HOLLINGSWORTH

(Levi[5], Thomas[4], Thomas[3], Thomas[2], Valentine[1].) Son of Levi[5] and
Mary (Harry) Hollingsworth. Born 1801. Died 1855. Married
Phœbe Kirk. She died 1874.

ISSUE

I. Lydia[7].   III. Rachel[7].
II. William[7].   IV. Phœbe[7].

F-6. ELI HOLLINGSWORTH

(Levi[5], Thomas[4], Thomas[3], Thomas[2], Valentine[1].) Son of Levi[5] and
Mary (Harry) Hollingsworth. Born 1807 at Xenia, Ind. First married Elizabeth Ellis. He then married . . . . . .

ISSUE 1ST MARRIAGE

I. Jonathan[7].   III. Isaac[7].
II. Mary Ann[7].   IV. John[7].

ISSUE 2ND MARRIAGE

V. Levi[7].   VII. Celia[7].
VI. Achsah[7].

C-3. JOSEPH HOLLINGSWORTH

(Thomas[2], Valentine[1].) Of Pennsylvania. Son of Thomas[2] and Grace
(Cook) Hollingsworth. Born March 11, 1709. Married Martha
Houghton, February 23, 1730. Removed to Virginia. Certificate
given to Hopewell Meeting, Virginia, March 2, 1741.

C-3. JACOB HOLLINGSWORTH

(Thomas[2], Valentine[1].) Son of Thomas[2] and Grace (Cook) Hollingsworth. Married Elizabeth Chandler, September 23, 1729. Born January 4, 1704. He died intestate, leaving 7 children. He purchased,
June 23, 1726, of James Logan, attorney for Letitia Aubrey, daughter
of William Penn, 225 acres of land in Mill Creek Hundred, New Castle
Co., Del.

ISSUE

I. Elias[4]—Born 1732. Married Susanna Pierce, October 25, 1753.
Was living at Fredericksburg, Va., 1769. More of Elias later.
II. David[4]—Born 1734. Married Sarah Green. Moved to Huntingdon Co., Pa. Purchased the old homestead, 1767. More
of David later.

III. Ruth⁴—Born 1739. Married John Way, June 16, 1763. He was born 1727.

IV. Jacob⁴—Born 1741. Married Susanna Haines, 1767.

V. Zebidee⁴—Born 1743. Married Lydia Allen, 1769. Moved to Virginia. More of Zebidee later.

VI. Jeptha⁴—Born 1745. First wife Miss Ray, and second wife, Nancy Gordon, 1768. Went South. More of Jeptha later.

VII. Rachel⁴—Born 1747.

D-4. JEPTHA HOLLINGSWORTH

(Jacob³, Thomas², Valentine¹.) Son of Jacob³ and Elizabeth (Chandler) Hollingsworth. Born 1745, New Castle Co., Del. Went South. Died 1816. First married 1768, Miss Ray, of Baltimore, Md. He then married, after the Revolutionary War, Nancy Gordon, a sister of Colonel Samuel Gordon, in whose regiment he served during the Revolutionary War.

ISSUE 1ST MARRIAGE

I. Rachel⁵.   II. Lydia⁵.

ISSUE 2ND MARRIAGE

III. Jeptha⁵—Born 1791, Greenville Dist., S. C. Died 1870, in Leavenworth Co., Kan. More of Jeptha later.

IV. Thomas K⁵.—Born April 29, 1798, Kentucky. Married March 1, 1819, Elizabeth Kennedy, Kentucky. More of Thomas K. later.

V. John⁵—Married Sarah Thompson.

VI. Enoch⁵—Born and lived in Union Co., S. C., moved to Pickens Co., about 1830 or '35. Married Rebecca Smith. Issue: 1. Robert⁶. 2. Wylie⁶—Daughter who married ...... Crane. 3. James Ivy⁶—Born 1811. Died 1859. Married 1834, Cynthia Clayton, born 1812. She died 1889. Both buried at Liberty Cemetery, Pickens Co., S. C. More of James Ivy later.

VII. Asenith⁵—Married W. Duncan.

VIII. Samuel⁵.

IX. Ruth⁵—Married Samuel Talkington.

E-5. JEPTHA HOLLINGSWORTH

(Jeptha[4], Jacob[3], Thomas[2], Valentine[1].) Son of Jeptha[4] and second wife, Nancy (Gordon) Hollingsworth. Born April 1791, Greenville District, S. C. Died Leavenworth Co., Kansas, 1870. Married Logan Co., Ky., December 1813, Mary B. Gordon, who was born December 5, 1793. Died, Todd Co., Ky., 1832. Jeptha[5] Hollingsworth came from Kentucky to Clay Co., Mo., in 1852 or 1853; went to Texas during Civil War, returned to Missouri year after war. He had moved from Clay to Bates County before going to Texas. Bought land in Kansas few years before his death. Occupation: farmer and slave owner.

Issue

I. Samuel Gordon[6]—Born December 14, 1814, Todd Co., Ky. Died in Kansas City, Mo., 1892. More of Samuel later.

II. Leander Fielding[6]—Born February 7, 1821, Todd Co., Ky. Died May 25, 1890. He was a lawyer. Lived in Missouri; moved to Colorado, and died at Silverton, Colo. Married 1847, Elizabeth Curd. Issue: 1. Mary[7]. 2. Leland[7]. 3. Edward[7]. 4. Emma[7]. All unmarried.

III. Benjamin Franklin[6]—Born June 20, 1824, Todd Co., Ky. More of Benjamin later.

IV. Jeptha Harrison[6]—Born March 17, 1828, Todd Co., Ky. Died 1880, Kansas. He was a lawyer. Married Sarah Jessups.

V. Virgil Christopher[6]—Born December 17, 1832, Todd Co., Ky. Died 1858. Married Margaret Swope.

F-6. SAMUEL GORDON HOLLINGSWORTH

(Jeptha[5], Jeptha[4], Jacob[3], Thomas[2], Valentine[1].) Son of Jeptha[5] and Mary B. (Gordon) Hollingsworth. Born December 14, 1814, Todd Co., Ky. Died at Kansas City, Mo., 1892. First married 1836, Susan Mimms. He married second, Mary Williams, September 1857. Occupation: lawyer.

Issue 1st Marriage

I. Helen[7]—Born December, 1838, Todd Co., Ky. Living 1918, Avon Park, Fla. Married David Gordon, 1858. Issue: 1. Gideon[8]—Born 1863. Married Jennie Kiebler. 2. Eva[8]— Born 1865. Married Edward Legg. 3. Hallie[8]—Born 1869. Married Alfred Buchanan. 4. Blanche[8]—Born 1871. First married ...... Ramsey. Second husband ...... Carter. 5. Stella[8]—Born 1874. Married ...... Ramsey. 6. David[8]— Born 1877.

II. Josephine[7]—Born April, 1842, Todd Co., Ky. Married Dr. Chas. Palmer, 1873. Issue: 1. Patti[8]—Born March, 1875. 2. Charlie[8]—Born 1877. Died 1900. 3. Grace[8]—Born December, 1879. Married Russell E. Neal. Living 1918, New York City, N. Y.

III. Susie[7]—Born December 17, 1855, Clay Co., Mo. Married Charles C. Faris, October 1882. Issue: 1. Daisy[8]—Born November, 1883. 2. Palmer[8]—Born April, 1885. Married Lillian Wolf. 3. Lieut. Frank Hollingsworth[8]—Born September, 1886. 1918 with U. S. Army in France. 4. Samuel Guy[8]—Born October, 1891.

ISSUE 2ND MARRIAGE

IV. Frank[7]—Born April 2, 1860, Clay Co., Mo. Unmarried. Living 1918, Avon Park, Fla.

E-5. THOMAS KENNEDY HOLLINGSWORTH

(Jeptha[4], Jacob[3], Thomas[2], Valentine[1].) Son of Jeptha[4] and Nancy (Gordon) Hollingsworth. Born April 29, 1798, in Garrett Co., Ky. Died October 26, 1857. First married March 11, 1819, Elizabeth Kennedy. He then married, December 6, 1843, Mrs. Amanda Harrell Wilson.

ISSUE 1ST MARRIAGE

I. William Kennedy[6]—Born February 16, 1820. Died June 10, 1892. Married March 9, 1843, Maria Gordon.

II. Jeptha Gordon[6]—Born July 7, 1822. Died 1878. Married June 1847, Maria Louisa Sherman. Issue: 8 children. More of Jeptha later.

III. Samuel Newton[6]—Born February 9, 1825. Died February 22, 1861. Married October 7, 1849, Martha Gray.

IV. John Lewis[6]—Born March 12, 1827. Died July 28, 1902. Married February 14, 1865, Emma Baugh. Issue: 1. Edward[7]. 2. Bessie[7].

V. Mary Ann[6]—Born December 30, 1829. Died May 5, 1911.

VI. Nancy Jane[6]—Born April 19, 1833. Died August 18, 1909. Married October 22, 1857, Thomas L. Gore. Issue: 1 son.

VII. Elizabeth*—Born December 1, 1839. Died March 18, 1892. Married May 10, 1859, John J. Hickman.

ISSUE 2ND MARRIAGE

VIII. Cornelia*—Born March 6, 1846. Married, ... Byers, McMinnville, Tenn.

F–6. BENJAMIN FRANKLIN HOLLINGSWORTH

(Jeptha⁵, Jeptha⁴, Jacob³, Thomas², Valentine¹.) Son of Jeptha⁵ and Mary B. (Gordon)·Hollingsworth. Born June 20, 1824, Todd Co., Ky. Died February 26, 1860, Bates Co., Mo., at the home of his father, Jeptha H⁵. Married, 1852, Mary Mimms, who was born February 10, 1828. She died at Platte City, Mo., April 4, 1884. Graduate of Medical College, Louisville, Ky.

ISSUE

I. Mary Catherine⁷—Born Platte City, Mo., January 9, 1854. Married October 3, 1876, Joseph McKee. Issue: 1. Mary⁸— Born August 28, 1877. Married G. Van Millett. 2. Frank⁸— Born July 28, 1879. Married Ida Geishler. 3. Eugene⁸—Born April 26, 1882. 4. Winifred⁸—Born October 24, 1889. Married Jas. Frederick Mervine. 5. Frances⁸—Born June 22, 1892. 6. Jeptha⁸—Born June 22, 1892. 7. Joseph⁸—Born December 31, 1898.

II. Jeptha Gideon⁷ (Dentist)—Born Platte City, Mo., February 16, 1856. Married October 2, 1884, Eliza Bush ·Park, born 1856, at Helena, Mont. Issue: 1. Kathleen⁸—Born October 20, 1888. Married October 7, 1911, Donald Davis, born 1887. Issue: a. Kathleen Hollingsworth Davis⁹. Born February 7, 1914. Living 1917, at Kansas City, Mo. 2. Park⁸—Born, August 5, 1892, in Missouri. Living 1917, Kansas City, Mo. Unmarried.

F–6. JEPTHA GORDON HOLLINGSWORTH

(Thomas Kennedy⁵, Jeptha⁴, Jacob³, Thomas², Valentine¹.) Son of Thomas Kennedy⁵ and Elizabeth (Kennedy) Hollingsworth. Born 1822. Died 1878. Married June, 1847, Maria Louisa Sherman, daughter of Edmund and Elizabeth Walton Sherman, of Virginia, and lived at Elkton, Ky.

Issue

I. Walter Otis⁷—Born September 17, 1848. (Twin.)
II. Lucy⁷—Born September 17, 1848. Living Decatur, Ill., 1917.
First married Jno. T. Montgomery, November 1875. No
issue. She then married Judge Wm. E. Nelson, June 1887.
No issue.
III. Ella⁷.
IV. Henry Gordon⁷.
V. Newton Elwood⁷.
VI. Nora Elizabeth⁷—Born Elkton, Ky. Died at Louisville, Ky.
Married George Braden, of Louisville, Ky. No issue.
VII. Granville Sherman⁷—Born ...... Living at Bowling Green,
Ky., 1917. Married Elma Lee Arnold. Issue: 1. Gordon
Arnold⁸. 2. Lieut. Granville Sherman, Jr⁸.
VIII. Edmund Ware⁷.

F-6. JAMES IVY HOLLINGSWORTH

(Enoch⁵, Jeptha⁴, Jacob³, Thomas², Valentine¹.) Son of Enoch⁵ and
Rebecca (Smith) Hollingsworth. Born ......, 1811. Died 1859.
Married 1834, Cynthia Clayton, who was born in 1812. Died 1889.
Daughter of Stephen and Hannah Watkins Clayton. Lived in Pickens
County, S. C. Buried in Liberty, S. C.

Issue

I. Columbus Lafayette⁷—Born 1836. Lawyer and planter. Died
1899. Married December 27, 1859, Malinda Anderson
McWhorter. Captain in the Confederate Army. Issue:
8 children. More of Columbus later.
II. Emily⁷—Born 1839. Died March 23, 1843.
III. Deborah Reid⁷—Born December 17, 1840. Died 1911. Married
December 4, 1859, Joab Mauldin, Pickens Co., S. C., who
died November 30, 1897. Issue: 1. Vesta⁸—Born October 7,
1860. 2. Frank Gratin⁸—Born August 16, 1864. 3. Thomas
Joab⁸—Born July 21, 1870. 4. Hortense⁸—Born August 23,
1872. 5. Ivy Milton⁸—Born December 17, 1875. 6. Leland
Osgood⁸—Born May 10, 1878. 7. Cleon Wirt⁸—Born July 31,
1880. 8. Wayne Fulton⁸—Born June 26, 1882. 9. Gregg
Twiller⁸—Born May 29, 1885.

IV. Stephen Franklin[7]—Born 1842. Died, 1867, Pilot Grove, Tex. Cadet at Citadel. Served in Confederate Army.

V. John Stark[7]—Born 1845. Died 1847.

VI. Susan[7]—Born 1847. Died 1899. Married Thomas Parkins. Moved to Texas. Left a family.

VII. Baylus Butler[7]—Born 1849. Died 1762.

VIII. Wm. Robinson[7]—Born 1853 Living 1917, Crosby, Tex. Married October 10, 1882, Lake E. Folger. Issue: 1. Ethel[8]. 2. Eula[8]. 3. Carl[8]. 4. Ivy[8]. 5. Olive[8]. 6. Lois[8]. 7. Columbus Lee[8].

IX. Martha[7]—Born 1855. Died at Charlotte, N. C. Married James Smith.

G–7. COLUMBUS LAFAYETTE HOLLINGSWORTH

(James Ivy[6], Enoch[5], Jeptha[4], Jacob[3], Thomas[2], Valentine[1].) Son of James Ivy[6] and Cynthia (Clayton) Hollingsworth. Born in South Carolina, 1836. Died Pickens, S. C., 1899. Married December 27, 1859, Malinda Anderson McWhorter, Pickens Co., S. C. He was a Captain in the Confederate Army.

ISSUE

I. Adelaide Rosamond[8]—Born Pickens Co., S. C., 1860. First married, December 24, 1882, Henry Ernest Harris, Albemarle Co., Va. Issue: Henry H[9]. She then married Martin F. Ansel, August 24, 1898, of Greenville, S. C. Living there 1918.

II. John Ivy[8]—Born Oconee Co., S. C., 1862. Physician. Died at Pickens Co., S. C., 1887. Never married.

III. Ida Jane[8]—Born Oconee Co., S. C., January 27, 1864. Living at Easley, S. C., 1918. Married August 22, 1888, Rufus Franklin Smith. He died 1915. Issue: 1. Velma H[9]. 2. Gladys H[9]. 3. Lloyd H[9]. 4. Frank H[9]. 5. Hugh H[9]. 6. Ralph H[9].

IV. Stephen Clayton[8]—Born Toxaway Plantation, Oconee Co., S. C. 1866. Died there 1868.

V. Eulola Eliza[8]—Born South Carolina, 1868. Living 1918, 1328 Lady St., Columbia, S. C. Married February 21, 1894, Dr. Robert Alexander Lancaster. Issue: 1. Annie H[9]. 2. Virginia H[9]. 3. Dorothy H[9]. 4. Margaret H[9].

VI. Aurora Malinda⁵—Born South Carolina, 1870. Married September 3, 1901, Jones Fuller, lawyer, of Greenwood, S. C., where they still lived in 1918.

VII. Columbus Eugene⁵—Born Pickens Co., S. C., 1873. Died Pickens Co., S. C., 1891.

VIII. Mary Vesta⁵—Born Pickens Co., S. C., 1876. Died 1877.

D–4. ZEBIDEE HOLLINGSWORTH

(Jacob³, Thomas², Valentine¹.)   Son of Jacob³ and Elizabeth (Chandler) Hollingsworth. Born in Pennsylvania, 1743.   Died at Winchester, Va., April 28, 1802.   Married Lydia Allen, 1769.   Born 1747.   Died 1828.

Issue

I. Rachel⁵—Born November 15, 1770. Died October 6, 1855. Married . . . . . . Hereford. Issue: A daughter, living at Plainville, Mich.

II. Isaac⁵—Born November 6, 1771. Died November 24, 1842. Married Hannah Parkins. More of Isaac later.

III. John⁵—Born November 15, 1773.

IV. Joshua⁵—Born June 15, 1779. More of Joshua later.

V. Thomas⁵—Born April 27, 1781. Married Rachel Jones, December 26, 1808. Died May 15, 1852. More of Thomas later.

VI. Lydia⁵—Born 1785. Died young.

VII. Jane⁵—Born April 19, 1790. Married Jonathan Smith, November 8, 1813. She died June 27, 1829.

F–6. JOSEPH P. HOLLINGSWORTH

(Isaac⁵, Zebidee⁴, Jacob³, Thomas², Valentine¹.) Son of Isaac⁵ and Hannah(Parkins) Hollingsworth. Born April 28, 1802, Frederick Co., Va. Died November 16, 1860. First married Louisa Holliday, 1823. He then married Ann E. Osbourn, December 20, 1856, Loudon Co., Va.

Issue 1st Marriage

I. Isaac⁷—Born April 21, 1825. Died June 2, 1831.

II. James H⁷.—Born November 13, 1827. Married Kate D. Gibbons, of Dayton, Ohio.

III. Elizabeth B⁷.—Born May 22, 1831. Died April 28, 1846.

IV. Harriett L⁷.—Born June 25, 1833. First married James Soeers, of Clark Co., Va. She then married Col. Henry Color, of Maryland.

V. Frank O[7].—Born November 21, 1857. Died 1861, near Winchester, Va.
VI. Louisa[7]—Born 1860. Died 1867, at Winchester, Va.
VII. Ada B[7].—Born 1862.
VIII. Roberta B[7].—Born 1865.

E-5. JOSHUA HOLLINGSWORTH

(Zebidee[4], Jacob[3], Thomas[2], Valentine[1].) Son of Zebidee[4] and Lydia (Allen) Hollingsworth. Born June 15, 1779. Married ....

Issue

I. Louisa[6]—Born 1803. Issue. Died 1863.
II. Henry Washington[6]—Born in Louden Co., Va., 1805. Died in Palmyra, Mo., April 20, 1873. Married Charlotte Louisa Clark, of New York, 1840. Issue: 1. Albert G[7].—Born in Lebanon, Ohio, 1842. Died 1842. 2. Mary E[7].—Born in Georgetown, Ky., 1844. 3. Samuel G[7].—Born in Palmyra, Mo., 1847. Died 1853. 4. Catherine C[7].—Born 1854. Died 1855. 5. Helen L[7].—Born 1854. 6. Henry Washington[7]—Born 1857. Died 1858. 7. Harold Wm[7].—Born 1858, Hannibal, Mo.

E-5. THOMAS HOLLINGSWORTH

(Zebidee[4], Jacob[3], Thomas[2], Valentine[1].) Son of Zebidee[4] and Lydia (Allen) Hollingsworth. Born 1781. Died May 21, 1842. Married Rachel Jones, 1808. Born 1787. Died October, 1869.

Issue

I. Isaac J[6].—Born 1809. Died 1821.
II. James W[6].—Born 1812. Married Nancy Mahohn, 1840.
III. Mary Jane[6]—Born 1815, Winchester, Va.
IV. Joseph G[6].—Born 1818, Ottumwa, Wappello Co., Iowa.
V. Catharine M[6].—Born 1822. Died 1856.
VI. I. Putnam[6]—Born 1825. Killed, second battle of Manassas, 1862.

F–6. JAMES W. HOLLINGSWORTH

(Thomas[6], Zebidee[4], Jacob[3], Thomas[2], Valentine[1].) Son of Thomas[6] and Rachel (Jones) Hollingsworth. Born 1812. Married Nancy Mahohn, 1840.

ISSUE

  I. Sarah E[7].
 II. Thomas W[7].—Married Sarah C. Baird. Issue: 2 children.
III. Francis Ann[7]—Married D. Gephart.
 IV. HenryC[7].
  V. James P[7].—Married Alice Carson, November 10, 1880.

E–5. ISAAC HOLLINGSWORTH

(Zebidee[4], Jacob[3], Thomas[2], Valentine[1].) Of Winchester. Son of Zebidee[4] and Lydia (Allen) Hollingsworth. Born November 6, 1771. Died November 24, 1842. First married Hannah Parkins, January 10, 1799. Born November 30, 1781. She died July 18, 1824. He then married Harriet Holliday, November 28, 1828. She died May, 1873.

ISSUE 1ST MARRIAGE

    I. Eliza[5]—Born September 19, 1800. Died August 26, 1860. Married Alfred Parkins, March 14, 1820.
   II. Joseph P[5].—Born April 28, 1802. Died November 16, 1870. First married Louisa Holliday, 1823. He then married Ann E. Osbourn, November 20, 1856.
  III. Charles[5]—Born December 2, 1803. Died in infancy.
   IV. Eleanor[5]—Born December 25, 1805. Died April 5, 1846. Married David Hollingsworth, 1833.
    V. John[5]—Born June 11, 1807. Died 1860. Married Dorothea Alphia Ayres.
   VI. Mary P[5].—Born July 15, 1809. Married A. H. Griffith, April 15, 1830.
  VII. William[5]—Born December 13, 1810. Died 1878. Married Caroline Luck. More of William later.
 VIII. Henry Clarkson[5]—Born August 31, 1812. Died August 16, 1835. Unmarried.
   IX. Lydia Ann[5]—Born July 1, 1814. Died February 8, 1845. Married James Richards, 1835.

X. Cyrus[6]—Born September 20, 1816. Died August, 1860. Married
    Delia .... No issue.
XI. Isaac Milton[6]—Born October 25, 1819. Married Mary Prichard,
    1843. More of Isaac Milton later.
XII. Alexander[6]—Born July 12, 1824. Died August, 1824.

ISSUE 2ND MARRIAGE

XIII. Isaac[6]—Born April 13, 1831. Died 1873. Married Alcinda Gib-
    son. More of Isaac later.

F-6. ISAAC HOLLINGSWORTH

(Isaac[5], Zebidee[4], Jacob[3], Thomas[2], Valentine[1].) Son of Isaac[5] and
Harriett (Holliday) Hollingsworth. Born April 13, 1831. Died 1873.
Married Alcinda Gibson.

ISSUE

I. Hattie[7]—Born 1855. Married Glisson Porter, May, 1877.
II. Gibson[7]—Married Clel Birch, August, 1880.
III. Boyd[7]—Married Gertie Lemley.
IV. Ida[7].
V. Delia[7].
VI. Holliday[7].

F-6. ISAAC MILTON HOLLINGSWORTH

(Isaac[5], Zebidee[4], Jacob[3], Thomas[2], Valentine[1].) Son of Isaac[5] and
Hannah (Parkins) Hollingsworth. Born October 25, 1819. Married
Mary Prichard, 1843. Resided at Woodstock, Va.

ISSUE

I. Harriett[7]—Born 1844. Married Henry Hannan.
II. Mary[7]—Born 1846. Married John H. Grubill.
III. C. Clarkson[7]—Born 1848. Married Mary ......
IV. Bettie[7]—Born 1849. Died young.
V. Stephen[7]—Born 1850. Married Artie Hiser.
VI. Alfred R[7].—Born 1852. Married Bettie Hockman.
VII. Annie C[7].—Born 1854.
VIII. Cornelius M[7].—Born 1856. Died young.
IX. Charles M[7].—Born 1857.
X. Edwin[7]—Born 1858.
XI. Fannie[7]—Born 1859. Died young.
XII. Lucie[7]—Born 1862.

F-6. WILLIAM HOLLINGSWORTH

(Isaac⁵, Zebidee⁴, Jacob³, Thomas², Valentine¹.) Son of Isaac⁵ and Hannah (Parkins) Hollingsworth. Born 1810. Died 1878. Married Carolina Luck, 1845.

ISSUE

   I. Wm. E⁷.—Born 1847. Died 1851.
  II. Clark⁷—Born 1849. Died 1850.
 III. Emma H⁷.—Born 1852.
 IV. Annie E⁷.—Born 1852.
   V. Adelia W⁷.—Born 1859.
 VI. Lavinia⁷—Born 1862. Died 1862.

D-4. DAVID HOLLINGSWORTH

(Jacob³, Thomas², Valentine¹.) Of New Castle Co., Del. Son of Jacob³ and Rachel (Chandler) Hollingsworth, of Pennsylvania. Born 1734. Died .... Married Sarah Green, 1757. He removed to Center Co., Pa., 1791, and died there.

ISSUE

   I. Israel⁵—Born November 20, 1757. Died 1842. More of Israel later.
  II. Elizabeth⁵—Born April 25, 1760. Married James Allen, 1778.
 III. Levi⁵—Born October 18, 1762. More of Levi later.
 IV. Hannah⁵—Born May 20, 1765. Married Jacob Taylor, 1779.
   V. David⁵—Born January 20, 1768. Married Catherine Murdock. More of David later.

E-5. ISRAEL HOLLINGSWORTH

(David⁴, Jacob³, Thomas², Valentine¹.) Son of David⁴ and Sarah (Green) Hollingsworth. Born 1757. Died 1842. Married Ann Pierce, 1796.

ISSUE

   I. Samuel⁶—Born January 7, 1797. Died 1850. More of Samuel later.
  II. Lydia⁶—Born 1798.
 III. Pierce⁶—Born 1800.

IV. Asaph⁶—Born 1802. Died 1846. More of Asaph later.
V. Jarius⁶—Born 1804. Married Eveline Gorham, 1827. More of Jarius later.
VI. Ann⁶—Born 1807. Died 1835.

E-5. LEVI HOLLINGSWORTH

(David⁴, Jacob³, Thomas², Valentine¹.) Son of David⁴ and Sarah (Green) Hollingsworth. Born October 18, 1762.

Issue

I. Joshua⁵.
II. Harriett⁵.
III. David⁵.
IV. Sarah⁵.

V. James⁵.
VI. Samuel⁵.
VII. Hannah⁵.

E-6. ASAPH HOLLINGSWORTH

(Israel⁵, David⁴, Jacob³, Thomas², Valentine¹.) Son of Israel⁵ and Ann (Pierce) Hollingsworth. Born 1802. Died 1846. Married Ann Wickershaw, 1827.

Issue

I. Valentine⁷—Born 1828. Died 1849.
II. Lydia⁷—Born 1830. Married Calvin Rockhill.
III. Enoch⁷—Born 1837. Married Hester A. Snider, Selma, Ohio.
IV. Pierce⁷—Born 1838. Married Sarah J. Whinery, Bangor, Iowa.
V. Rachel⁷—Born 1840. Married Chas. W. Kirk.
VI. Israel⁷—Born 1840. Married Rachel E. Wildman, Selma, Ohio.

F-6. JARIUS HOLLINGSWORTH

(Israel⁵, David⁴, Jacob³, Thomas², Valentine¹.) Son of Israel⁵ and Ann (Pierce) Hollingsworth. Born 1804. Married Eveline Gorham, September 20, 1827.

Issue

I. Levi⁷—Born 1828.
II. Eliza J⁷.—Born 1831.
III. Jas. Pierce⁷—Born 1833.
IV. Israel⁷—Born 1833.
V. Lydia⁷—Born 1839.

VI. Eva Maria⁷—Born 1841.
VII. Caroline⁷—Born 1844.
VIII. Asaph⁷—Born 1847.
IX. Mary⁷—Born 1850.

E-5. DAVID HOLLINGSWORTH

(David⁴, Jacob³, Thomas², Valentine¹.) Of Pennsylvania. Son of David⁴ and Sarah (Green) Hollingsworth. Born January 20, 1768. Married Catherine Murdock, 1789.

Issue

    I. William⁶—Born 1790. Died 1875. Unmarried.
    II. Sarah⁶—Born 1792. Died 1810.
    III. Henry⁶—Born 1794.
    IV. Levi⁶—Born 1796. Died young.
    V. Mary⁶—Born 1798. Married John Wall.
    VI. Elizabeth⁶—Born 1801. Married Jonathan Sleeper. Died 1834.
    VII. Hannah⁶—Born 1803. Married Azel Babb.
    VIII. David⁶—Born 1806. Died 1859. Unmarried.
    IX. Sarah⁶—Born 1810. Married John Grant, 1850.

F-6. SAMUEL HOLLINGSWORTH

(Israel⁵, David⁴, Jacob³, Thomas², Valentine¹.) Son of Israel⁵ and Ann (Pierce) Hollingsworth. Born January 7, 1797. Died 1850. First married Jane A. McMillan, 1823. He then married Emily Kirk, 1841.

Issue 1st Marriage

    I. Israel⁷—Born 1824. Married Susanna Johns, Xenia, Ohio. More of Israel later.
    II. Jonathan⁷—Born 1827. Married ...... Died 1867.
    III. Harman F⁷.—Born 1828. Married Mary M. Lindsey.
    IV. Sarah A⁷.—Born 1831.
    V. Elizabeth⁷—Born 1832.
    VI. Phœbe⁷—Born 1834. First married Ezekiel Jackson. She then married Wm. Wilson.
    VII. Samuel⁷—Born 1837. Died 1837.

Issue 2nd Marriage

    VIII. Mary W⁷.—Born 1842. Died 1861.
    IX. David⁷—Born 1843. Died 1868.
    X. Harriett⁷—Born 1845. Married Wm. Milner.
    XI. Josiah⁷—Born 1847. Married Eunice A. Stansfield, New Sharon, Ia.

G-7. ISRAEL HOLLINGSWORTH

(Samuel⁶, Israel⁵, David⁴, Jacob³, Thomas², Valentine¹.)   Son of Samuel⁶
and Jane A. (McMillan) Hollingsworth. Born 1824. Married Susanna Johns, of Xenia, Ohio.

   I. Henry H⁸.   III. Sarah Jane⁸.
  II. Eli W⁸.

E-5. NATHANIEL HOLLINGSWORTH

(Thomas⁴, Thomas³, Thomas², Valentine¹.)   Son of third Thomas⁴ and
Jane (Smith) Hollingsworth. Born August 4, 1755. Died September
2, 1834. Married Abigail, daughter of Robert Green, October 22, 1783.
Settled in Harford Co., Md., coming from Center Co., Pa., 1806.

ISSUE

    I. Robert⁶—Born May 7, 1784. Married Elizabeth West. More of
        Robert later.
   II. Hannah⁶—Born 1786. Married Joel Carter, 1823. Died 1872.
  III. Aaron⁶—Born 1788. Died 1806.
  IV. Mary⁶—Born 1790. Died young.
   V. Thomas⁶—Born 1791. Married Eliza Garrett, 1819. He died
        1820.
  VI. Eli⁶—Born 1793. Married Edith Carter, 1831. More of Eli
        later.
 VII. Jesse⁶—Born 1796. Married Guilelma Maria Spicer, 1821. Died,
        1863. More of Jesse later.
VIII. Abigail⁶—Born 1798. Unmarried. Living 1884.
  IX. Nathaniel⁶—Born 1801. Married Mary Warner, 1834. Died
        1851. More of Nathaniel later.
   X. John⁶—Born 1805. Married Rachel Benson, 1834. Died 1874.
        More of John later.

Nathaniel⁵ was a highly respected member of the Society of Friends.
With a temper unruffled by the storms of this life, he passed quietly
along through the trials of the world, and has left an example worthy
of imitation by all. All his actions were regulated by the precepts of
Christianity. He was an affectionate husband and parent, a benevolent
and truly valuable neighbor, and a shining ornament of the society of
which he was a member.

E-6. NATHANIEL HOLLINGSWORTH

(Nathaniel⁵, Thomas⁴, Thomas³, Thomas², Valentine¹.)   Son of Nathaniel⁵ and Abigail (Green) Hollingsworth, Harford Co., Md.   Born February 20, 1801.   Died March 19, 1851.   Married 1834, Mary Warner, of Deer Creek, Md.

Issue

I. Silas Warner⁷—Born November 23, 1835. Died May 7, 1902. Married May 5, 1879, Olivia J. Lewis, of Jerusalem, Harford Co., Md. No issue.

II. Thomas⁷—Born June 16, 1837. Died December 14, 1911.

III. Sarah⁷—Born July 12, 1839. Died June 30, 1899.

IV. Rebecca Garrett⁷—Born January 1, 1841. Living 1918.

V. Mary⁷—Born December 20, 1842. Living 1918.   Married January 1903, at Darlington, Harford Co., Md.

VI. Nathaniel⁷—Born May 11, 1845. Died September 23, 1889.

VII. Edward⁷—Born July 15, 1847. Died January 16, 1918. Married January 7, 1874, Elizabeth Lewis, at Baltimore, Md. Issue: Lewis Edward⁸—Born March 6, 1875. Living 1918, Joppa, Harford Co., Md. Married January 9, 1901, Alice Lee Barnes, Harford Co., Md. No issue.

G-7. ISAIAH HOLLINGSWORTH

(Robert⁶, Nathaniel⁵, Thomas⁴, Thomas³, Thomas², Valentine¹.)   Son of Robert⁶ and Elizabeth (West) Hollingsworth. Born November 29, 1814. He married Martha Hoskins, 1839.

Killed on his way to California. Wife and family living in Texas, 1884.

Issue

I. Elizabeth Mildred⁸—First married Wm. Cole, 1856. She then married Geo. C. Neill, 1863.

II. Robert Barclay⁸—Married Julia A. Whittington, 1868.

III. Martha Elmira⁸—Died . . . .

IV. William Henry⁸—Married Mary L. Stone, 1874. Died 1877.

V. Phœbe Jane⁸—Married Jacob J. Wirts, 1875.

VI. Mary Eliza⁸—Died . . . .

VII. Sallie Rebecca⁸—Unmarried.

H–8. ROBERT B. HOLLINGSWORTH

(Isaiah[7], Robert[6], Nathaniel[5], Thomas[4], Thomas[3], Thomas[2], Valentine[1].)
Son of Isaiah[7] and Martha (Hoskins) Hollingsworth. Born about 1843.
He married Julia Ann Whittington, 1868.

ISSUE

    I. Dora Eugene[9]—Born 1869. Died young.
    II. James Barclay[9]—Born about 1871.
    III. Phœbe[9]—Born about 1872.
    IV. Henry Nathaniel[9].

G–7. MAHLON W. HOLLINGSWORTH

(Robert[6], Nathaniel[5], Thomas[4], Thomas[3], Thomas[2], Valentine[1].) Son of
Robert[6] and Elizabeth (West) Hollingsworth. Born February 7, 1817.
Died August 18, 1888. Married February 12, 1840, Ophelia Foote.
Moved to Freeport, Ill. Afterwards settled in Iowa.

ISSUE

    I. Mary E[8].—Married Albert M. Tull.
    II. Hiram F[8].—Married Cynthia Armstrong.
    III. Ellen[8]—Married John A. Wilson.
    IV. Charles Henry[8]—Married Lizzie Mite. Issue: 1. Samuel W[9].
            2. Lizzie May[9].
    V. Alice[8]—Married David Vought.

H–8. HIRAM F. HOLLINGSWORTH

(Mahlon[7], Robert[6], Nathaniel[5], Thomas[4], Thomas[3], Thomas[2], Valentine[1].) Son of Mahlon W[7]. and Ophelia J. (Foote) Hollingsworth.
Married Cynthia Armstrong.

ISSUE

Mahlon[9].

F-6. ROBERT HOLLINGSWORTH

(Nathaniel[5], Thomas[4], Thomas[3], Thomas[2], Valentine[1].) Of Harford
Co., Md. Son of Nathaniel[5] and Abigail (Green) Hollingsworth. Born
May 7, 1784. Died October 16, 1863. Married November 21, 1809,
Elizabeth West, who was born April 17, 1792, and died March 12, 1861.

ISSUE

I. Mary[7]—Born September 8, 1810. Married January 6, 1831,
   Josiah Brown. Died . . . .

II. Hannah W[7].—Born August 9, 1812. Died August 22, 1814.

III. Isaiah B[7].—Born November 29, 1814. Married August 15, 1839,
   Martha J. Hoskins. Killed on his way to California. Family
   living in Texas, 1884. More of Isaiah later.

IV. Mahlon W[7].—Born February 7, 1817. Died August 18, 1888,
   Hampton, Ill. Married February 12, 1840, Ophelia Foote.
   Moved to Freeport, Ill. Afterwards settled in Iowa. More
   of Mahlon later.

V. Amos West[7]—Born Aug. 29, 1820. Died February 1, 1884.
   Married February 20, 1845, Lois Pope Clement. Lived near
   Fallston, Md. More of Amos later.

VI. Elizabeth H[7].—Born August 26, 1821. Died March 12, 1861.
   Married September 6, 1838, Edward Cunningham. Issue: 1.
   Elizabeth Caroline[8]. 2. Susan Jane[8]. 3. Robert Hollingsworth[8].

VII. Jane S[7].—Born November 30, 1823. Died May 17, 1842. Unmarried.

VIII. Susan W[7].—Born July 8, 1826. Died 1914. Married November 11, 1847, Dr. Frederick Converse Robinson, Uniontown,
   Pa. Issue: 1. Ada[8]. 2. Harry[8]. 3. Charles[8]. 4. Elizabeth[8].

IX. Henry[7]—Born March 8, 1829. Died May 28, 1902, Mt. Carroll Co.,
   Ill. Married, October 28, 1849, Emily Parkinson, of Baltimore,
   Md. She died Mt. Carroll, Ill., November 4, 1900. Issue: 1.
   James Henry[8]. 2. Chas. Carroll[8]. 3. Emma Francis[8]. 4. Harry
   Lee[8].

X. Rebecca S[7].—Born March 20, 1831. Died December 25, 1860.
   Unmarried.

XI. Charles Robert[7]—Born March 1, 1833. Died June 5, 1907.
   Married May 29, 1856, Sarah Longstreth, of Philadelphia,
   Pa. More of Charles later.

G-7. CHARLES ROBERT HOLLINGSWORTH

(Robert⁶, Nathaniel⁵, Thomas⁴, Thomas³, Thomas², Valentine¹.) Son of Robert⁶ and Elizabeth (West) Hollingsworth. Born March 1, 1833. Died June 5, 1907. Married May 29, 1856, Sarah Longstreth (daughter of Daniel and Hannah Townsend Longstreth, of Philadelphia, Pa). She was born September 4, 1834, and died March 14, 1901. Both buried at Fallston Friends' burying ground. He was a merchant and farmer.

ISSUE

I. Anna Turner⁸—Born March 12, 1857, Harford Co., Md. Living 1918, at Fallston, Md. Married October 25, 1882, Joseph B. Hoskins, of Harford Co., Md., son of Jesse and Angeline Johnson Hoskins. He was born November 7, 1852. Issue: Raymond Hollingsworth⁹—Born December 6, 1889. Died December 10, 1910.

II. John Longstreth⁸—Born June 9, 1858, Harford Co., Md. Living, 1918, 2341 North 57th St., Seattle, Wash. Married, November 28, 1880, Matilda Jones, of Rush Co., Kansas, daughter of Matthew W. and Sarah Brouse Jones. She was born December 26, 1860, Taylor Co., Iowa, and died February 6, 1909, at Seattle, Wash. Issue: 1. George Edward⁹—Born October 7, 1881. Died January 9, 1909. 2. Ethel Olivia⁹—Married Walter Bruce Gamble. 3. Sarah Myrtle⁹—Married Oscar Warren Anderson. 4. Walter Longstreth⁹.

III. William⁸—Born April 18, 1861, Harford Co., Md. Living, 1918, 3400 W. North Ave., Baltimore, Md. Maufacturer. Married, June 1, 1882, Laura E. Starr, daughter of George and Vallurea Carter Starr, who was born July 15, 1859. Issue: 1. Edith Belle⁹—Married Dr. Gilbert Haven Alford, of Baltimore, Md.

IV. Walter Longstreth⁸—Born August 29, 1863, Harford Co., Md. Died September 4, 1876.

V. Robert ⁸—Born December 23, 1865, Harford Co., Md. Died September 28, 1906. First married September 22, 1887, at Baltimore, Md., Fannie Barber, born 1869. She died February 3, 1888. He then married, March 12, 1890, at Baltimore, Elizabeth Jane Riley, born October 25, 1869, at Baltimore, daughter of Wm. Leonidas and Mary Rice Riley. Issue: 1. Edna Florence⁹. 2. Elizabeth⁹.

VI. Martha Townsend⁸—Born February 28, 1873. Living 1918, Baltimore, Md. Unmarried. Treasurer of Pikesville Dairy Co.

G-7. AMOS WEST HOLLINGSWORTH

(Robert[6], Nathaniel[5], Thomas[4], Thomas[3], Thomas[2], Valentine[1].) Of
Harford Co., Md. Son of Robert[3] and Elizabeth (West) Hollingsworth.
Born August 29, 1820. Died February 1, 1884. Married February 20,
1845, Lois Pope Clement. She was born November 21, 1823, Woodstock, Vt. Died March 13, 1903. Farmer at Fallston, Md. Very
highly respected by all who knew him.

ISSUE

    I. Daniel Pope[8]—Born January 7, 1846. Died January 14, 1907.
        Married December 18, 1878, Katharine A. Hoskins. No
        issue. 2 adopted children. 1. Mary Catherine[9]. 2. Chas.
        Pope[9]—Major, U. S. A., France, 1918.

    II. Elizabeth[8]—Born February 23, 1848. Living 1918, Fallston,
        Md. Married October 7, 1873, Wm. S. Preston ,of Fallston,
        Md. He died November 23, 1904. Issue: 1. Lois H[9].—
        Married Edgar W. Cleaver. 2. Edgar W[9].—Married Cecelia
        Estelle Howard. 3. Phœbe Alice[9]—Married Walter Rabell.

    III. Edward Price[8]—Born December 12, 1849. Died March 19, 1918,
        Ambler, Pa. Married December 21, 1871, Hannah Moore,
        of Pennsylvania. More of Edward later.

    IV. Rebecca[8]—Born May 31, 1852. Unmarried. Living 1918,
        Fallston, Md.

    V. Cyrus Clement[8]—Born May 28, 1854. Died March 3, 1903.
        Married October 30, 1883, Virginia R. Hanway. Issue:
        1. Mary Ann[9]—Married October 9, 1902, Wm. E. Thompson,
        of Baltimore, Md. Issue: 2 children. 2. Clement W[9].—Liv-
        ing 1918, Baltimore, Md., 2317 N. Charles St. Married
        December 13, 1911, C. Edna Long. Issue: Clement War-
        ner, Jr[10].—Born August 25, 1913.

    VI. Dr. Chas. Amos[8]—Born May 7, 1856. Lived at Bel Air, Md.
        Died November 10, 1915. Married October 25, 1888,
        Roberta A. Young. Issue: 1. Charles Amos[9]. 2. William
        Young[9]—U. S. A., Medical Corps, France, 1918. 3. Edward
        West[9]. 4. John Young[9]. 5. Elizabeth Young[9]. 6. Roberts
        Lois[9].

H-8. EDWARD PRICE HOLLINGSWORTH

(Amos[7], Robert[6], Nathaniel[5], Thomas[4], Thomas[3], Thomas[2], Valentine[1].)
Son of Amos[7] and Lois Pope (Clement) Hollingsworth. Born December 12, 1849. Died March 19, 1918, Ambler, Pa. Married December 21, 1871, Hannah Moore, daughter of ......· Moore, of Pennsylvania.

Issue

I. Robert Amos[8]—Born February 8, 1872. Living 1918, Ambler, Pa. Married, October 16, 1895, Elizabeth Atkinson, daughter of Albert and Phœbe Atkinson. She was born March 17, 1872. Issue: 1. Robert[10]—Born August 22, 1897. Died July 18, 1898. 2. Elizabeth Marie[10]—Born July 14, 1896. 3. Albert A[10].—Born August 30, 1898. In Radio Service, U. S. A., 1918. 4. Edward P., Jr[10].—Born December 31, 1900. 5. Phœbe A[10].—Born October 13, 1902. 6. Hannah M[10].—Born December 19, 1906.

II. David Faulke[8]—Born January 19, 1878. Living 1918, Shelby-ville, Del. Married, October 26, 1905, Virginia Dennis, daughter of ...... and ...... Dennis. Issue: 1. Edward F[10]. 2. Eleanor[10]. 3. Virginia[10].

F-6. ELI HOLLINGSWORTH

(Nathaniel[5], Thomas[4], Thomas[3], Thomas[2], Valentine[1].) Son of Nathaniel[5] and Abigail (Green) Hollingsworth. Born 1793. Married 1830, Edith Carter, daughter of Joel and Margaret Carter, of Pennsylvania. Died ......

Issue ·

I. Joel C[7].—Born December 26, 1831. Living 1918, Harford Co., Md. Married May 1, 1856, Hannah Carter. More of Joel later.

II. Nathaniel T[7].—Died 1898. Married Hannah S. Carter. More of Nathaniel T. later.

III. Jeremiah[7]—Died ......

G-7. JOEL C. HOLLINGSWORTH

(Eli⁶, Nathaniel⁵, Thomas⁴, Thomas³, Thomas², Valentine¹.)   Of Harford Co., Md.   Son of Eli⁶ and Edith (Carter) Hollingsworth.   Born December 26, 1831.   Living 1918, Harford Co., Md.   Married May 1, 1856, Hannah Carter, of Chester Co., Pa., daughter of Amos and Sophia Carter.   Manufacturer.

ISSUE

I. Curtis A⁸.—Born March 18, 1857.   Died October 28, 1882.   Unmarried.

II. Barclay Eli⁸—Born September 18, 1858, Harford Co., Md.   Living 1918, Hagerstown, Md.   Manufacturer.   Married at Philadelphia, Pa., January 10, 1883, Alice Anna Stubbs, daughter of Cooper and Anna Stubbs, of Lancaster Co., Pa.   She died June 5, 1907.   Issue: 1. Curtis Amos⁹.   2. Anna Muriel⁹.   3. Barclay Edwin⁹.   4. Edith Margaret⁹.   5. Norman Stubbs⁹.   6. Edmond Amos⁹.   7. Lydia Eliza⁹.   8. Alice Elizabeth⁹.

III. Harrie Joel⁸—Born August 29, 1861, Harford Co., Md.   Living 1918, Hagerstown, Md.   Manufacturer.   Married January 21, 1885, Irene M. Patterson, daughter of Amentis T. and Ellen Hanna Patterson, Harford Co., Md.   Issue: 1. Webster Patterson⁹—Born January 16, 1886.   Living 1918, Baltimore, Md.   Married February 19, 1916, Rhoda Bell Troup, of Hagerstown, Md.   2. Helen Carter⁹—Born July 27, 1888.   Living 1918, Hagerstown, Md.

IV. Maggie B⁸.—Born October 7, 1866.   Living 1918, Harford Co., Md.   Married January 18, 1888, William F. Stubbs, of Delta, Pa.   He was the son of Vincent and Elizabeth Stubbs.   Issue: 4 children.

G-7. NATHANIEL T. HOLLINGSWORTH

(Eli⁶, Nathaniel⁵, Thomas⁴, Thomas³, Thomas², Valentine¹.)   Son of Eli⁶ and Edith (Carter) Hollingsworth.   Died 1898.   Married Hannah S. Carter, daughter of John and ...... Carter, of Belmont Co., Ohio.

ISSUE

I. Eli⁸—Died.
II. Mary⁸—Died.
III. Samuel Howard⁸—Born July 15, 1875.

F-6. JESSE HOLLINGSWORTH

(Nathaniel⁵, Thomas⁴, Thomas³, Thomas², Valentine¹.) Son of Nathaniel⁵ and Abigail (Green) Hollingsworth. Of Harford County. Born 1796. Died 1863. Married Guilelma Maria Spicer, 1821.

ISSUE

I. Thomas O⁷.   III. James⁷.
II. John H⁷.   IV. Henry Eugene⁷.

F-6. NATHANIEL HOLLINGSWORTH

(Nathaniel⁵, Thomas⁴, Thomas³, Thomas², Valentine¹.) Son of Nathaniel⁵ and Abigail (Green) Hollingsworth, of Harford County. Born 1801. Died 1851. He married 1834, Mary Warner, of Deer Creek Md.

ISSUE

I. Silas W⁷.   VI. Nathaniel⁷.
II. Thomas⁷.   VII. Edward⁷—Married Elisa-
III. Sarah⁷.   beth L. Lewis. Issue:
IV. Rebecca G⁷.   Lewis E⁸. Living 1918,
V. Mary⁷.   Joppa, Harford Co., Md.

F-6. JOHN HOLLINGSWORTH

(Nathaniel⁵, Thomas⁴, Thomas³, Thomas², Valentine¹.) Son of Nathaniel⁵ and Abigail (Green) Hollingsworth. Born 1805. Died 1874. Married Rachel Benson, 1834.

ISSUE

I. Margaret⁷.   IV. John⁷.
II. Lydia⁷.   V. Amos B⁷.
III. Eliza⁷.   VI. William⁷.

B-2. VALENTINE HOLLINGSWORTH

Of Kennett, Pa. Son of Valentine¹ and Ann (Calvert) Hollingsworth. Born November 12, 1677. Died 1757. Will dated November 30, 1749. Proven March 25, 1757. Married Elizabeth Heald, 1713.

I. James²—Married Mary .... More of James later.
II. Rachel²—First married ...... Hope. He then married ......
Barnes, 1737.
III. Valentine, Jr³.—Married Elizabeth Harlan, 1743, daughter of
Aaron (died 1732) and Sarah Harlan. Sarah left will, dated
February 5, 1747. Proven March 3, 1747. Mentions sons:
George, Samuel, and Aaron Harlan, and daughters: Charity
Baldwin, Mary Evans, and Elizabeth Hollingsworth.
IV. Elizabeth²—Married Samuel Harlan, 1746. Moved to North
Carolina, 1753.
V. Sarah²—Married Aaron Harlan, 1746. Moved to Cane Creek,
N. C., 1753.

E-5. ISIAH HOLLINGSWORTH

(Valentine⁴, James³, Valentine², Valentine¹.) Of Chester Co., Pa. Son
of Valentine⁴ and Deborah (Harlan) Hollingsworth. Born 1777. Died
July 30, 1829. Married Jane Morrison, 1798.

I. Deborah⁶—Born 1799. Died 1872. Married James Richards.
II. Mary⁶—Born 1800. Died 1855. Married Jacob Flack.
III. David⁶—Born 1802. Died 1863. First married Margaret Ma-
hon. He then married Hester Coleman. More of David
later.
IV. Harlan⁶—Born 1804. Died 1855. Married Mary Johnson.
More of Harlan later.
V. Hannah⁶—Born 1806. Died 1865. Married John Murray.
VI. Abner⁶—Born 1809. First married Nancy Coleman. More of
Abner later.
VII. John⁶—Born 1811. Died 1811.
VIII. Benjamin⁶—Born 1813. Died 1846. Married Jane Montgom-
ery. More of Benjamin later.
IX. Hiram⁶—Born 1816. Died 1841. Married Jane Mahon. More
of Hiram later.
X. George⁶—Born 1818. Married Sarah Morris. More of George
later.
XI. Sarah Jane⁶—Born 1823. Married George Parsons.

F–6. DAVID HOLLINGSWORTH

(Isaiah[5], Valentine[4], James[3], Valentine[2], Valentine[1].) Son of Isaiah[5] and Jane (Morrison) Hollingsworth. Born 1802. Died 1863. First married Margaret Mahon. He then married Hester Coleman.

ISSUE 1ST MARRIAGE

I. Roland[7]—Born 1830. II. Wm. Valentine[7]—Born 1832.

ISSUE 2ND MARRIAGE

III. Elizabeth[7]. VI. Isaiah[7].
IV. Lavinia[7]. VII. Ellen[7].
V. George[7]. VIII. Alice[7].

G–7. ROLAND HOLLINGSWORTH

(David[6], Isaiah[5], Valentine[4], James[3], Valentine[2], Valentine[1].) Of Woodstock, Va. Son of David[6] and first wife, Margaret (Mahon) Hollingsworth. Born June 21, 1830. Married Sarah Best, 1857.

ISSUE

I. Francis[8]. IV. Emma[8].
II. Richard B[8]. V. Margaret[8].
III. George W[8].

F–6. HARLAN HOLLINGSWORTH

(Isaiah[5], Valentine[4], James[3], Valentine[2], Valentine[1].) Son of Isaiah[5] and Jane (Morrison) Hollingsworth. Born 1804. Died 1855. Married Mary Johnson.

ISSUE

I. Ellen[7]. VI. Decatur[7].
II. Isaiah[7]. VII. Desdemona[7].
III. Jane[7]. VIII. Elizabeth[7].
IV. William[7]. IX. Belle[7].
V. David[7]. X. Josephine[7].

F-6. ABNER HOLLINGSWORTH

(Isaiah⁵, Valentine⁴, James³, Valentine², Valentine¹.) Of Ohio. Son of
Isaiah⁶ and Jane (Morrison) Hoolingsworth. Born June 9, 1809.
First married Nancy Coleman. He then married Amanda Bending.

ISSUE 1ST MARRIAGE

I. Samantha⁷.	IV. George⁷.
II. Jane⁷.	V. Hezron⁷.
III. Mary⁷.	VI. Lafayette⁷.

F-6. BENJAMIN HOLLINGSWORTH

(Isaiah⁵, Valentine⁴, James³, Valentine², Valentine¹.) Son of Isaiah⁶
and Jane (Morrison) Hollingsworth. Born 1813. Died 1846. Married
Jane Montgomery.

ISSUE

I. Sarah A⁷.	IV. Mary⁷.
II. Hiram⁷.	V. John⁷.
III. Isaac⁷.	

F-6. GEORGE W. HOLLINGSWORTH

(Isaiah⁵, Valentine⁴, James³, Valentine², Valentine¹.) Son of Isaiah⁶
and Jane (Morrison) Hollingsworth. Born 1818. Married Sarah
Morris.

ISSUE

I. Angeline⁷.	III. Mary⁷.
II. Desdemona⁷.	IV. Lorenzo⁷.

F-6. HIRAM HOLLINGSWORTH

(Isaiah⁵, Valentine⁴, James³, Valentine², Valentine¹.) Son of Isaiah⁶
and Jane (Morrison) Hollingsworth. Born 1816. Died 1841. Married
Jane Mahon. Issue: Mary Jane⁷.

C–3. JAMES HOLLINGSWORTH

(Valentine², Valentine¹.) Son of Valentine² and Elizabeth (Heald) Hollingsworth. Born .... Will dated February 2, 1763. Proven March 5, 1763. Married Mary ......, in 1747.

ISSUE

I. Valentine⁴—Born 1748. Married Deborah Harlan.
II. Abner⁴—Born 1750. Married Phœbe Hall, 1788. More of Abner later.
III. Betty⁴.
IV. Ann⁴.
V. Sarah⁴.
VI. Susanna⁴
VII. Mary, Jr⁴.
VIII. Hannah⁴.
IX. Rebecca⁴.

D–4. ABNER HOLLINGSWORTH

(James³, Valentine², Valentine¹.) Son of James³ and Mary ...... Hollingsworth. Born 1750. Married Phœbe Hall, January 10, 1788.

ISSUE

I. Abner⁵—Married Louisiana Kay. More of Abner later.
II. Elizabeth⁵—Married Daniel Hoopes.
III. Mary⁵—Married Samuel Newlin.
IV. Stephen⁵—Married. More of Stephen later.
V. James⁵—Married ...... Hoopes. More of James later.
VI. Sarah⁵—Married Amor Chandler. Issue: Eli⁶.
VII. Hayes⁵—Married Rachel C. Garrett. Issue: 1. Eli⁶. 2. Howard⁶.

E–5. ABNER HOLLINGSWORTH

(Abner⁴, James³, Valentine², Valentine¹.) Son of Abner⁴ and Phœbe (Hall) Hollingsworth. Married Louisiana Kay.

ISSUE

I. Martha⁶—Married Thomas Rowey. Issue: Rufus⁷.
II. James⁶—Married Philena Johns. Issue: 1. Enos⁷. 2. Maris⁷.

E-5. STEPHEN HOLLINGSWORTH

(Abner⁴, James³, Valentine², Valentine¹.) Son of Abner⁴ and Phœbe
(Hall) Hollingsworth. Married ......

Issue

I. James⁶—Married Elizabeth Newlin.
II. Lydia⁶—Married James Chambers.
III. Maria⁶—Married ......
IV. Alburtes⁶—Married ...... Lived in Ohio.

F-6. JAMES HOLLINGSWORTH

(Stephen⁵, Abner⁴, James³, Valentine², Valentine¹.) Son of Stephen⁵
and Phœbe (Hall) Hollingsworth. Married Elizabeth Newlin.

Issue

I. James⁷.   III. Sallie⁷.
II. William⁷.

E-5. JAMES HOLLINGSWORTH

(Abner⁴, James³, Valentine², Valentine¹.) Son of Abner⁴ and Phœbe
(Hall) Hollingsworth. Married Miss Hoopes.

Issue

I. William⁶—Died.
II. John⁶—Married Hannah Pyle. Issue: 1. William⁷. 2. David⁷.
    3. Sallie⁷. 4. Hannah⁷. 5. Abner⁷. 6. Ralph⁷.
III. Abner⁶—Married Mary E. Springer. Issue: 1. Emma C⁷.
    2. Everett⁷—Married ...... Wilson. 3. Hawley L⁷.

B-2. SAMUEL HOLLINGSWORTH

Of Birmingham, Chester Co., Pa. Son of Valentine¹ and his second
wife, Ann Calvert. Born in Ireland, January 27, 1672. Came to
America from Belfast, Ireland, with his father, 1682. He married Han-
nah Harlan, daughter of George and Eliza Harlan, 1701. He died 1748.
His will dated August 30, 1748. Proven October 1, 1748. Executors:
His son, Enoch, and son-in-law, Henry Green. He mentions his wife
Hannah and 4 children.

I. Enoch[1]—First married Joanna Crowley, October 23, 1725. He
then married Betty . . . . . ., a widow.
II. John[1]—Married Mary Reed, 1732.
III. Samuel Jr[2].—Married Barbary Shewin, 1738.
IV. George[1]—Living 1731 to 1737; died before his father.
V. Betty[1]—Married Henry Green, 1734.

C–3. SAMUEL HOLLINGSWORTH

(Samuel[2], Valentine[1].) Son of Samuel[2] and Hannah (Harlan) Hollingsworth. Died 1751. Married Barbary Shewin, 1738. Samuel made
will dated October 2, 1751. Proven November 11, 1751. Mentions
wife and 2 sons.

I. Samuel[4]—Moved to Fayetteville, N. C. More of Samuel later.
II. Jacob[4]—Moved to North Carolina and Georgia. More of Jacob
later.
Both had large families.   .

C–3. ENOCH HOLLINGSWORTH

(Samuel[2], Valentine[1].) Son of Samuel[2] and Hannah (Harlan) Hollingsworth. First married Joanna Crowley, 1722. Second wife, Betty
. . . . . ., a widow. His will dated August 11, 1752, and proven September 17, 1752. He left "To my son Jehu, my plantation in Kennett.
To my son Enoch, my plantation in Birmingham, when 21 years of age."
Also mentions his wife Betty, and daughters Abigail and Hannah.

I. Hannah[4]—Born August 16, 1727. Married John Moore, April
13, 1749.
II. Abigail[4]—Born November 27, 1729. Married William Harlan,
October 1, 1748.
III. Jehu[4]—Born October 27, 1731. First married Ann Pyle, May 20,
1752. He then married Deborah Phillips, February 22, 1779.
She died April 9, 1793.
IV. Enoch, Jr[4]

D-4. JEHU HOLLINGSWORTH

(Enoch³, Samuel², Valentine¹.) Son of Enoch³ and Joanna (Crowley) Hollingsworth. Born 1731. Died 1819, age 87 years. Jehu first married Ann Pyle, May 20, 1752. He then married Deborah Phillips, of Lancaster, Pa., February 22, 1779. She died April 9, 1793.

Issue 1st Marriage

I. Samuel⁵.
II. Jehu⁵—Married Hannah Shallcross.

E-5. JEHU HOLLINGSWORTH

(Jehu⁴, Enoch³, Samuel², Valentine¹.) Son of Jehu⁴ and Ann (Pyle) Hollingsworth. Married Hannah Shallcross, daughter of Joseph and Orpha (Gilpin) Shallcross.

Issue

I. Samuel⁶—Married Jane P. Smith, daughter of John Smith.
II. Thomas G⁶.—Married Hannah, daughter of Chas. Wharton, Sr.
III. Anna Maria⁶—Married Chas. Wharton, son of Chas. Wharton, Sr. More of Anna later.
IV. Ann Caldwell⁶.

F-6. SAMUEL HOLLINGSWORTH

(Jehu⁵, Jehu⁴, Enoch³, Samuel², Valentine¹.) Son of Jehu⁵ and Hannah (Shallcross) Hollingsworth. Married Jane P. Smith.

Issue

I. Jehu⁷—Married Francis E. Schorie. More of Jehu later.
II. Samuel L⁷.—Married Anna Pemberton. More of Samuel L. later.
III. John⁷—Died.
IV. Elizabeth P⁷.—Died.
V. Anna M. Wharton⁷—Married Dr. John Neill.
VI. Caroline Town⁷—Married Henry Pemberton.
VII. Thomas Gilfillan⁷—Died at sea.

F–6. THOMAS G. HOLLINGSWORTH

(Jehu[5], Jehu[4], Enoch[3], Samuel[2], Valentine[1].) Son of Jehu[5] and Hannah (Shallcross) Hollingsworth. Married Hannah, daughter of Charles Wharton, Sr.

ISSUE

- I. Hannah R[7].—Died.
- II. Elizabeth S[7].—Married Charles A. Lyman.
- III. Fanny[7]—Married Crawford Arnold.
- IV. William Wharton[7]—Married Caroline Newbold. More of William later.
- V. Charles Wharton[7].

G–7. WILLIAM WHARTON HOLLINGSWORTH

(Thomas[6], Jehu[5], Jehu[4], Enoch[3], Samuel[2], Valentine[1].) Son of Thomas[6] and Hannah (Wharton) Hollingsworth. Married Caroline Newbold.

ISSUE

I. Wharton[8].   II. Josephine[8].

F–6. ANNE MARIA HOLLINGSWORTH WHARTON

Daughter of Jehu[5] and Hannah (Shallcross) Hollingsworth. Married Charles Wharton, Jr.

ISSUE

I. Elizabeth[7].   III. Anne Maria[7].
II. Charles[7].   IV. Edmund[7].

G–7. JOHN HOLLINGSWORTH

(Samuel[6], Jehu[5], Jehu[4], Enoch[3], Samuel[2], Valentine[1].) Son of Samuel[6] and Jane P. (Smith) Hollingsworth. Married Frances E. Schorie.

ISSUE

- I. Samuel Schorie[8]. More of Samuel later.
- II. Jane Porterfield[8].

H–8. SAMUEL S. HOLLINGSWORTH

(Jehu[7], Samuel[6], Jehu[5], Jehu[4], Enoch[3], Samuel[2], Valentine[1].) Son of Jehu[7] and Frances E. (Schorie) Hollingsworth. Married Nancy P. Pleasants. He was an attorney-at-law in Philadelphia, Pa., 1884.

ISSUE

I. Esther[9].   II. Samuel[9].

G–7. DR. SAMUEL L. HOLLINGSWORTH

(Samuel[6], Jehu[5], Jehu[4], Enoch[3], Samuel[2], Valentine[1].) Son of Samuel[6] and Jane P. (Smith) Hollingsworth. Married Anne C. Pemberton.

ISSUE

I. Rebecca P[8].   IV. Samuel[8]—Died.
II. J. Pemberton[8].   V. Anna[8]—Died.
III. Clifford[8]—Died.

DR. JOHN NEILL

Born 1829. Died February 11, 1880, age 60 years. Married Anna M. Wharton Hollingsworth[7], daughter of Samuel Hollingsworth[6], son of Jehu[5].

ISSUE

I. Caroline M[8].   III. Patty D[8].
II. Hollingsworth[8].   IV. John[8], Jr.

D–4. SAMUEL HOLLINGSWORTH

(Samuel[3], Samuel[2], Valentine[1].) Of Fayetteville, N. C. Son of Samuel[3] and Barbara (Shewin) Hollingsworth, of Pennsylvania. Born about 1740 to '42. Died from the bite of a snake, 1814. One of the Signers of the Cumberland County Association, June 20, 1775, opposing the English Government. Living at Fayetteville, N. C., 1775. He was twice married. Names of wives unknown.

ISSUE

I. Samuel[5].
II. Stephen[5]—More of Stephen later.
III. Enoch[5].—Died 1809. More of Enoch later.
IV. John[5]—Born 1795. Married Eliza McNaill, North Carolina, 1813. Moved to Macon, Ga., 1825. Issue: 1. John[6]—Born 1822. Issue: 2 sons. 2. Walter T[6].—Born 1824. Issue: 1 son, Macon, Ga., 1878.

E-5. ENOCH HOLLINGSWORTH

(Samuel[4], Samuel[3], Samuel[2], Valentine[1].) Son of Samuel Hollingsworth[4] and ...... Hollingsworth. Died 1809. Married Elizabeth Thames.

ISSUE

I. William[6]—Born .... Died, Fayetteville, 1873. Issue: 1. Isaac[7]. 2. Wm[7]. 3. James[7]. 4. Stephen[7].

II. James[6]—Born 1801. Married Miss Jessup. He died 1852. More of James later.

III. Jonathan[6]—Born July 29, 1803. Died 1855. More of Jonathan later.

IV. Joseph[6]—Born 1805. Married Miss C. F. Shipman, of Bladen County. She died in 1874. Issue: 1. Mary[7]. 2. Joseph W[7]. 3. Theo. B[7]. and Emma[7], living 1882. 4. Daniel W[7].—Died. 5. Virginia D[7].—Died. 6. Hays F[7].—Died. 7. Albert D[7].—Died. 8. Edmond H[7].—Died. 9. Andrew F[7].—Died.

V. Richard[6]—Born 1807 or '08. Moved to Arkansas, 1859. Died 1880. Issue: 1. Judson[7]—Killed. 2. Addison[7]. 3. Luther[7].

VI. May H[6].—Married J. C. Ellis.

F-6. JAMES HOLLINGSWORTH

(Enoch[5], Samuel[4], Samuel[3], Samuel[2], Valentine[1].) Of Fayetteville, N. C. Son of Enoch[5] and Elizabeth (Thames) Hollingsworth. Born 1801. Died 1852. He married Miss Jessup, 1835. Born 1807. Died 1848.

ISSUE

I. James[7]—Born 1837. Died 1855; age 18 years.

II. Benjamin G[7].—Born 1840. Married Miss Royall. More of Benjamin later.

III. Sue[7].

IV. Kate[7].

G-7. BENJAMIN G. HOLLINGSWORTH

(James[6], Enoch[5], Samuel[4], Samuel[3], Samuel[2], Valentine[1].) Son of James[6] and ...... (Jessup) Hollingsworth. Born in 1840. Married Miss Royal, of Sampson Co., N. C., 1869.

ISSUE

I. Joseph G[8].

II. Bessie[8].

III. Frank[8].

F-6. JONATHAN HOLLINGSWORTH

(Enoch⁵, Samuel⁴, Samuel³, Samuel², Valentine¹.) Of Fayetteville, N. C. Son of Enoch⁵ and Elizabeth (Thames) Hollingsworth. Born July 29, 1803. Died October 20, 1855. Married Rebecca Carter.

ISSUE

I. Jonathan⁷—More of Jonathan later.   IV. James R⁷.
II. William Henry⁷.   V. Mary E⁷.
III. Josephus⁷.

G-7. JONATHAN HOLLINGSWORTH

(Jonathan⁶, Enoch⁵, Samuel⁴, Samuel³, Samuel², Valentine¹.) Son of Jonathan⁶ and Rebecca (Carter) Hollingsworth. Born July 14, 1842. Married Mary Eliza Battley, 1870.

ISSUE

I. Edgar B⁸.—Born 1872. Died 1873.
II. Nellie L⁸.—Born 1873.
III. Walter G⁸.—Born 1875.
IV. Willie T⁸.—Born 1877.

E-5. STEPHEN HOLLINGSWORTH

(Samuel⁴, Samuel³, Samuel², Valentine¹.) Son of Samuel⁴ and ...... Hollingsworth. Married Annie Smith.

ISSUE

I. Stephen⁵—Married Mary Edwards. He died September, 1840. More of Stephen later.
II. William⁵—Unmarried. Moved West, 1810.
III. John⁵—Married twice. Issue: Twins. More of John later.

F-6. STEPHEN HOLLINGSWORTH

(Stephen⁵, Samuel⁴, Samuel³, Samuel², Valentine¹.) Of Cumberland Co., N. C. Son of Stephen⁵ and Annie (Smith) Hollingsworth. Grandson of Samuel⁴. Born .... Died September, 1840. He married Mary Edwards.

ISSUE

I. Augustus J⁷.—Married Elizabeth Fisher.   V. Susan⁷.
II. Alexander McNeill⁷—Died.   VI. Isabella⁷.
III. Sarah⁷.   VII. Mary⁷.
IV. Rebecca⁷.

Stephen⁵ was a member of the Legislature in 1838.

F-6. JOHN HOLLINGSWORTH

(Stephen⁵, Samuel⁴, Samuel³, Samuel², Valentine¹.) Son of Stephen⁵
and Annie (Smith) Hollingsworth. Had two wives; names unknown.

ISSUE 1ST MARRIAGE

I. William⁷.   II. Sarah⁷.

ISSUE 2ND MARRIAGE

III. John⁷.   V. Mary⁷.
IV. Edward⁷.   VI. Susan⁷.

D-4. JACOB HOLLINGSWORTH

(Samuel³, Samuel², Valentine¹.) · Son of Samuel Hollingsworth³ and
Barbar (Shewin) Hollingsworth. Died in Georgia, about 1826. Married Mary Brooks, of Pennsylvania, about 1768.

ISSUE

   I. Samuel⁵—Born 1770. Died in Georgia, 1817. Issue: 3 sons.
      More of Samuel later.
  II. Jacob⁵—Born 1773. Died at Caddo Parish, La., 1849. More of
      Jacob later.
 III. Thomas⁵—Born 1775. Died at Lawrenceville, Ga., 1820. More
      of Thomas later.
 IV. James⁵—Born 1777. Died in Franklin, now Grundy Co., Tenn.,
      1824. More of James later.
  V. Benjamin⁵—Born 1779. Died 1844, age 65, Benton Co., Ala.
      More of Benjamin later.

This family came from Pennsylvania to Rutherford Co., N. C., and
moved to Franklin Co., Ga., in 1790.

E-5. SAMUEL HOLLINGSWORTH

(Jacob⁴, Samuel², Samuel², Valentine¹.) Of North Carolina and Georgia. Son of Jacob⁴ and Mary (Brooks) Hollingsworth. Born 1770.
Died in Georgia, 1817. Name of wife unknown.

ISSUE

   I. John⁵—Raised large family. Lived on the Black Warrior River,
      Tuscaloosa Co., Ala.
  II. Henry⁵—Issue: 1. John⁷. 2. Joshua⁷.
 III. Jacob⁵—More of Jacob later.

F-6. JACOB HOLLINGSWORTH

(Samuel[5], Jacob[4], Samuel[3], Samuel[2], Valentine[1].) Son of Samuel[5] and
...... Hollingsworth. Grandson of Jacob[4] and Mary (Brooks) Hollingsworth. Married Diana .... Resided at one time at Spartan-
burg, S. C., then St. Clair Co., Ala., and finally Pickens Co., Ala.

Issue

I. Abraham[7]—Leon Co., Texas.
II. Thomas[7]—Lived at Gadsden, Ala., and later in Texas.
III. David[7].
IV. Jacob[7]—Had large family. Lived and died in Pickens Co., Ala.
V. Daniel I[7].—Pickens Co., Ala.
VI. Wm. P[7].—Born 1828, Gadsden, Ala. Died April 23, 1879. More
of Wm. P[7]. later.

E-5. THOMAS HOLLINGSWORTH

(Jacob[4], Samuel[3], Samuel[2], Valentine[1].) Son of Jacob[4] and Mary
(Brooks) Hollingsworth. Born 1775. Died at Gainesville, Ga., 1820.
Married Miss Terrell.

Issue

I. James [6]—Died about 1877. Family at Augusta, Ga.
II. Thomas[6].
III. John[6].
IV. Henry[6].
V. Dr. William T[6].—Living at Madison, Ga.
VI. Mrs. C. L. Williams[6]—White Co., Ga.
VII. Mrs. C. B. Day[6]—Augusta, Ga.
VIII.
IX. } Two other daughters.

G-7. WILLIAM P. HOLLINGSWORTH

(Jacob[6], Samuel[5], Jacob[4], Samuel[3], Samuel[2], Valentine[1].) Of Gadsden,
Ala. Son of Jacob[6] and Diana (......) Hollingsworth. Born April 22,
1828. Died April 23, 1879. Married November 27, 1851, Mary
Josephine Lewis, daughter of Joel and Anne Charlotte Lewis. Born
.... Died Gadsden, Ala., November 14, 1917. Wm. P. served 4
years in the Confederate Army. Merchant at Gadsden, Ala. A man
of rare character and great force. One of the most successful business
men of Alabama.

ISSUE

I. Annie Dorothy[2]—Born October 18, 1852. Died June 21, 1909.
Married John S. Paden, of Gadsden, Ala. Issue: 1. John S[3].
2. W. Clifford[3]. 3. Anne Josephine[3]. 4. Maude[3].

II. Laura Josephine[2]—Born May 10, 1856. Living 1917. Married
April 27, 1876, to W. P. Lay, of Gadsden, Ala. Issue: 1. Wm.
Earl[3]. 2. Carl[3]. 3. Tracy[3]. Tracy Lay was Vice-Consul at
Paris, France, 1917.

III. Katie M[2].—Born June 2, 1858. Living 1917. Married November 7, 1877 to W. S. Standifer, of Gadsden, Ala. Issue: 1.
Fred[3]. 2. Edward Marion[3]. 3. May[3]. 4. Katie M[3]. 5. Charles[3].
6. Goetner[3].

IV. Willie[2]—Born May 30, 1861. Living at Gadsden, Ala., 1917.
Married August 26, 1880, Wm. P. Johnson, of Gadsden. Issue:
1. Josephine[3]. Wm. P. Johnson was Mayor of Gadsden, Ala.,
1917.

V. Edward Tracy[2]—Born February 18, 1866. Living 1919, Gads-
den, Ala. Married January 18, 1886, Julia R. Parrot, at
Newman, Ga. She died December 3, 1916, at Gadsden, Ala.
Issue: 1. Edward Tracy Jr[3]. 2. Armir[3]. 3. Florence[3]. Edward
Tracy Hollingsworth[2] is President Gadsden National Bank,
President Hollingsworth Realty Co., President Gadsden Loan
& Trust Co., and City Treasurer, of Gadsden, Ala.

VI. Mary Alice[2]—Born April 11, 1869. Died July 6, 1908. Married
R. C. George, of Gadsden, Ala. Issue: 1. Robt. F[3]. 2. William
P[3]. 3. John F[3]. 4. Marguerite Tracy[3].
Wm. P. George was Vice-Counsul at Grenoble, France, 1917.

E–5. JAMES HOLLINGSWORTH

(Jacob[4], Samuel[3], Samuel[2], Valentine[1].) Son of Jacob[4] and Mary
(Brooks) Hollingsworth. Born 1777. Died at Franklin, now Grundy
Co., Tenn., 1824. Issue: 1 daughter, who married Gen. A. E. Patton,
Tracy City, Tenn.

E–5. BENJAMIN HOLLINGSWORTH

(Jacob[4], Samuel[3], Samuel[2], Valentine[1].) Son of Jacob[4] and Mary
(Brooks) Hollingsworth. Born 1779. Died 1844, age 65 years, Benton Co., Ala.

ISSUE

I. Stephen Perry[6]—Born Franklin Co., Tenn., March 10, 1814.
    Died December 9, 1879.   More of Stephen later.
II. Wyly B[6].—Born 1816.   Died in Alabama, 1841.   Wyly had one
    son, Thomas W[7]. who married Mary, daughter of S. P. Hol-
    lingsworth.   Issue: *a*. Wyly C[8]. *b*. S. P., Jr[8].
III. Benjamin P[6].—Born 1822.   Died in Texas, 1867.
IV. J. B[6].—Born 1824.   Living in Rusk Co., Texas.   Issue: 1. S. H[7].
    2. Wyly C[7]. 3. Wat[7]. 4. James B[7].
V. O. W[6].—Born 1825.   Living at Austin, Texas.

F-6. STEPHEN PERRY HOLLINGSWORTH

(Benjamin[5], Jacob[4], Samuel[3], Samuel[2], Valentine[1].)   Son of Benjamin[5]
and ...... Hollingsworth.. Born Franklin Co., Tenn., March 10,
1814. Died December 9, 1879. Moved to Calhoun Co., Ala., 1832,
and to Texas, 1837. Married; name of wife not known.

ISSUE

I. John E[7].—Born Rusk Co., Texas, 1874; afterwards lived at
    Graham City, Young Co.
II. Mary[7].—Married Thomas W. Hollingsworth, son of Wyly B.

E-5. JACOB HOLLINGSWORTH

(Jacob[4], Samuel[3], Samuel[2], Valentine[1].) Son of Jacob[4] and Mary
(Brooks) Hollingsworth. Born 1773. Died in Caddo Parish, La.,
1849. Married Miss Jones.

ISSUE

I. Samuel[6]—More of Samuel later.
II. Jacob[6]. Issue: 4 children. More of Jacob later.
III. Thomas[6]—Issue: 1. Osmus[7]. 2. Thomas[7].

Also 8 daughters. All lived and had families, except 4 of the daughters.

F-6. SAMUEL HOLLINGSWORTH

(Jacob[5], Jacob[4], Samuel[3], Samuel[2], Valentine[1].) Of Shreveport, La.
Son of Jacob[5] and ...... Jones Hollingsworth.

ISSUE

   I. Col. James[7]—Issue: 1. Samuel[8]. 2. Lillian[8]. 3. Hearsey[8].
  II. Benjamin[7].
 III. Jacob[7].
 IV. Elizabeth[7].
  V. Amanda[7]—Married ...... Gray. Issue: 4 children.

F-6. JACOB HOLLINGSWORTH

(Jacob[5], Jacob[4], Samuel[3], Samuel[2], Valentine[1].) Of Shreveport, La.
Son of Jacob[5] and ......Jones Hollingsworth.

ISSUE

    I. Robert Bruce[7]—Pleasant Hill, P. O., De Soto Parish, La.
   II. Wm. Wallace[7].
  III. Susan[7].
  IV. Thomas[7].
   V. Richard[7].
  VI. Jacob[7].

F-6. JAMES H. HOLLINGSWORTH

(Thomas[5], Jacob[4], Samuel[3], Samuel[2], Valentine[1].) Of Atlanta. Son
of Thomas[5] and ...... (Terrell) Hollingsworth, a grandson of Jacob[4],
who died 1843.

ISSUE

   I. Charles T[7].—Born 1850. Augusta, Ga.
  II. Edward H[7].—Augusta, Ga.
 III. John B[7].—Savannah, Ga.
 IV. William J[7].—Augusta, Ga.
  V. James T[7].—Augusta, Ga.
    And 3 daughters.

D-4. HENRY HOLLINGSWORTH

(Stephen³, Henry², Valentine¹.) Of Duplin Co., N. C., son of Stephen³ and Anne ...... Hollingsworth, of Cecil Co., Md., and Orange Co., Va., after 1734. Henry was living in Duplin Co., N. C., in 1764. Married Mary Murrah.

Issue

    I. Nancy⁵—Married ...... Wright.

    II. James⁵—Married Betsey Merritt. More of James later.

    III. Henry⁵—Married Betsey Griggs. More of Henry later.

    IV. Zebulon⁵—Married Elizabeth Chesnutt. More of Zebulon later.

    V. Elizabeth⁵—Married Alexander Chesnutt.

    VI. Mary⁵—Born September 17, 1753. Married Jas. Faison. She died September 19, 1822, age 69 years.

    VII. Charity⁵—Married Cannon Caison.

    VIII. Sarah⁵—Married David Chesnutt.

    IX. Lydia⁵—Married Hardy Carroll.

E-5. JAMES HOLLINGSWORTH

(Henry⁴, Stephen³, Henry², Valentine¹.) Son of Henry⁴, of Duplin Co., N. C., and Mary (Murrah) Hollingsworth. Married Betsey Merritt.

Issue

    I. James⁶—Married Mary Carroll.

    II. Jacob⁶—Married Elizabeth Hollingsworth. More of Jacob later.

    III. Nancy⁶—Married John Carroll (first wife).

    IV. Charity⁶—Married John Swinson.

    V. Jane⁶—Married Joseph Chesnutt.

    VI. Mary⁶—Married Needham Chesnutt.

F-6. JACOB HOLLINGSWORTH

(James⁵, Henry⁴, Stephen³, Henry², Valentine¹.) Son of James⁵ and Elizabeth (Merritt) Hollingsworth and grandson of Henry⁴, of Duplin Co., N. C. Married Elizabeth Hollingsworth, daughter of Henry⁵ and granddaughter of Henry⁴ Hollingsworth, Duplin Co., N. C.'

Issue

    I. Henry⁷—Born January 24, 1824. Married ......, May 24, 1857. No issue. Wife died August 10, 1877. He was living at Magnolia, N. C., 1881.

    II. Francis M⁷.—Married. Issue.

    III. Catherine⁷—Married. No issue.

IV. Nancy⁷—Married. Issue.
V. Elizabeth⁷—Married. Issue.
VI. Margaret⁷—Married. No issue.
VII. James⁷—Married. Issue: 3 children.

E-5. HENRY HOLLINGSWORTH

(Henry⁴, Stephen³, Henry², Valentine¹.) Son of Henry⁴ and Mary
(Murrah) Hollingsworth, of Duplin Co., N. C. Married Elizabeth
Griggs.

Issue

I. Zebulon⁵—Married Mary Winters.
II. Leonard⁵—Married Catherine Carlton.
III. Guilford⁵—Married Rebecca Carlton.
IV. Francis⁵—First married Wm. Smith. She then married Uriah
Bass.
V. Elizabeth⁵—Married Jacob Hollingsworth, son of James⁵ Hol-
lingsworth.
VI. Nancy⁵—Married Bennett Ballard.

E-5. ZEBULON HOLLINGSWORTH

(Henry⁴, Stephen³, Henry², Valentine¹.) Son of Henry⁴ and Mary
(Murrah) Hollingsworth, of Duplin Co., N. C. Married Elizabeth
Chesnutt, 1792.

Issue

I. Stephen⁵—Born 1794. Married Elizabeth Colwell.
II. Henry⁵—Born 1798. Married Mary Carroll, 1825.
III. Jacob⁵—Born 1806. Married Catharine Treadwell.
IV. Edith⁵—Born .... Married Joseph Carroll, Thomasville,
Ga.
V. Jane⁵—Born .... Married Richard Colwell, Sampson Co.
VI. Mary⁵—Born .... Married Thomas Vann.
VII. Annie⁵.
VIII. Elizabeth⁵—Born .... Married John Kelley. Living in
Florida.

F-6. STEPHEN HOLLINGSWORTH

(Zebulon⁶, Henry⁴, Stephen³, Henry², Valentine¹.) Son of Zebulon⁵ and Elizabeth (Chesnutt) Hollingsworth. Born in Duplin Co., N. C., 1794. Married Elizabeth Colwell. Removed from North Carolina to Tampa Bay, Fla.

ISSUE

I. John H⁷.

II. Wm. W⁷.

III. Stephen T⁷.

IV. Timothy H⁷.

V. Catharine⁷.

VI. Margaret A⁷.

F-6. HENRY HOLLINGSWORTH

(Zebulon⁶, Henry⁴, Stephen³, Henry², Valentine¹.) Of Koscuisco, Miss. Son of Zebulon⁵ and Elizabeth (Chesnutt) Hollingsworth. Born December 25, 1798, Sampson Co., N. C. Married January 18, 1825, Polly Carroll. Occupation: farmer. Died July 7, 1880. Man of high integrity and respected by all who knew him. Polly Carroll Hollingsworth died May 25, 1889, age 82, Attala Co., Miss.

ISSUE

I. Margaret E⁷.—Born 1826. Married D. T. Patterson. She died in North Carolina, 1842. No issue.

II. Mary J⁷.—Born 1828. First married J. R. Ezzell. He died 1865. She then married David Stephens, Faisons, N. C. No issue.

III. Lewis H⁷.—Born May 23, 1830. Died February 22, 1901. Married 1855, Martha C. Mallett, in Attala Co., Miss. More of Lewis later.

IV. Priscilla⁷—Born May 1, 1832. Married August 1850, M. H. Gregory. She died July 18, 1851. Issue: Priscilla A⁸.

V. Jesse J⁷.—Born August 20, 1834. Married February 15, 1866, Pauline Gilliland. Died December 30, 1899. More of Jesse later.

VI. James T⁷.—Born May 26, 1837. Married July 8, 1866, Mary R. Pettigrew. Died March 13, 1917. More of James T. later.

VII. Electa C⁷.—Born September 23, 1839. Died November 20, 1890. Married December 18, 1866, William S. Gilliland⁸. More of Electa later.

VIII. Hosea H⁷.—Born October 25, 1841. Died in the Confederate Army, September 10, 1862.

IX. George Zebulon[7]—Born November 10, 1844. Living 1918. Married February 27, 1870, Florence Dulin. More of George Zebulon later.

X. William Wright[7]—Born April 3, 1847. Married February 28, 1869, Sarah E. Pettigrew. More of William later.

Henry Hollingsworth moved from Sampson Co., N. C., 1848, to Attala Co., Miss. (Koscuisco, P. O.)

Lucy Hollingsworth (colored) left her own mother to follow her mistress, Mrs. Henry Hollingsworth from North Carolina to Mississippi. She was born in 1837. Living 1917, and though 80 years of age is still faithful to this family.

G–7. LEWIS HENRY HOLLINGSWORTH

(Henry[6], Zebulon[5], Henry[4], Stephen[3], Henry[2], Valentine[1].) Son of Henry[6] and Polly (Carroll) Hollingsworth. Born May 23, 1830. Married Martha C. Mallett, 1855. Died September 22, 1901, at Koscuisco, Miss. Widow living 1917, at Laurel, Miss. He was a merchant. Captain in the Confederate Army.

Issue

I. Celeste C[8].—Born 1857. Died 1862.
II. Theodosia E[8].—Born 1858. Died 1885.
III. James H[8].—Born 1860. Married May 11, 1888, Carrie Mae Land, of Shreveport, La. Living 1917, Greenwood, Miss. Issue: 1. Mary Theodosia[9]. 2. Lewis Henry[9]. 3. Floyd[9]. 4. James, Jr[9].—Enlisted U. S. Army, 1916.
IV. Lewis H[8].—Born May 21, 1862, Attala Co., Miss. Married Lena Allen, of Leak Co., Miss. Issue: 1. Nancy[9]—Married R. S. Roby, Surgeon U. S. Army. 2. George A[9].—Married Lena Gunter. 3. Lattie C[9]. 4. Frank C[9]. 5. Lewis Haywood, Jr[9]. 6. Mary[9]. 7. Lucille[9]. 8. Blanche Elizabeth[9]. 9. John Donald[9].
V. Baker M[8].—Born 1867. Died July 23, 1893.
VI. Katie H[8].—Born January 9, 1877. Married December, 1896, C. I. Depew. Living 1917, Laurel, Miss. Husband a merchant. Issue: 1. Alice Katherine[9]. 2. Elsie H[9].

G-7. JESSIE J. HOLLINGSWORTH

(Henry[6], Zebulon[5], Henry[4], Stephen[3], Henry[2], Valentine[1].) Son of Henry[6] and Polly (Carroll) Hollingsworth. Born August 20, 1834, Sampson Co., N. C. Died December 25, 1899. Married February 15, 1866, Pauline Gilliland, who died December 30, 1899. Was a planter, near Kosciusko, Miss.

ISSUE

I. Hosea[8]—Born March 26, 1867. Died Aug. 6, 1893.

II. Esther A[8].—Born July 22, 1870.

III. Mary R[8].—Born December 15, 1874. Died January, 1902. Married June 6, 1899, Dr. W. M. Turnage. Issue: 1. Joe B[9]. 2. Mary E[9].

IV. Henry[8]—Born January 24, 1876. Married December 12, 1899, Susie J. Jamison. Living 1918, Kosciusko, Miss. Planter and saw mill owner. Issue: 1. Hosea S[9]. 2. Charlie[9]. 3. Jessie J[9]. 4. Ruth E[9]. 5. Helen L[9].

V. Electa C[8].—Born May 18, 1881. Married December 24, 1903, E. E. Pickle, planter, at Dossville, Miss. Living 1918. Issue: 1. Mary C[9]. 2. David L[9]. 3. Margaret E[9]. 4. James H[9]. 5. George W[9].

VI. Pauline[8]—Born April 11, 1884. Married December 20, 1914, J. E. Purr, planter at Lambert, Miss. Living 1918. Issue: 1. Francis P[9]. 2. Mary S[9].

G-7. JAMES T. HOLLINGSWORTH

(Henry[6], Zebulon[5], Henry[4], Stephen[3], Henry[2], Valentine[1].) Son of Henry[6] and Polly (Carroll) Hollingsworth, of Kosciusko, Miss. Born May 26, 1837. Died March 13, 1917. Married July 8, 1866, Mary R. Pettigrew. Planter.

ISSUE

I. Ella[8]—Born March 19, 1868. Married September 5, 1891, W. R. Gannaway, druggist, Fort Smith, Ark. Issue: 1. Thomas B[9]. 2. Ethel[9]. 3. Louis[9]. 4. John[9].

II. Mary George[8]—Born December 19, 1869. Married June 1, 1901, James Watson, teacher. Issue: 1. Doree Ella[9]. 2. Hue E[9]. 3. Jessie E[9]. 4. James F[9].

III. John Lewis[8]—Born November 24, 1876. Married January 27, 1907, Daisy Funk, at Seldin, Tex. Planter. Issue: Christine[9].

IV. James T[8].—Born August 14, 1878. Married Mita .... Occupation: Traveling Salesman. Issue: James Remington[9].

G-7. GEORGE ZEBULON HOLLINGSWORTH

(Henry⁶, Zebulon⁵, Henry⁴, Stephen³, Henry², Valentine¹.)   Son of
Henry⁶, of Kosciusko, Miss. Born November 10, 1844, North Caro-
lina. Living 1918, at Stephensville, Tex. Married February 27, 1870,
Florence Dulin. Retired planter, Mason, and Confederate Veteran.

ISSUE

I. Sallie May⁸—Born May 16, 1871. Died October 13, 1872.

II. Carrie Ella⁸—Born November 8, 1872. Living 1918, Stephenville, Tex. Married December 6, 1896, A. T. Alkison,
planter. Issue: 1. Mary⁹. 2. George⁹. 3. Verna Ruth⁹.
4. Almabel⁹. 5. Albert⁹. 6. Louise⁹. 7. Catherine⁹. 8. Lura⁹.

III. Bettie Cockburn⁸—Born June 5, 1874. Married September 13,
1894, James Winters, planter. Living 1918, Stephenville,
Tex. Issue: 1. Harvey⁹. 2. Jimmie⁹ (daughter). Living
1918, Brady, Tex.

IV. Mary Etta (Polly)⁸—Born May 10, 1877. Died December 1,
1904. Married July 27, 1902, Arthur Clifton Ferguson,
educator. Issue: Juanita May⁹—Living 1918, with her
father, at Marlin, Tex.

V. George⁸—(Daughter)—Born June 24, 1879. Living 1918, Stephenville, Tex. Married April 15, 1910, Ed. Bryant, Jour-
nalist. Issue: 1. Boy⁹—Born September 4, 1912. Died in
infancy. 2. Florence Ione⁹—Born August 1, 1914. 3. and 4.
Edward⁹ and George⁹ (twins)—Born August 30, 1917.

VI. Susie Belle⁸—Born March 28, 1881. Living 1918, Stephensville,
Tex. Writer.

VII. John Carroll⁸—Born August 31, 1884. Living 1918, Stephens-
ville, Tex. Married November 7, 1912, Lura Durham.
Demonstration Agent of Somervell County. United States
Government work, and a planter. Issue: John Carroll, Jr⁹.

G-7. WM. WRIGHT HOLLINGSWORTH

(Henry⁶, Zebulon⁵, Henry⁴, Stephen³, Henry², Valentine¹.) Son of
Henry⁶ and Polly (Carroll) Hollingsworth, of Kosciusko, Miss. Born
April 3, 1847, Sampson Co., N. C. Living 1917, at Kosciusko, Miss.
Merchant and planter. Married February 28, 1869, Sarah E. Petti-
grew, Attala Co., Miss.

Issue

I. Emma Eugenia⁶—Born July 27, 1870.   Living 1917.   Married
   May 8, 1894, J. H. Jamison, of Kosciusko.   Planter.   Issue:
   1. Hugh⁹—Born April 15, 1895.   2. Eugene Henry⁹—Born
   December 24, 1897.   3. Lidd Corinne⁹—Born May 19, 1903.

II. Henry Ebbie⁶—Born November 7, 1872.   Died October 16, 1905.
   Married October 17, 1895, Lula C. Smith, of Dossville, Miss.
   Issue: 1. Wm. Henry⁹—Born January 18, 1897, 1st Lieuten-
   ant, 61st Co., U. S. Marine Corps, Brooklyn, N. Y. 2. Joseph
   N⁹.—Born January 19, 1899. 3. Samuel Thomas⁹. 4. James
   Lewis⁹. 5. George Ebenezer⁹.

III. William Joseph⁶—Born November 8, 1874.   Living 1917, Louisville, Miss.   Married February 15, 1903, Emma E. Hays.
   Issue: 1. William Edward⁹. 2. Joseph, Jr⁹.

IV. Thomas L⁶.—Born January 30, 1877.   Living 1917.   Married
   February 8, 1906, Lennie U. Smith, of Dossville, Miss. Issue:
   1. Robert Wright⁹. 2. Sarah Louise⁹.

V. Mary Theodosia⁶—Born January 6, 1879.   Living 1917, Delhi,
   La.   Married June 1903, C. H. Hooker, of Clinton, Miss.
   A merchant. Issue: 1. Annie E⁹.   2. Charles Hollingsworth⁹.
   3. Dodie Mae⁹. 4. George P⁹.

VI. Ida Mae⁶—Born March 19, 1882.   Living 1917.   Married March
   1, 1904, Dr. J. E. Turnage, of Kosciusko, Miss.   Issue: 1. William Edward⁹. 2. Wade Hollingsworth⁹.   3. Johnson Lee⁹.
   4. Claude Eugene⁹.

VII. Camilla Elizabeth⁶—Born March 18, 1884.   Living 1917.   Married April 24, 1913, L. A. Ward, of Kosciusko, Miss. Issue:
   1. Mary Mae Elizabeth⁹.

VIII. Samuel Valentine⁶—Born February 18, 1886.   Living 1917, Attala Co., Miss.   Married December 24, 1909, Kittie D. Kelly.
   Issue: William Wright, Jr⁹.

G-7.   ELECTA C. (HOLLINGSWORTH) GILLILAND

Daughter of Henry⁵ and Polly (Carroll) Hollingsworth.   Born September 23, 1839.   Died November 20, 1890.   Married December 18, 1866,
William S. Gilliland.   Planter.

Issue

I. Anna⁶—Born August 4, 1874.   Married August 3, 1896, C. C.
   Bailey, of Kosciusko, Miss.   Planter.   Issue: 1. Everett⁹.
   2. Mary⁹. 3. Electa⁹. 4. Ella⁹. 5. Annie⁹. 6. Kate⁹.

II. Haywood Harvey⁶—Born April 12, 1876. Living 1918, Attala
Co., Miss. Married January 26, 1898, Betty Harvey, of
Lexington, Miss. Sheriff of County. Issue: 1. Haywood
Harvey⁹. 2. Electa⁹.

III. James Wilson⁸—Born September 8, 1878. Living 1918, Attala
Co., Miss. Married December 22, 1909, Bessie Furr, of
Smyrna, Miss. Issue: 1. Catherine⁹. 2. Willie Furr⁹.

F-6. JACOB HOLLINGSWORTH

(Zebulon⁵, Henry⁴, Stephen³, Henry², Valentine¹.) Of Duplin Co.
N. C. Son of Zebulon⁵ and Elizabeth Chesnutt. Born 1806. Died
about 1865. Married Catharine Treadwell.

ISSUE

I. Jacob⁷.
II. Amelia⁷—Married Mr. Cashwell.
III. Eliza⁷.
IV. Charlotte⁷.

E-5. JAMES HOLLINGSWORTH

(George⁴, Abraham³, Thomas², Valentine¹.) Son of George⁴ and Jane
(Elwell) Hollingsworth, and half-brother of Abraham⁵, of Taurens, S. C.
Born 1758. Died .... First married Sarah Wright. Name of
second wife unknown.

ISSUE 1ST MARRIAGE

I. James⁶.
II. Joseph⁶—Born August 4, 1789. Died November 1, 1849. Mar-
ried Elizabeth Hutchins, July 5, 1815. More of Joseph later.
III. William⁶.
IV. Sarah⁶.

ISSUE 2ND MARRIAGE

V. Carter⁶.
VI. Ira⁶.
VII. Henry⁶.

VIII. Katurah⁶.
IX. Rachel⁶.

F-6. JOSEPH HOLLINGSWORTH

(James⁵, George⁴, Abraham³, Thomas², Valentine¹.) Son of James⁵
and Sarah (Wright) Hollingsworth. Born August 4, 1789. Died
November 1, 1849. Married Elizabeth Hutchins, July 5, 1815.

Issue

  I. Sarah⁷—Born 1816. Died 1839.
 II. Anderson Hutchins⁷—Born December 29, 1818. Died January
       14, 1865. More of Anderson later.
III. Horatio⁷—Born 1821. Died May 5, 1852.
 IV. Johnson⁷—Born 1823. Died October 23, 1824.
  V. Amanda⁷—Born 1825. Died 1870.
 VI. James⁷—Born 1828. Died May 29, 1862.
VII. Keziah⁷—Born 1833. Died August 19, 1863.

G-7. ANDERSON HUTCHINS HOLLINGSWORTH

(Joseph⁶, James⁵, George⁴, Abraham³, Thomas², Valentine¹.) Son of
Joseph⁶ and Elizabeth (Hutchins) Hollingsworth. Grandson of James
and Sarah (Wright) Hollingsworth. Born December 29, 1818. Died
January 14, 1865. Married Parmelia Key, of South Carolina (she was
born 1827), Bienville Parish, La., January 6, 1847.

Issue

   I. Gibson⁸—Born August 19, 1849. Living Texas.
  II. Joseph⁸—Born March 11, 1851. Died June 15,
        1853.
 III. Horatio A⁸.—Born May 14, 1853. Died 1870.
  IV. Mary⁸—Born January 17, 1855. Died 1862.
   V. Sarah⁸—Born December 20, 1856. Died 1857.   All born
  VI. Emma⁸—Born December 18, 1857. Died 1862.   in Rosier
 VII. Jackson⁸—Born December 26, 1859. Living   Parish, La.
        Texas.
VIII. Preston D⁸.—Born December 18, 1861. Living
        Texas.
  IX. Delula L⁸.—Born November 27, 1864. Died
        1865.

G–7. JAMES HOLLINGSWORTH

(Jesse[6], Nathaniel[5], Thomas[4], Thomas[3], Thomas[2], Valentine[1].) Son of Jesse[6] and Guilema Mary (Spicer) Hollingsworth. Born 1795. Married Elizabeth Newberry, about 1812.

Issue

    I. Mary Ann[8]—Born June 15, 1813. Married ......

    II. John M[8].—Born December 25, 1814. Married ......

    III. Jefferson[8]—Born March 22, 1817. Married ......

    IV. Eliza[8]—Born March 7, 1819. Married ......

    V. Deborah[8]—Born November 18, 1821.

    VI. David Marshall[8]—Born March 10, 1823. More of David later.

    VII. Isaac[8]—Born May 5, 1825. Married ......

    VIII. James[8]—Born March 20, 1828. Married ......

    IX. Benjamin F[8].—Born September 24, 1832. Married ......

H–8. DAVID MARSHALL HOLLINGSWORTH

(James[7], Jesse[6], Nathaniel[5], Thomas[4], Thomas[3], Thomas[2], Valentine[1].) Son of James[7] and Elizabeth (Newberry) Hollingsworth. Born at Macon, Ga., March 10, 1823. First married Caroline Bower, at New Orleans, La., May 11, 1848. Second wife, Rosina Prague Hollingsworth, Signal Mountain, Tenn., May 9, 1868.

Issue 1st Marriage

    I. Louis Bower Hollingsworth[9]—Born 1850. More of Louis Bower later.

    II. Jefferson Davis[9]—Born January 18, 1851, at Yazoo City, Miss. Married Alice ...... Issue: 1. Myrtle[10]. 2. Maud[10].

    III. William Leake[9]—Born October 4, 1852, Yazoo City, Miss. Married at Minneapolis, Minn.

    IV. Warren[9]—First married Lillie Irwin. She died without issue, at Yazoo City, Miss. He then married Cordelia Calkins, at Ocean Springs, Miss., 1909. Issue: 1. Ada[10]. 2. Harvey[10]. 3. William[10]. 4. Bessie[10]. 5. Robert[10].

    V. Kate[9]—Born Yazoo City, Miss. Married David M. Hollingsworth, at New Orleans, La., April 30, 1895. She died at Yazoo City, Miss., January 10, 1897. No issue.

VI. David Marshall[9]—Born July 26, 1871, New Orleans, La. Married May Gwinner, at Canton, Miss., November 8, 1894. Both living 1918. Issue: 1. May[10]. 2. Harry B[10]. 3. Edith M[10].

VII. Edith[9]—Born June 21, 1874, New Orleans, La. Married James A. Wiggs, at New Orleans, La., December 3, 1901. Husband died April 4, 1912, at Chattanooga, Tenn. Issue: 1. Edith[10]. 2. James A[10]. 3. Lucy Carol[10].

I-9. LOUIS BOWER HOLLINGSWORTH

(David M[9]., James[7], Jesse[6], Nathaniel[5], Thomas[4], Thomas[3], Thomas[2], Valentine[1].) Son of David Marshall[8] and Caroline (Bower) Hollingsworth. Born 1850.

ISSUE

I. Annie Caroline[10]—Born April 5, 1875. Married January 19, 1898, Reuben Shotwell Cross. Both living at 111 Regina Ave., Mobile, Ala. Issue: 1. Harlan Eugene[11]—Born October 20, 1898. 2. Dorothy Claire[11].

II. Louis Cotton[10]—Born September 25, 1877. Married Lelia Gibson. Both living at 103 Regina Ave., Mobile, Ala., 1918. Issue: 1. Louise[11].

III. John Cotton[10]—Born October 25, 1879. Married December 21, 1905, Maude Snyder. Both lived at 279 Audubon Blvd., New Orleans, La., 1918. Issue: 1. John Cotton[11]. Dead. 2. Shirley Elizabeth[11]—Born October 12, 1910.

IV. Sallie Seward[10]—Born November 26, 1884. Married July 5, 1906, Joseph Wynn. Both living at Rayne, La., 1918. Issue: 1. Vivian Hughes[11]. 2. Sallie Averill[11].

V. Gwynne Hughes[10]—Born August 16, 1894. Unmarried 1918.

1. JOSEPH HOLLINGSWORTH

Ancestors not given.   Lived in Huntingdon Co., Pa.

ISSUE

I. Jesse².   III. Mary².
II. Jacob².   IV. Elizabeth².

2. JACOB HOLLINGSWORTH

Son of Joseph¹ Hollingsworth.   Died August 17, 1844.   Married Catharine Pinkney, Huntingdon Co., Pa.

ISSUE

I. Alexander M².
II. John S².—Died 1855.
III. Jesse H².—Married.   Living at Dubuque, Iowa.
IV. Eliza J².—Married Richard Passmore, Keithsburg, Ill.
V. Amos D².—Married ...... Issue: 4 children.
VI. Calvin S².—Married ...... Monmouth, Ill.
VII. Anna²—Married James Monroe, Illinois.
VIII. Catharine²—Married Abraham Stokes, Mt. Vernon, Ohio.

3. ALEXANDER M. HOLLINGSWORTH

(Jacob², Joseph¹.) Of Zanesville, Ohio.   Son of Jacob² and Catharine (Pinkney) Hollingsworth.   Born October 11, 1821.   First married Margaret Logan.   He then married Alcinda Rush.

ISSUE 1ST MARRIAGE

I. Joseph H⁴.—Born December 25, 1843.   Married Sallie McDermott.
II. Jesse S⁴.—Born August 14, 1845.   Married C. Musselman.
III. John S⁴.—Born January 2, 1847.   Married Leila C. Graves.
IV. James A⁴.—Born October 11, 1850, Cincinnati.
V. Mary J⁴.—Born September 1852.   Married Lewis ......, of Zanesville.
VI. Edw. J⁴.—Born March 1, 1854.   Married Maggie Kerner, of Zanesville.
VII. William L⁴.—Born October 13, 1855.   Married Maggie Kilen, of Zanesville.
VIII. Margaret A⁴.—Born September 1857.

ISSUE 2ND MARRIAGE

IX. Samuel F⁴.—Chicago, Ill.
X. Lewis M⁴.—Newark, Ohio.
XI. Charles H⁴.—Zanesville, Ohio.
XII. Caroline⁴.—Married Martin Miller, Zanesville, Ohio.

1-a. WILLIAM HOLLINGSWORTH

Emigrated from South Carolina, 1805, with six other families of the same name. At Crab Orchard, Ky., they divided; three families went to Ohio, and the rest to Indiana. Levi, Thomas, and Daniel, to Ohio; Joseph, Peter, John and William, to Indiana. William probably born in Virginia or North Carolina. Died in Indiana, 1809, age about 80 years.

Issue

I. William(b)—Born .... Married ...... Crosby. He died
    1815, age 40 years. Issue: 1. Barnett G(c). 2. Joseph(c).
    3. Mattie(c).
II. Joseph(b)—Born ...... Died 1841, age about 75 years.
III. Peter(b)—Born .... Died 1846, age about 60 years. Issue:
    1. William(c). 2. Ferdinand(c). And 4 daughters.
IV. John(b)—Born .... Died 1853. Married, 1807, Nelly Polk,
    of Kentucky. Issue: 1. George W(c). 2. Joseph(c). 3. Isaac(c).
    4. Spear S(c). And 4 daughters. More of Isaac later.

3-c. ISAAC HOLLINGSWORTH

(John(b). William(a)), Son of John(b) and Nelly (Polk) Hollingsworth. Born December, 1821. Married Nancy E. Wilson. Born May, 1823.

Issue

I. Thaddius C(d).	IV. John T(d).
II. Alonzo(d).	V. Sarah E(d).
III. Arrabella(d).	VI. Frank(d).

3-c. BARNETT G. HOLLINGSWORTH

(William(b), William(a.) Son of William(b) and (...... Crosby) Hollingsworth. Went to Indiana, and then to Texas, 1849. Died 1874.

Issue

I. Joseph(d)—Wounded in the Battle of Sharpsburg, Md. Died at
    Winchester.
II. William(d)—Killed in battle.

  III. Robert(d)—Living at Ft. Worth, Tex.   Law partner of John E.
  IV. Roland(d)—Lives in Navoo Co., Tex.
   V. George(d)—Lives in Anderson Co., Tex.
  VI. Daniel(d)—Lives in Anderson Co., Tex.
 VII. Lucy(d).
VIII. Sarah(d).
  IX. Mattie(d).
   X. Caroline(d).

AMHERST CO., VA. AND NORTH CAROLINA

William Hollingsworth and Joseph Hollingsworth.   Brothers.   William
went to Nashville, Tenn.

1-a. JOSEPH HOLLINGSWORTH

Ancestors unknown.   Born in Amherst Co., Va., about 1765 to '70.
Died 1819, Stokes Co., N. C.   Married Mary Matthews, 1793.

ISSUE

   I. Aquilla(b)—Born ...... Died 1837.
  II. James(b)—Born 1797.   Died 1857.   More of James later.
 III. Tandy(b)—Born 1800.   Went to Kentucky.
  IV. Mary(b)—Born 1802.
   V. Daniel(b)—Born 1804.   Died 1833.
  VI. William(b)—Born 1807.

2-b. JAMES M. HOLLINGSWORTH

Son of Joseph(a) and Mary (Matthews) Hollingsworth.   Born March 4,
1797.   Died 1857.   Married Elizabeth Golding, 1819.   Went to Surry
Co., N. C.

ISSUE

    I. Joseph(c)—Born February 27, 1820.   More of Joseph later.
   II. Mary(c)—Born 1821.   Died 1875.
  III. Eliza(c)—Born 1824.   Died 1858.
   IV. Sallie(c)—Born 1826.
    V. James(c)—Born 1829.   Died 1839.
   VI. Edwin(c)—Born 1832.   Died 1859.   More of Edwin later.
  VII. Martha(c)—Born 1834.
 VIII. William(c)—Born 1836.   More of William later.
   IX. Nannie(c)—Born 1838.   Died 1877.
    X. John(c)—Born 1840.   Died 1858.
   XI. Isaac(c)—Born 1842.   Died 1871.

3–c. Dr. JOSEPH HOLLINGSWORTH

(James M.(b), Joseph(a).) Of Mt. Airy, Surry Co., N. C. Son of James M(b). and Elizabeth (Golding) Hollingsworth. Born February 27, 1820. Married Mary L. Banner, 1848, Mt. Airy, N, C.

Issue

I. Virginia E(d).—Born 1849.
II. Katie(d)—Born 1850. Died 1857.
III. James(d)—Born 1852. Died 1861.
IV. M. Letitia(d)—Born 1855. Married Richard L. Gwyn, November 13, 1879.
V. John B(d).—Born 1858.
VI. S. Kate(d)—Born 1860. Died 1864.
VII. Anna(d)—Born 1862.
VIII. Joseph(d) —Born 1865.
IX. Edwin (d).

3–c. Dr. EDWIN S. HOLLINGSWORTH

(James M.(b), Joseph(a).) Son of James M(b). and Elizabeth (Golding) Hollingsworth. Born 1832. Died 1859. Mt. Airy, N. C. Married Sarah R. Banner, 1858. Issue: Edwin T(d). Born 1859.

3–c. Dr. WILLIAM R. HOLLINGSWORTH

(James M(b)., Joseph(a).) Son of James M(b). and Elizabeth (Golding) Hollingsworth. Born January 14, 1836, Mt. Airy, N. C. Married Susan Davis, 1865.

Issue

I. Elizabeth D(d).—Born 1866. Died 1867.
II. Kate(d)—Born 1868.
III. James M(d).—Born 1869.
IV. Saida E(d).—Born 1871.
V. Robert E(d).—Born 1873.
VI. J. Frank(d)—Born 1875.
VII. M. Maggie(d)—Born 1877.

HOLLINGSWORTHS OF NORTH CAROLINA

1-a. WILLIAM T. HOLLINGSWORTH

Son of ......, of Virginia. Born 1788. Died 1859. He settled in Franklin Co., N. C.   Married about 1814, Miss Crawley, of Franklin Co. She was much over 90 years of age at the time of her death. Issue: 4 children; the name of only 1 is known.

ISSUE

    I. William F(b).—Born Franklin Co., 1818. Married Miss Babbitt, of same county, South Carolina. She was born 1822. They moved to Nash Co., N. C., and were living there at the time of their death.

1-b. WILLIAM F. HOLLINGSWORTH

Son of William T(a). and ...... (Crawley) Hollingsworth. Born Nash Co., N. C. Married Lucinda ......, about 1845.

ISSUE

    I. J. T(c).—Born 1849. Lived in Nashville, N. C.
    II. J. H(c).—Born 1851.
    III. Lucy(c)—Born 1845.
    IV. Louisa(c)—Born 1860.

JOHN M. HOLLINGSWORTH

Son of James and ...... Hollingsworth. Born .... Married Miss Cunningham, 1833.

    They had 13 children and only 5 lived.

ISSUE

I. Ada.	IV. Philip W.
II. Lizzie.	V. Willis.
III. Georgia.	

HOLLINGSWORTHS OF EDGEFIELD

(By SALLIE STROTHER HOLLINGSWORTH)

James Hollingsworth came from Winchester, Va., about 1786, and settled in the Meeting Street Section of Edgefield Co., S. C. He left one brother in Virginia, another went to North Carolina, a third to Ohio, a fourth to Kentucky, and one to Mississippi.

James Hollingsworth—Born ...... Died September 12, 1821, in Edgefield County. Married Agnes Evans—Born ...... Died 1812.

ISSUE

 I. John—Born in Virginia, 1773. Died in Florida, 1841.
 II. Alexander—Born 1775. Died 1804. Issue: 1. James. 2. Alexander. 3. Isaac. 4. Daughter Jane, or Ginsey. She married Jacob Miller. Isaac died 1813.
 III. James—Born 1778. Issue: James, Jr. James, Sr., died 1805. His wife, Barbery, married second husband, Hugh Mosely.
 IV. Lucy—Born 1780. Married Enoch Walton. She died before 1818. Issue: John.
 V. Sarah—Born 1782. Married James Carson. She died before 1822.
 VI. Mary—Born 1786. Married 1808, James Harrison. He was born June 6, 1781. Died 18...... A son of James and Susannah Harrison, of Virginia.

John Hollingsworth, the eldest child, married Beersheba Oliphant, third daughter of John and Nancy (Fraser) Oliphant. Born 1786. Died 1876.

ISSUE

 I. William F. Hollingsworth—Born 1809. Died October 23, 1831.
 II. John Hampton Hollingsworth—Born February 15, 1811. Died July 31, 1887.
 III. Eliza A. Hollingsworth—Born September 3, 1813. Died September 19, 1903.
 IV. Emily D. Hollingsworth—Born May 20, 1816. Died June 26, 1900.
 V. Diomede F. Hollingsworth—Born June 25, 1819. Died February 25, 1857.
 VI. Mansfield F. Hollingsworth—Born August 2, 1821. Died October 23, 1853.

William Hollingsworth, the eldest son, married, but left no heirs.

John Hampton Hollingsworth (son of John H. and Beersheba Oliphant) was married twice.

He married Elizabeth Richardson, November 15, 1853, and Lucinda Brunson, December 23, 1858. The latter was born 1836 and died May 16, 1883.

Issue 1st Marriage

I. Elizabeth Richardson Hollingsworth—Born August 24, 1855. Married January 15, 1880, to William Hayne Folk. Issue: Julia Folk—Born September 8, 1895. Col. Folk died May 16, 1898.

Issue 2nd Marriage

II. Diomede—Born 1859. Died 1862.

III. Lucretia Helen—Born 1861. Died 1865.

IV. John Hampton—Born 1864. Died 1867.

V. Daniel Brunson—Born July 14, 1868. Still living. Daniel Brunson Hollingsworth—Married October 19, 1889, Sallie Strother—Born April 25, 1871. Issue: 1. John Hampton—Born April 24, 1891. Unmarried. 2. Anna Ball Strother—Born February 24, 1894. Married Wad. D. Allen, June 1915. Issue: Horde, Jr.—Born March 4, 1916. 3. Elizabeth Folk—Born February 23, 1896. Married William S. Anderson. Issue: Elizabeth—Born November 1920. 4. Diomede Franklin—Born July 12, 1898. Unmarried. 5. William Strother—Born February 18, 1900. Unmarried.

Eliza Ann Hollingsworth, third child of John Hollingsworth and his wife, Beersheba Oliphant, married Alexander Walker, December 15, 1831.

Issue

I. Virginia—Married Mr. Harmon.

II. Caroline—First husband, Mr. Freeman; second husband, Mr. Williams. Has children by both.

III. John H.—Died without issue.

IV. Alexander Spann—Died in Iowa; left daughters.

V. Milton Scott—Died without issue.

VI. Emma E.—Died unmarried.

VII. Herbert W.—Living, but unmarried.

Emily D. Hollingsworth, fourth child of John Hollingsworth and his wife, Beersheba Oliphant, married Ezra G. Talbert. Issue: 1. Cornelia. 2. John. 3. Ezra. Ezra only had children. They live now in Edgefield County.

Diomede Franklin, fifth child of John Hollingsworth and his wife, married Eliza Griffin. They had one son, who died in childhood.

Mansfield Emilius, sixth child of John Hollingsworth and his wife, Beersheba Oliphant, married Margaret Gomillian, May 10, 1843.

Issue

I. Margaret Cornelia—Born August 26, 1846. Died March 13, 1906. She was twice married. First to Robert D. Brunson. Born December 11, 1841. Died October 1, 1870. And second to Artemus Lowe Brunson. Born January 28, 1846; left two children by each marriage. Issue: 1. Susan Brunson—Born February 2, 1869. Married J. Walter Hill. No issue. 2. Cornelia—Born June 6, 1870. Married Wade S. Cothran, and has a son, James S. Cothran, born October 20, 1895, unmarried, and a daughter, Margaret Cornelia, born December 25, 1900, who was married March 15, 1921, to Julian D. Holstein, Jr. 3. Cleora—Born January 17, 1881. Married Wallace C. Tompkins, November 25, 1908. No issue. 4. Artemus Lowe, Jr.—Born October 28, 1886. Married Virginia L. Thomason, August 9, 1917. Issue: 1. Artemus Lowe. 2. Idalia Walker Brunson.

II. Mansfield E. Hollingsworth, Jr., child of Mansfield and Margaret (Gomillian) Hollingsworth. Married Jane Holcomb, and has eight children (I do not know their ages). They are: 1. Jane—Married Manton McCutcheon. She has four daughters. 2. Thomas Thomason—Married, but no children. 3. Margaret—Married William Addy. 4. Septima—Married Roy Gillerland. 5. William Grover Mansfield, Jr. 6. Laurence. The last two are unmarried. Cornelia married Mr. Creech.

JAMES HOLLINGSWORTH, Jr. WILL

Brother, John Hollingsworth, Administrator, Wife, Barbery. Married second husband, Hugh Mosely, 1807 or 1808. Issue: James. Witnessed, Henry Shelnut, William Gordon. Date of will, June 21, 1805. Recorded February 19, 1806. James Harrison also mentioned as one of the administrators. Jeremiah Thorton's name is mentioned.

ALEXANDER HOLLINGSWORTH. ESTATE

John Hollingsworth and John Kerkesy. November 1804. Wife, Sarah. Issue: James, Isaac, Alexander and Jane. Witnessed, James Hollingsworth and Phillip Inlow. Bondsmen, Drury Hern, James Hollingsworth, Young Allen and Dyonicius Oliver. Daughter, Jane married Jacob Miller. He died December, 1849. Issue: John H. Miller, Wiley Miller, Alexander Miller, James Miller and Hugh Miller. H. B. Meade was paid a share, and William Quattlebaum was also paid a share of Jacob Miller's estate. Young Isaac Hollingsworth died September 24, 1813. The medical bill for same was $34.00, paid to Dr. Thomas Powell; his burial expenses were $20.00. Articles are given as bought in Charleston, S. C., and Augusta, Ga., at this time. Paid James Hollingsworth, Sr., money appropriated to Dr. Adams, $53.00. Recorded in book B, pages 217 to 219. James Blocker, Clerk for John Simkins, Ordinary of Edgefield County. Dated November 19, 1804.

JAMES HOLLINGSWORTH, Sr. WILL

November 3, 1818. Witnessed, Henry Capeheart, John Terry, Sr., and John Moss. The will was proven by Henry Capehart, Hughes Moss and John Terry, Sr., September 24, 1821. John Hollingsworth, James Carson, James Harrison, Executors. To John Hollingsworth he gives 700 acres of land, on little Turkey Creek. To James Carson and James Harrison, 336 acres on Hard Labor Creek, in Abbeville District, to be equally divided. To grandchildren, James Hollingsworth, Jane (or Gency) Miller, Alexander Hollingsworth, James, the son of James Hollingsworth, deceased, and John Walton, the son of Enoch, a tract containing 800 acres, also fifty dollars to be paid each grandchild of his three children, John Hollingsworth, Sarah Carson and Polly Harrison, to receive all his personal estate. David Richardson, Trustee, for his grandchildren, heirs of Alexander Hollingsworth, James Hollingsworth, and Lucy Walton, deceased. Sarah Hollingsworth, it seems, died between 1818 and 1822.

GEORGE HOLLINGSWORTH

Of Wythe Co., Va. Son of ...... Born 1780. Married Jane Carr, 1812.

8 boys and 4 girls, of whom only 2 (boys) are known.

ISSUE

I. William O.—Born 1813.
II. George O.—Born 1815. Married Sarah Jackson, 1841. Issue: 14 children.

COLLIN F. HOLLINGSWORTH

Of Queen Anne's Co., Md.

ISSUE

I. John A.
II. A daughter—Married Thomas H. Hammond, of Frederick Co., Md.

JOHN HOLLINGSWORTH

Son of John L. and Rosina Eldridge Hollingsworth, of Massachusetts, First married Miss Howard, Alexandria, Va., 1796. Born 1759 or '60. Died 1836 or '37, age 77 years. Was at St. Clair's defeat, 1791. He married Margaret Baker, 1812. He was at Fort McHenry, 1814.

ISSUE 1ST MARRIAGE

I. Thomas Howard—Born at Alexandria, Va., 1797. Died 1841. More of Thomas Howard later.

ISSUE 2ND MARRIAGE

II. Charles—Lived at Xenia, Ohio.
III. Frank—Lived at Xenia, Ohio.
Also daughters; names unknown.

THOMAS HOWARD HOLLINGSWORTH

Son of John and ...... (Howard) Hollingsworth. Born in Alexandria, Va., 1797. Died 1841. Lived at Baltimore, Md., until 1818, at Waynesboro, Franklin Co., Pa., until 1834, and at Smithsburg, Washington Co., Md., until his death, 1841.

ISSUE 1ST MARRIAGE

I. John.
Also 5 daughters. Name of wife unknown.

II. Thomas—Lived at Waynesboro, Franklin Co., Pa.

III. Franklin—Lived near Smithsburg, Washington Co., Md.

IV. Augustus—Died.

V. Mary E.—Lived at Waynesboro, Franklin Co., Pa.

VI. Martha Jane—Lived at Waynesboro, Franklin Co., Pa.

JOHN HOLLINGSWORTH

Son of Thomas Howard Hollingsworth. Born August 17, 1821, Smithsburg, Washington Co., Md.

ISSUE

I. George.	V. Alice.
II. John F.	VI. Elizabeth.
III. Charles.	VII. Hannah.
IV. William G.	VIII. Ella.

ZEBULON HOLLINGSWORTH

Son of James. Born in Maryland, April 12, 1782. Died February 17, 1827. Had 2 brothers, William and Caleb.

Zebulon Hollingsworth, son of James and Edith Strickland, who were married in 1804, were living in Sampson Co., N. C., and moved to East Tennessee, 1806, and from there to North Alabama.

Zebulon—Born 1816, in North Alabama. Issue: 7 girls and 5 boys. John and 1 sister lived in North Alabama, 1878.

Zebulon Hollingsworth—Lived in St. Louis, Mo., 1878. His son, Zebuon David, born 1844.

FAMILY LISTS OF LATER EMIGRATION, ETC.

ENGLISH

JAMES HOLLINGSWORTH

Deceased, came from Melbourne, Derbyshire, England, in 1848.

ISSUE

I. F. S.—Winona, Minn.

II. James—Beatrice, Gage Co., Neb.

III. Joseph—Beatrice, Gage Co., Neb.

IV. Henry—DeWitt, Saline Co., Neb.

V. Robert—Oak, Nackolls Co., Neb.

F. K. HOLLINGSWORTH

Of Chicago. Son of F. S., of Winona, Minn.

Issue

I. James.
II. Joseph.
III. Henry.
IV. Robert.
All have families.

JOHN HOLLINGSWORTH

Of Sussex Co., Del. Ancestors not traced. Born 1760. Died Kent Co., Del., 1830, age 70 years. Married Elizabeth Harper.

Issue

I. Thomas—Died at Philadelphia, Pa. No issue.
II. William—Married; moved to Indiana. Died 1846. Issue: 5 children.
III. Mary—Married ...... Starling. Went to Minnesota. Issue: 1 child.
IV. Ann—Married Wilson Legg. Died. No issue.
V. Elizabeth—Died. Unmarried.
VI. John—Married Mary Merick. Died at Philadelphia, Pa. Issue: 5 children.
VII. James—Born December 14, 1810. Married Prudy Morris, of North Carolina. No issue.

GEORGE HOLLINGSWORTH

Of Sandford Parish, Lancaster Co., England.

Issue

I. George R.

GEORGE R. HOLLINGSWORTH

Of "Boken Hall." Son of George Hollingsworth, of Lancaster Co., England. Died August 20, 1878. Came to America, 1818. Wood Sta-:ion, Ala.

Issue

I. George R.—Married .... Issue: 1. Maud. 2. Eugene. 3. Minnie.

...... HOLLINGSWORTH

Born in Lancashire, 7 miles from Manchester, England. Died 1853, in his 51st year. Came from England to Philadelphia, Pa.

Issue

    I. George—Born 1823. Died 1862.
   II. James—Born 1826. Died 1863.
  III. Thomas—Born 1836. Lived at Mt. Vernon, Ind.
  IV. John—Born 1841. Lived in Indiana.
   V. Robert—Born at Philadelphia, Pa., 1844. Lived at St. Louis, Mo.
    Also 3 daughters.

ROBERT HOLLINGSWORTH

Born in England. Died at Philadelphia, 1860.

Issue

    I. William—Born in England, February 27, 1823. Died at Philadelphia, Pa., 1877. Married Elizabeth Newton, born in England, 1825. Issue: 1. Robert Newton—Roxbury, Philadelphia, Pa. 2. Samuel T.—Roxbury, Philadelphia, Pa. 3. Milton J.—Roxbury, Philadelphia, Pa.

DANIEL HOLLINGSWORTH

Issue

    I. Samuel—Married Margaret Fernely.
   II. Edmond Valentine—Born February 14, 1830. Married Eliza Jane Wilson, June 4, 1857. No issue.

JOHN HOLLINGSWORTH

Issue

    I. William—Norristown, Pa.
   II. Henry—Germantown, Pa.

JOHN HOLLLINGSWORTH, Esq.

Of Ballinakill, Wexford Co., Ireland. · Died December 16, 1877, age
88 years. Pure Anglo-Saxon stock; came from England about 1665.
Since this date the family has lived there.

EDWARD T. HOLLINGSWORTH

Son of John. Born December 15, 1823. Came to the United States,
1849. Residence: Cincinnati Enquirer Office, Cincinnati, Ohio. Only
one of his family in the United States. His brothers still lived at Ballinakill, Wexford Co., Ireland, 1878.

WEXFORD, IRELAND, FAMILY
JOHN HUMBER HOLLINGSWORTH

Son of John H., Jr., and grandson of John H., Sr. Born 1789.

JOHN H. HOLLINGSWORTH

Born at Wexford, Ireland, 1836. Issue: William—Born 1860.

INDEX TO HOLLINGSWORTHS

(For Hollingsworths, not traced, see pages 160 thro 172.)

INDEX TO OTHER SURNAMES

#992